$4.—

JACK'S SKILLET

Jack's Skillet

PLAIN TALK AND SOME RECIPES FROM A GUY IN THE KITCHEN

JACK BUTLER

ALGONQUIN BOOKS OF CHAPEL HILL   1997

Published by
ALGONQUIN BOOKS OF CHAPEL HILL
Post Office Box 2225
Chapel Hill, North Carolina 27515-2225

a division of
WORKMAN PUBLISHING
708 Broadway
New York, New York 10003

Portions of this book, in different form, first appeared in the *Arkansas Times*.

"Preserves" from *The Kid Who Wanted to Be a Spaceman* by Jack Butler. © 1984 by Jack But-ler. Reprinted by permission of the author. Excerpt from *Living in Little Rock with Miss Lit-tle Rock* by Jack Butler. © 1994 by Jack Butler. Reprinted by permission of the author. Excerpt from *Jujitsu for Christ* by Jack Butler. © 1986 by Jack Butler. Reprinted by permis-sion of the author.

Library of Congress Cataloging-in-Publication Data
Butler, Jack, 1944–
    Jack's skillet : plain talk and some recipes from a guy in the kitchen / by Jack Butler.
        p.   cm.
    Includes index.
    ISBN 1-56512-149-X (hardcover)
    1. Cookery.   I. Title.
  TX652.B883   1997
  641.5–dc21   97-15925
                                                                              CIP

10 9 8 7 6 5 4 3 2
First Edition

For my mother, Dorothy Niland Butler

CONTENTS

JACK'S SKILLET

INTRODUCTION

I'm the original improvisational cook. Hardly ever look at recipes, except to get ideas or maybe to refresh my grasp of the principles involved in a soufflé, a sauce, a stir-fry. But I certainly don't cook with the instructions at my elbow, and I'm never happier than when I'm wheeling and dealing, slicing and dicing, rolling the dough and rolling my own.

You understand, I don't have anything *against* cooking by the rules. There are some culinary geniuses out there who measure to the milliliter and time to the split second. More power to them. It's just not what I do, and it's not what this book is about. I'm a *cook,* not a chef. And besides, food is too wonderful for absolute rules.

This book is about food as pleasure, food as ritual, food as communication. It's about health, satisfaction, celebration, the giving and receiving of sustenance and delight.

None of which is to say there aren't any recipes in here. There are plenty, and I think you'll have fun with them. Some of the recipes are family secrets — from my mother, my grandmother, some all the way up from Alligator, Mississippi. Some I must have gotten out of books a long time ago, or talked a chef out of, or imitated from a fine restaurant till I got it right. Some I just plain made up. Those of you who cook will recognize variations on a few old favorites. Those of you who are thinking about getting into cooking will find you can use this book not only for its recipes, but also as a traveler's companion in the new territory, a freehand map of the countryside.

Cooking for yourself is infinitely rewarding, but if you haven't grown up doing it, getting started can be pretty intimidating and modern American life doesn't do much to encourage you. I grew up in a big-time food tradition, but

I didn't learn how to cook for myself till I was a grown man. Had to start from scratch, literally. I'm here to tell you it was worth it.

I'm a cook, and I can't help thinking about food. I'm a novelist, and I can't help telling stories. I'm a poet, and I can't help singing out from time to time. As a result, you should think of this book as a story, a story with occasional bursts of paean and dithyramb. The story is the story of our lives with food. I say *our*.

Stories have characters, and this one is no exception. I can't write about food without writing about people. One of the main characters in this story is Jayme Tull, my closest friend and the person to whom I am married. The names of our daughters—Sarah, Lynnika, Catherine, and Sherri—float in and out of the narrative, as do the names of cats and relatives. Lynnika, in fact, is personally responsible for one of these chapters.

Stories also have settings and backgrounds. I spent roughly the first twenty years of my life in Mississippi, mostly in the cotton-growing Delta. Then I spent twenty-five or so in Arkansas—so many that I began to think of myself as a native, so many that I root for the Razorbacks to this day. It was in Arkansas that Jayme and I met (she's a native of Little Rock). And finally, in 1993, we moved to a place we had visited for years—Santa Fe, New Mexico.

You are what you eat, and all my life I've eaten Southern. But sort of nouvelle Southern, with pluralistic influences. Semi-enlightened good old boy, you might say. I can't imagine writing about food and not at some point talking about the absolute best breakfast on earth, which is not, I'm sorry to say, garlic-and-cheese grits, or even pork chops, scrambled eggs, and hot biscuits with strawberry preserves, but *novy mit a schmeer*—a toasted bagel slathered with cream cheese and layered with capers, thin slices of smoked Nova Scotia salmon, tomato, and onion.

You get the idea. We've all done some traveling nowadays. Even us deep-fried types have gone out into the world, and the world has come our way, and we've learned to like Ethiopian in Washington, D.C., Continental in Connecticut, and Thai in Panama City, Florida.

You can expect a streak of health consciousness in here. I love to eat and I hate to be fat, so I've spent a lot of time thinking about the problem. And food affects your mood and your thought processes and the way your body feels, so there's a lot to think about there. And Jayme, who loves to eat, too, is allergic to almost everything with DNA, so we've had to do some heavy-duty pondering on balanced nutrition and the best emotional equivalents to ice cream.

I'm sure there are lingering influences from my hippie days: I still don't see any point in store-bought white bread or degerminated cornmeal or milled rice, and I can't eat black-eyed peas and cornbread without thinking how nice it is to be getting my complementary amino acids. Even so, I'm no purist. Food is too wonderful, remember? You *can't* make a good biscuit with whole wheat flour, and biscuits are good for you, if only through sheer force of delectability. Same for pie crusts and same for gravy. Our bones know grease is right, and it's hard to trust somebody who can turn down a slice of fresh warm pecan pie.

It has occurred to me that one of the ways I stay healthy is by sublimating my love of eating. I cook, which lets me hang around food without actually ingesting it. I shop, I practice inventory control. I write about food. I think about food.

I think about it all day long. I go to sleep at night wondering whether to have an omelet or eggs over easy for breakfast. I wake up in the morning deciding what to pull out of the freezer for supper that evening. I think about food at work. I think about it when I'm writing, when I'm running or playing basketball or skiing. The kinds of friends I have, we all sit around the table after a grand meal remembering other feasts and planning the menu for the next one. I can be stuffed so full of lemon icebox pie that I feel like I couldn't eat another bite till Thanksgiving and still have a high old time yakking about hot blackberry cobbler with globs of vanilla ice cream.

It took me a long time to realize that nothing which was that much and that completely a part of my daily existence could possibly be too unimportant to put into words. So I put some of it into words, and here they are. I hope you enjoy. I hope these words remind you of favorite meals and favorite times, and make you look forward to the next time you sit down to eat.

And remember, this book contains absolutely *no* calories.

A NOTE ON THE RECIPES

This book provides you two kinds of recipes. The first, what I call action recipes, take you through a typical cooking session, the dynamics of the process so to speak, and you'll find one or two in almost every chapter. At the end of the chapters are the recipes from that chapter (plus a few extras sometimes) in a standard recipe format for you to use if you prefer.

Cooking conditions vary widely, and you would do well to take your own unique situation into account. Most of these recipes are designed for relatively humid climates and for cooking at altitudes under a thousand feet above sea level. Especially for baking, I'd recommend increasing temperatures five degrees for every thousand feet above sea level. You may also need to increase baking times at higher altitudes (be sure to keep an eye on whatever you're making if you increase baking time, to keep the added time from drying out your dish).

The number of people each recipe will serve has been calculated for moderate eaters. Light eaters will find themselves with leftovers. With heavy eaters—more common in our household than not—you had perhaps better invite fewer guests.

I almost always prefer to use fresh herbs if I have them around. In most recipes, I've indicated whether I'm using fresh or dried. But if you have fresh on hand and I've called for dried (or vice versa), just convert the measurement (*Joy of Cooking* has a good fresh–dry herb conversion chart). Be sure to convert, though, as you don't need as much of a dried herb for flavoring as you do of a fresh herb.

Likewise, I will refer to cooking with oil throughout this book. For clarity's sake, let me explain that when I am frying or cooking at high temperatures, I use canola oil, corn oil, peanut oil, or a mixed vegetable oil. When I want more flavor and am cooking at lower temperatures, I use extra virgin olive oil.

Common themes run through these recipes, so that once you master a few of them, many others will come more and more easily, and once you are familiar with many of them, you will have developed an ample repertoire of cooking strategies for use in any situation. You'll be prepared to whip up something delicious and satisfying from what's on hand, and on a moment's notice when you come in exhausted at the end of the day. You'll also be ready to tackle a full-scale formal dinner, requiring a day's preparation.

Finally, I would also note that most of these recipes are designed not only to produce a wide range of basic dishes, but also to provide very forgiving general guides for your own experiment and variation. I can't overemphasize the importance of trying new approaches.

Don't be afraid to play with your food!

TOMATO GRAVY AND BISCUITS

We were six months married, Lynnice and I, and it was a cold snowy January in Sedalia, Missouri, a quarter century ago. We lived in a freezing little two-room walk-up. We were a long way from our families, we were out of food, and we were stone-cold broke. That's how I remember it, anyway.

We were complete innocents. Somehow I had managed to get through high school and college and out into the world with no more idea how to take care of myself than a baby frog on a rainy blacktop. She wasn't any better. We had been given five hundred dollars as a wedding present, which seemed an enormous sum back then, enough to set up a young couple in style for years. But the door came off our little white Volkswagen, and I took the car in to the shop. And then there was a serious problem with the brake linings. And then the carburetor was shot.

The repair shop was just down the street and we didn't have a phone, so they sent one of the boys trotting over to tell me what else was wrong. I can still see the messenger standing there on the second-floor stoop, panting, delivering the bad news with a smile.

Well, what could we do? They were the mechanics, not us. Our good Christian upbringings had taught us to just be nice to people and probably they would be nice to you. After all, these were *neighbors*. Surely the times weren't so corrupt, not even way up north in Missouri, that a fellow American could just smile and lie and cheat a pair of earnest newlyweds out of their last dime?

I declare, if I could think of the name of that auto shop I'd write it down right now.

Anyway, that's how the five hundred dollars went. And come to think of it, pretty much how the marriage went too, though that process took a lot longer and was more painful.

So anyway, like I was saying, we were broke. Oh, I had an incredibly tiny stipend coming in from working as a graduate assistant thirty miles away in Warrensburg. And you could get milk for eighty-five cents a gallon. Seems I remember some extremely yellow sort of margarine that went four sticks for twenty-five cents. They practically paid you to take the lettuce, and I think all canned vegetables available in the continental United States sold for the same price, three for thirty-seven cents.

But even with all of those breaks, we couldn't afford much. We needed something hot and filling. Steak was out of the question. Even hamburger ran outrageously high, nearly a dollar a pound. And then I remembered tomato gravy and biscuits. Flour was cheap, canned tomatoes were cheap, onions were cheaper than the dirt they grew in.

I had grown up eating biscuits, of course. And biscuits need gravy, of course. I was probably five years old before I realized it was more than one word: biscuitsandgravy. The thing was, we didn't always have meat. Sometimes, in the middle of winter, we'd run out of ham scraps for the redeye gravy, or the farmers who paid my preacher father with tablefare would decide they'd better hang on to the rest of the hens till spring. Now there was nothing wrong with eggs and fried Spam for breakfast, but Spam doesn't make good gravy. And a Sunday dinner of canned butterbeans, crowder peas, chowchow, cornbread sticks, sweet potato pudding, and turnip greens was just fine, the heck with the poultry. But what did you put on the biscuits?

What my mother did, as you will have deduced by now, was make tomato gravy. She'd chop an onion, break out a quart jar of canned tomatoes, grab a cast-iron skillet, and Presto! The marvelous sauce ladled out hot, savory, ruddy, and redolent, and suddenly the blessing was heartfelt instead of routine. And that's what we newlyweds did, there in far Missouri. We laid in supplies, and we made tomato gravy and biscuits. There was an entire month when that was our supper night after night, because five dollars had to get us to the next payday. It's a wonder we didn't get kwashiorkor. I don't blame you if you suppose my memory's skipped a few things, and we must have gotten some meat in our victuals somehow. You may be right. But what good is a memory that only remembers things the way they really happened?

What isn't fiction is how I felt when I got home with the onions and the sixty-nine-cent sack of bleached white flour and the cans of peeled tomatoes and the packs of margarine—my one extravagance since, as cheap as they were, they were much more expensive than the time-honored can of lard. But of course you have to butter the biscuits before you put gravy on them, so I would have had to get the margarine anyway, so really I was saving the cost of the lard . . .

When I got home, I say, I realized I didn't know how to *cook* tomato gravy and biscuits. I didn't, in fact, know how to cook much of anything. You can imagine my shock. This food was my *birthright*. It wasn't that I wasn't familiar with kitchens. I'd been washing dishes since I was six. The kitchen was where you did all your serious talking, it was where you drew tanks and airplanes in your homework notebooks. Now here I was, miles and years away, stranded in the frozen tundra of the Show-Me State, and I needed somebody to show me. I was already salivating; I was the victim of intense olfactory visitations. And neither my bride nor I had the least idea how to produce the dish we had in mind.

I will pass over those first few terrible days of trial and error. Suffice it to say that finally I taught myself to replicate my mother's tomato gravy and my grandmother's biscuits, and went on to learn other specialties. I went on until I had reconstructed my entire childhood diet, and then I went on further, experimenting. I went on practicing cooking until, somewhere in there, it quit being practice and started being just cooking. I went on past even that point until it became play. Now my favorite way to unwind after work is to spend an hour in the kitchen—an icy martini at hand, things bubbling or sizzling while I wash and peel and chop yet other things or roll out a rich crust, leaving, when I take a sip, floury fingerprints on my cold and beaded glass. It's usually about six-thirty, Jayme has *Wheel of Fortune* running in the next room. I step to the doorway every few minutes, hands covered in flour or chicken fat, trying to guess the answer before the blue-haired lady from Georgia, the Chinese American accountant from Bemidji, the would-be actor fresh out of Hunter College. Not infrequently the smell of sautéed garlic fills the air.

My kitchen is warm, and my marriage to Jayme has proven durable. The evening is just beginning, we've got hours and hours together—what Jayme calls Wide Time. We look forward to a good hot meal together. Our mortgage is under control. The cars are old, but when they break down we know a mechanic we can trust.

Cooking, I want to say now, is a way of taking responsibility. And taking responsibility leads to satisfaction. It is, I sometimes think, the only path to satisfaction. I am sure there are more significant ways of taking responsibility than cooking. But perhaps not all that very many.

I will never forget the dismay I felt twenty-five years ago, or the absolutely vivid realization, that my ignorance of cooking was part and parcel of my general ignorance of life. Six or seven years after my realization, in connection with a church visitation program, I met a recent widower. He seemed older then than he does in retrospect—he was only sixty-five—but even so I felt he should have looked forward to years of life and vigor. Instead, he was a shell, a ruined pathetic thing. It wasn't grief that he was feeling but the panic of a small child on the first day of school. His wife had always done all the sewing, all the shopping, all the ironing, washing, sweeping, saving.

All the cooking.

Even before there was a political movement to guide me, I had a distaste for the stupidity of our cultural divisions. It wasn't that the man I was visiting didn't know how to care for himself. It was that he never *would* know how to. After all those years frozen into his role, he found change inconceivable. What I felt, I remember quite clearly, was not pity but revulsion.

Several years after that, Jayme let me know that she had been impressed, the first time she visited, to find me in the kitchen whipping up a meal. She informed me that it had been a definite determining factor. She didn't mean a simple reversal of the old cliché, either. She's an excellent cook, thank you very much. No, what she meant, she said, had a lot more to do with sex appeal than with the prospect of a reduced workload.

And see, I never even knew it at the time.

So what I'm telling you, it was a close call. A word to the wise, if you're in the hunt for love. Male or female, maybe you might think about skipping the crowd scene at the local bar. Getting out the old skillet. Brushing up on a few recipes.

And naturally I'm going to start you out with tomato gravy and biscuits.

First get your biscuits in the oven. You can make the gravy while they rise, and it will be hot and ready when they are. Biscuits are easy. Just remember the two-to-one rules.

YOU CAN MAKE perfect, wonderful biscuits nearly every time if you remember three sets of two-to-one ratios. Here they are:

USE 2	FOR EVERY 1
TEASPOONS OF BAKING POWDER	CUP OF FLOUR
TABLESPOONS OF SHORTENING	CUP OF FLOUR
CUPS OF FLOUR	CUP OF LIQUID

Two cups of flour will make six to nine fairly large biscuits, so let's assume those are the proportions you're working with. For that amount of flour, according to the rules, you'll need four teaspoons baking powder. You'll also need a pinch of salt and a quarter teaspoon of baking *soda*, not powder—really, that's all, a quarter teaspoon. Too much soda makes the biscuits taste funny. I use, nowadays, unbleached white flour. The liquid in this recipe should be a cup of buttermilk, but I've made fine biscuits with the old vinegar-and-sweet-milk trick. Heck, I've even made good biscuits with thinned-down yogurt. The point of these liquids is their slight acidity, which reacts with the baking soda to release carbonic acid. The acid immediately breaks down into water and carbon dioxide, which makes the biscuits rise. Most of the rise comes from the heat-activated baking powder, true, but the soda-buttermilk combo provides just the right fillip of fluffiness, and the buttermilk makes for a wonderful texture.

Mix all the dry ingredients in a bowl, like they always say. What do they think, you're going to mix them in a plate? I confess I usually toss in an extra pinch of baking powder. One to grow on. Now the shortening. The classic biscuit is made with true animal-fat white lard, but I use margarine. I would use butter, but Jayme's allergic to milk products. The oleo gives the biscuits a slight golden hue that I have come to feel is all to the good. They tell you to "cut in" the shortening until the mixture is the consistency of cornmeal, meaning with a table knife or one of those plastic scraper blades. I do that, and it takes a while. Sometimes I cut it in with my fingertips. It bruises the flour a little, but take my word for it, no problem. Pinch those patties of margarine or butter, squeeze those dollops of Crisco. Voila! Cornmeal consistency!

Now add the buttermilk. Wait, not so much! Don't put the whole cup in, save back a tablespoon or two. You don't want to get the dough too moist. (If you do, though, just sprinkle in a little more flour.) Mix as well as you can with a large spoon. See if you think you need more buttermilk. Forget the spoon, you've got to put your hands in again. Don't work the dough too much. What you're after is a soft spongy mix that will ball up easily, a dough that is moist and affectionate, but not tacky like wet plaster. Judging the texture requires experience, so don't feel bad if you don't get it perfect the first few times. It's a sensual process. Your fingers learn to know when the batch is right. At this point, you'll probably want to pinch off a bite and eat it. *Mmm,* those are going to be some *good* biscuits.

Or don't you eat dough? The world falls pretty evenly into those who do and those who don't. There are some people at our house, if I don't leave a few scraps over, they get upset.

If you have the time, you can let the dough rest up in the fridge, retracting its gluten. Mixing the dough with your hands, you were of course kneading it, which is good for chewy bread but not good for flaky fluffy fall-apart biscuits.

Next roll the dough out—with an oiled wood rolling pin, please, not one of those plastic monstrosities. Pat the dough flat, then dust it lightly with flour to keep it from sticking to the rolling pin or countertop. I like high biscuits, so I roll the batch to about a finger's thickness (I don't have big hands). Cut the biscuits out with a round biscuit cutter. No cute shapes. They show a lack of respect, and I promise you, the biscuits won't taste as good. You can use the top of a water glass, though the dough seals perfectly and will resist like a pump-flange. My mother always used the bottom of one of those cup-shaped tin funnels through which you pour hot stewed fruit into canning jars. But why not go ahead and get yourself a stainless-steel, three-inch biscuit cutter, complete with a slot to release the air pressure? The tool for the job.

Once you've cut them, plop the biscuits onto a cookie sheet, brush with melted butter if you like (I usually don't), and bake at 350°F for about twenty minutes. You'll have to play around to find the right cooking time, since every oven cooks differently and every climate affects the way things cook.

Mainly, what you need to do is check carefully in the last five minutes or so.

On to the tomato gravy. What you do now, when the biscuits are in the oven, is heat some oil in your black iron skillet, four or five tablespoons' worth. Add some fresh-ground black pepper to the oil first, and don't let it get smoking hot. I say *oil*. My mother used lard. I used to use butter or margarine, though they scorch pretty quickly. Olive oil does just fine. Stir the pepper and oil with a spatula, and toss in the whole onion you've just chopped. Keep stirring. Browned onions are simply glorious, and the odor is your first reward. (Actually, nowadays, I use garlic—Jayme's allergic to onions.)

When the onions have just begun to turn translucent, sprinkle in a couple of heaping teaspoons of flour and stir to get a smooth, velvety mix. Cajun aficionados will recognize that we are creating a roux. You want to brown the roux just slightly but without scorching the onions, an operation that requires practice and delicacy.

When you've got the roux just right, turn the heat down to low and open one of those cans of tomatoes. Pour in the juice gently, a bit at a time, stirring to blend in the roux. If the sauce seems too thick, add water. When you've added all the liquid, add the tomatoes, which you should gleefully chop and mash and stir with your spatula. Bring the heat back up to medium or medium-high and linger over the skillet, mashing and stirring. You want the gravy to simmer, not bubble. This is when I add salt to taste. I don't believe in adding salt too early. It dries things up and interferes with the osmosis. Simmer and stir, keeping the bottom of the skillet clean, until the gravy is as thick and rich as you like. For me, that's pretty thick and rich.

By now the biscuits should be ready, golden brown on top but not hard on the bottom. Take them out and butter them, all of them, while they're hot. (Sure, I butter my biscuits before I put the gravy on them. Doesn't everybody?) I forgot to tell you, you should have a big old glass of cold milk standing by because you're about to eat one of these suckers right there and then. It will be piping hot, dripping with butter, and you're going to eat it plain — no jam, no gravy. It's the cook's responsibility to make sure they came out right, isn't it?

You heap a nice linen-covered basket with your creations. You pour the gravy into a gravy boat. Before you pour, you notice with pleasure that a nice skin has formed on the surface. It's cold outside. Your friends in the dining room are going crazy. How much longer do you plan to keep them waiting?

Buttermilk Biscuits

2 cups unbleached white flour
4 teaspoons baking powder
¼ teaspoon baking
   soda

Pinch of salt
4 tablespoons butter or
   margarine
1 cup buttermilk

You may substitute a cup of milk curdled with a teaspoon of vinegar, or a cup of plain yogurt thinned with water, for the buttermilk.

TOTAL PREPARATION AND BAKING TIME: 35 to 45 minutes.

1. Preheat oven to 350°F.
2. Mix dry ingredients in a medium bowl. Cut in butter or margarine until mix is consistency of cornmeal. Add buttermilk gradually, blending with spatula or large metal spoon. *Do not knead.*
3. Turn out onto floured board, dust both sides with flour, and roll out lightly to a finger's thickness (thicker if higher biscuits are desired).
4. Cut into individual biscuits with a 3" biscuit cutter. Roll out remaining dough as above and cut into biscuits, repeating until all the dough is used.
5. Place biscuits on cookie sheet and bake in oven until just golden brown on top, 20 to 25 minutes. (If you're planning to serve these with tomato gravy, start preparing it now while the biscuits are baking. The recipe follows.)
6. When the biscuits are ready, remove from oven, cut open, and butter immediately.

MAKES 6 TO 9 FAIRLY LARGE BISCUITS

Tomato Gravy

4 to 5 tablespoons shortening
Freshly ground pepper, to taste
1 onion, finely chopped
2 teaspoons unbleached white
  flour

1 can stewed tomatoes
  (28 to 32 ounces)
Salt, to taste

If you have them, substitute a quart of home-canned tomatoes for the commercially canned variety. Garlic lovers may substitute 4 to 6 cloves minced garlic for the onion. For shortening you may use leftover bacon grease, pure lard, butter or margarine, olive oil, or other good cooking oil.

TOTAL PREPARATION AND COOKING TIME: 30 to 35 minutes.

1. Heat shortening in skillet on high heat till just before smoking. Reduce heat to medium. Mill generous portions of pepper directly into the skillet. Add chopped onion and sauté till slightly translucent, stirring constantly with a spatula. Sprinkle flour over shortening-onion mix. Stir with spatula until flour begins to form a brown roux. Add tomatoes (with juice) gradually, stirring to blend with roux. Mash tomatoes with spatula and continue blending. If roux is too thick, dilute with water. Add salt to taste.
2. Reduce heat to low and simmer till ready, about 20 minutes.

MAKES ENOUGH GRAVY FOR 6 TO 9 BISCUITS

THE CARE AND FEEDING OF THE
BLACK IRON SKILLET

I've been around black iron skillets all my life without thinking about them much. In fact, really, that phrase "black iron skillet" is redundant. I can't remember saying it before about 1975, which is a comment on the sad decline of modern standards. All you really ought to have to say is "skillet." But I'm getting ahead of myself.

There are a lot of good people out there who, through no fault of their own, weren't born in the rural South and so haven't grown up just sort of *knowing* about skillets. I'm a liberal in these matters. I think my neighbors have just as much right to enjoy black iron skilletry as I do, regardless of taste, greed, or Nashville origins. Herewith, a brief dissertation on the basics with this one caveat: No list of rules can tell you everything you need to know. What you do with a black iron skillet, you get acquainted over time. You *live* with it. It's the relationship that counts, not your first-time-out technique.

It bears repeating: A black iron skillet is made of iron. Black. Iron. Aluminum will not do. You can find some beautiful-*looking* aluminum skillets out there, and if you use them you might find that what you thought was arthritis in your wrists has miraculously cleared up. But the sacrifice is too great. Don't get me wrong. Aluminum's a good metal. I got nothing against aluminum. Some of my best pans are aluminum.

But in a skillet, aluminum just won't do. It's too dry. It won't take oil the way iron will, so you can't cure it. And it doesn't conduct heat the way iron does. It's too light a metal. Iron not only conducts heat rapidly and evenly, it *holds* heat. Which is why the best way to cook eggs in a black iron skillet, whether you want them scrambled or over easy, is to get the skillet nice and hot but not sizzling hot, and then turn the heat off not long after you slide the eggs in.

That's the point of the fancy copper-bottomed stuff favored by chefs, I know. Mate a highly conductive metal with a highly durable metal, and have the best of both. High technology trying to approximate the virtues of old reliable iron. Why bother? And you can't cure copper worth a flip either.

I presume you understand Teflon is out of the question? We don't talk Teflon in polite company. It may be OK for unimportant things like presidents or ball bearings or valves in artificial hearts, but we're talking *cooking* here. For one thing, Teflon is another example of unnecessary technology. A well-cured iron skillet is as slippery as anything needs to get. Your heart will soar at the delicacy of gravy coming away clean from all that smooth black iron, all that family history. Whereas with Teflon, even if the stuff doesn't stick, all you're looking at is Teflon. Besides, Teflon *always* scratches, and then it's worse than useless. You think it won't scratch, you think you'll be careful to use only wooden or plastic or Teflon-coated spatulas, but the next thing you know your skillet looks like you used it to play jai alai in a blackberry patch. And did you ever try to turn an egg or a potato pancake with a wooden, plastic, or Teflon-coated spatula?

Oh, but you're worried about your heart, your intake of low-density lipoproteins, all that grease you have to use with a black iron skillet. Now you know better than that. It's not the skillet's fault. Just don't put so much of it in your *mouth*, hey?

And really you don't have to use that much grease. Once you get the skillet cured, less than half a pat of butter will set you up just fine for a delicious one-yolk, three-egg omelet.

OK, so we've got the question of materials settled. Iron, and nothing else. Let's talk workmanship. Nowadays, there are a lot of iron skillets showing up in the housewares section of supermarkets and in the various X-, Y-, and Z-marts. But that doesn't mean you can just grab something off the rack and walk straight into skillet heaven. Many of these are quickie jobs, rough-cast and unevenly cooled, which means they're prone to cracking and, even if they don't crack, to patchy cooking. You can tell these rip-offs because they seem lighter and cleaner and because their surfaces are minutely pebbled and pitted.

The outside of a good iron skillet should be a nice smooth matte. The inside, the cooking surface, should be smoother, about the texture of a watermelon that has just been washed down with cold water from a garden hose.

If you're buying your skillet new, it won't be black, of course. Yet. Curing and cooking and history is what turns it black. If you're buying your skillet new, it'll be, well, iron-colored. If it is black already, they've painted it. Don't buy it. But I don't recommend buying your skillet new. Your skillet ought to be roughly as old as you are, is my opinion.

So where do you get a good old black iron skillet? Flea markets, probably. Like I say, I grew up with the creatures so naturally never gave a thought to where they came from. They were just there. They came with the family. A child is born, a black iron skillet appears in the cupboard under the sink. The steady state theory of black iron skillets.

We have a dozen or so now, all shapes and sizes. We hang them on the skillet sculpture, which is a whole other story. I've had one skillet since I can remember, since even that Missouri winter I was telling you about, during my first marriage, when neither of us knew how to cook. I must have gotten it from my mother. It was probably what I slept in for the first year of my life. I know I pulled another one out of a pile of ashes behind my house in Fayetteville seventeen years ago. Tossed out by the previous tenant, I suppose. Criminal, throwing away a good black iron skillet. Nothing at all wrong with it, either, except an agglomeration of melt material, the anthracitic canker of some sort of burned-on black polycarbon. A few dozen hours with a chisel and a rotary sander and it was almost as good as new.

All the others we've gotten at estate sales and flea markets. Jayme collects things. Everything I didn't have when we met, we now have six of, and everything I had one or two of, we've got twenty. We have 6" black iron skillets, we have slope-shouldered, rounded-bottom regulation 10¼" skillets, we have steep-walled, flat-bottomed regulation 10¼-inchers. We have one truly impressive 14-incher. We have a square black iron skillet, which is great for frying bacon. We haven't found a square lid to fit it yet, but there's years of shopping ahead of us.

Once you've found your skillet, you take it home, rub the rust away with kitchen cleanser and steel wool, rinse, and dry. It's time for the cure. I've mentioned curing several times, and if you're not familiar with black iron skillets,

YOU TAKE YOUR chances at flea markets. Every now and then you buy a skillet that has a hairline crack. The crack's invisible, but when you try to cook, oil seeps through and sets the gas flame to flaring yellow, or smoke to billowing off the electric coil:

Then, too, skillets are beginning to be collectible. I hate that word, with its strangely passive attribution, its abstract nomination of a supposed value—a value that has no particular correspondence in delight or utility. Things are collectible not because they are beautiful or useful but because they are being collected. But there you are. You have to speak the argot of your time. Skillets, which *are* both beautiful and useful, are also collectible, so prices are going up. Still, if you're patient, there's no reason to pay more than five to ten dollars for a perfectly serviceable lifelong cooking companion. The same rules of selection apply as apply to new skillets. A couple of brand names to watch for: Martin Stove and Range Company, in Florence, Alabama, has made some

mighty fine skillets. With a name like that, you would think so. I have no idea whether they're still in business or whether I've been collecting the necroferric version of out-of-print first editions. Wagner, for which I have no address, does pretty well, too. The latter company is also responsible for that nice sixties-ish magnalite stuff, itself getting pretty collectible now.

Don't worry if the skillet's coated in a fine powdery rust. It just means you've got a handful of good iron. If the rust is rough, or has knotted up like a scratched mosquito bite, or has eaten down into the metal, that's another matter and you should move on to some other collectible.

And finally, just to put a lid on this discussion: You might as well shop for a skillet lid while you're at it—though, in my experience, the right lid is much harder to find than the right skillet. It's nicer aesthetically if you can come up with a matching black iron lid, but it isn't really necessary. I've been making double use of the lid from our old aluminum Dutch oven for years. It's a perfect fit for my favorite skillet and does a fine job.

you may have been puzzled. But there's nothing mysterious about the process. A couple tablespoons of oil or solid shortening, a good soft cloth. Rub the skillet with the grease inside and out. Make sure you get every square inch of it. Make that black *shine*. Then put the skillet in the oven and bake it slowly at 250°F to 300°F, for a couple or three hours. You may have to do this several times. What are we up to? Iron is friendly to lipids. It seems to have pores. It seems to absorb the slippery stuff and that's how you get your famous smooth nonstick surface.

Now try cooking. Start with something simple like pancakes. If they stick, clean the skillet out with a plastic scrubber—no steel wool this time!—and hot water, and cure it again. Now this is very important. You must *never*, under any circumstances, clean a black iron skillet with soap or detergent. I mean, it won't ruin the skillet, but it will completely strip your cure and you'll have to start all over. Once you get a black iron skillet well cured, even if food does stick a bit, all you have to do is soak the skillet briefly in hot water and scrub it out with your plastic scrubber, and it will shine like Satan's own heart.

Some food *will* stick. Sugary recipes, if you cook them down too far. Most vegetables are sugary. If you scorch them, they stick. Meat sticks if you try to cook it dry—that is, without some sustaining medium like oil or wine or water. Black iron skillets make good griddles but lousy grills. It's wise to be careful but let's face it, at some point in your life you're going to forget and leave your skillet on the burner too long, carbonizing your bananas Foster. And carbon loves to bond with iron. The situation can be remedied even so, but be ready for some serious long-term work with rubber gloves, steel wool, and the powdered cleanser.

But enough negatives. The point of this dissertation after all *is* pleasure. Understand your skillet, keep a friendly eye on its moods, and your troubles will be few, your satisfactions manifold.

What can you cook in a black iron skillet? What *can't* you cook in a black iron skillet!

Gravy. The French say sauce, and we think it's fancy. Our liquors may be plain, but I say it's all gravy. Fried chicken with milk or cream gravy, redeye gravy with ham scraps, sausage gravy white and brown. Thickened gravy with roast beef and onions, or clear concentrated gravy with roast beef and onions. Tomato gravy you already know about.

Which puts me in mind of an exception. No art is one-dimensional. I warned you how to keep things from sticking, but sometimes you *want* things to stick, right? Because then when you deglaze, with wine or coffee or whatever, you get all that glorious flavor. And after deglazing, the skillet is still cured, will come clean with a wipe and a rinse. But I should save something for later. For now, let me simply say that the black iron skillet is *the* instrument for gravy.

The black iron skillet makes a great griddle, as I've said, so think corncakes, flapjacks, crepes, omelets, salmon croquettes, French toast, grilled cheese sandwiches . . .

Soups. Vegetable soups, bean soups, thickened broths. Soups do wonders in a black iron skillet—which should be deep shouldered, of course. Cooking soup in a black iron skillet is like aging whiskey in a charred oak barrel. What you get is character.

And casseroles. And chili. I can't imagine why anyone would want to cook chili any other way. All those once-regional tomato-and-meat dishes. Spaghetti sauce, which now in America means hamburger meat, tomato sauce, and oregano. Sure, in a flash.

But don't feel you have to stay down-home. One of our favorites is when the oyster mushrooms come in. I grab a bowlful off the stump in the front yard, clean and slice them, simmer with garlic and fresh-ground black pepper in a little olive oil, and Presto! Pasta sauce! Grate some real Parmesan over all and you have a feast to warm the heart. A black iron skillet isn't a wok in the park, but it does a beautiful job of stir-frying. Put a lid on the thing and you can simmer a beef Bourguignonne worthy of the name.

I love to make crusts for the black iron skillet. Quiches. Deep, savory, masterful quiches, cheesy and rich. You make your quiche in a black iron skillet and you won't be getting any snide remarks about not being a real man. Or if you do, you can bonk the offender with the weapon at hand. Pot pies. Chicken pot pies, with dill, rosemary, garlic, carrots, mushrooms, and dumplings, baked till the crisscross strips on top are golden brown . . .

It's dark outside, and I'm getting hungry. Time to be thinking of supper. Don't know what I'll cook, but you can guess what I'm going to be cooking it *in*.

Universal Black Iron Skillet Pie Crust

This is a flaky yet robust pie crust, larger and deeper than those prepared in the average pie pan. It makes a wonderful crust for a wide variety of dishes, from quiche to pot pies to tarts and cobblers. With appropriate variations in amount of ingredients, it can be fitted in casserole dishes, standard pie pans, and a variety of other serving dishes. I include the pinch of salt even for dessert crusts, but leave it out if you prefer.

If you're concerned about the fat content of this crust, your only reasonable strategy is to avoid it or to eat very little of it. Whatever you do, do not attempt to produce a crust with less shortening in it. Excessive as the 3-to-1 ratio may seem, the butter or margarine together with a minimum of handling is what produces the exquisite flakiness, which is the only justification for a pie crust in the first place. Use too little butter or margarine and you'll likely wind up with shoe leather.

Above all, be patient with yourself—a great deal of the secret to a good pie crust is in the handling, and it may require a bit of practice before you are satisfied. But the results are definitely worth the time and trouble. Commercial crusts simply don't compare.

1½ cups unbleached white flour	½ cup margarine or butter
Pinch of salt	½ cup ice water

You may substitute lard or vegetable shortening for the margarine or butter. Do not use oils or liquid shortenings. If you want to have sufficient crust left over to make dumplings for deep-dish cobbler, increase the amount of flour to 2 cups and the margarine or butter to ⅔ cup, and otherwise follow the procedures described below.

PREPARATION TIME: 20 to 30 minutes (you get faster with experience), not including baking.

1. Mix flour and salt in a bowl. Cut in margarine or butter with a table knife or rubber spatula until mix has the consistency of cornmeal. Trickle in ice water gradually, mixing with spatula until dough will ball up. You probably won't need all of the water. Do *not* knead the dough.
2. Roll dough out on floured board, dusting both sides as needed to keep it

from sticking to the board or the rolling pin. Roll out to desired thinness. (For a truly flaky rather than stout crust, usually $\frac{1}{16}$" or less.) Roll out evenly in all directions, forming a rough circle. When the circle is 3" or 4" wider in diameter than is necessary to fill a 2"-deep, $10\frac{1}{4}$" black iron skillet, it is about the right thickness.

3. Lift the crust and fit into the skillet, then trim the edges with a knife. (The crust may tear as you lift it into the skillet. No problem. It tears because it is fragile, which means it will be truly crisp and delicate in texture. Make patches from the remnant dough, moisten the edges with ice water, and press the patches into place in the skillet.)

4. Press a dinner fork repeatedly around the edges of the crust to provide a decorative crenellation. Depending on the filling, the leftover dough may be used for stripping for the top, as with a cobbler, or as dumplings for the interior.

5. Bake as needed for particular filling. With any given dish, you generally don't want the crust to bake more than 40 to 50 minutes. If the filling is cooked ahead of time and requires less baking time, brown the crust at 375°F for 10 minutes before adding the filling.

MAKES A SINGLE PIE CRUST

REFRIGERATOR SOUP

I'm sitting here thinking about refrigerator soup. You know what I mean. You look in the refrigerator. On the meat side, half a flank steak and that left-over burger from the cookout late last week. A microwave-scarred Tupperware dish full of two-day-old green beans. Wrinkled turnips in the veggie drawer. Half a can of cream of mushroom soup. And suddenly you're overcome with a passion for salvage, neatness, resolution.

You grab the black iron skillet, pour in some olive oil, grind some black pepper, chop some garlic, mince the burger and the steak, and let's throw in that lonesome drumstick, too, the one angling from the door shelf, sheathed in crumpled aluminum. Sauté everything, so far so good. The turnips? Sure. Peel them, cube them, sauté them, too. They'll come out browned and sweet, not at all musky. Normally you wouldn't think garlic and turnips in the same dish, but this way it'll work, the flavors joining in a slightly caramel piquancy. Sprinkle in some flour, brown it.

Deglaze with a cup or two of that box wine nobody would drink at New Year's, the blush stuff—the way this is headed, the touch of sweetness is all to the good. Think better of the cream of mushroom soup? Nah, what the heck, throw it in. Add water or wine to get the mix more souplike. Gonna need more color, though. Carrots. Always a carrot or two languishing in a corner of the drawer, putting out pale yellow sprouts in the cold darkness. Clean, chop, add to the simmering brew. The green beans later, because they're already cooked almost to pieces.

Spices. Bay leaves? No, no, no, too angry for this, better with beef-and-tomato stew. Dill, no. Thyme, why bother? Marjoram? Marjoram? OK, marjoram, just a touch, and that's enough in the way of spices, don't get too enthusiastic and overwhelm all the nice commingles you've already set to commingling. Know when to say when. Time to uncork a Chardonnay or a Sauvignon Blanc and sit back and sip and think and get your digestion ready while the meal simmers and reorganizes itself like life coming into existence in the bottom of a primordial sea.

You know what I mean. Refrigerator soup.

It may seem the humblest sort of eating. It may seem a long way from the exotic international cuisines offered up in New York City or San Francisco or Miami. But I would argue that the leap is not so great as it seems. What are we after when we go out to eat Bulgarian or Polish or Zimbabwean food? (Assuming of course that we aren't Bulgarian, Polish, or Zimbabwean.) The very word *exotic* is a clue. It means, quite simply, "outside."

We're after revivification of the senses. Perhaps the greatest of all pleasures is that new awareness, to feel oneself alertly and vividly alive. It's what a fine book or movie can do for us, a splendid piece of music, a grand painting. "Everything looks so clear and sharp," my daughter Sarah said once, fresh from our visit to the National Gallery's Bierstadt exhibit, those huge canvases full of unlikely light.

For some people, food can never seem terribly important. Gustation is the lowest and most comedy prone of the senses. But it's also the most basic, the most closely connected to survival. Dining might not be high art, but it is art. And in any art, vitality counts.

Do you see where I'm headed? It may have been three hundred years ago, it may have been three thousand, but for every minestrone, every cassoulet, somewhere back there some adventurous soul looked in his or her cruse of oil, checked out the granary or the dried herbs on the wall, inspected the springhouse, and then went back to the fire and whomped up a big batch of the moral equivalent of refrigerator soup.

Some may look on the recycling of leftovers as defeat. The answer to the question the ovenbird frames in Robert Frost's poem: *What to make of a diminished thing?* I personally refuse to submit to care and boredom. I am the master of my plate, I am the captain of my *sole meunière!* Maybe all you have is cornmeal, an egg, lard, and the vegetables aren't even ripe yet. Would you have believed fried green tomatoes if you had never eaten them?

Necessity may be the mother of invention, but why so much grim emphasis on the necessity part and so little on the grand possibilities of the off-spring? Maybe because we think the birth is illegitimate. Invention wouldn't be invention if it didn't surpass the boundaries, if it didn't upset our expectations and conventions. Nothing I cook ever comes out exactly the same way twice. For me, that's the fun of cooking, trying things out. Inventing.

I admit the risks. With trial and error, you get a lot of error. One of my darkest days occurred when I was living in the Ouachita river bottoms near Arkadelphia, working as a writer-in-residence. Writers-in-residence are depressed anyway. They shouldn't be allowed near the kitchen. What happened, I decided maybe I could save some chicken livers I was a little doubtful of by sautéing them with cardamom. Listen, don't ever put cardamom and chicken livers together. It just doesn't work. Not even with good livers.

But see, even that wasn't a total loss because I returned from the horror with good advice for my fellow humans. Here's some more good advice. Don't try to rescue chicken livers. If you have even the tiniest bit of doubt, throw them to the coyotes.

I probably get my penchant for wild-card experimentation from my father, the Southern Baptist preacher. He's the one who created jalapeño chocolate cake. The way he tells it, he knew this fellow who went on and on about how much he loved jalapeño peppers. The man just couldn't get enough peppers. No matter how hot you made the dish, it didn't have enough peppers in it. So one day, for the man's birthday, Dad baked a jalapeño chocolate cake. The way my father tells it, it was a big hit. Everybody in the office loved it, and the man begged him for the recipe. That's the way my father tells it, but I don't know. He is a Baptist preacher.

Everything worth doing has risks. And suppose things do go totally wrong, what have you lost? What were you going to do with the stuff anyway, watch it turn blue-green and grow fur? Write a monograph on hitherto undiscovered icebox fungi? A few simple principles will help you avoid the worst catastrophes.

The first principle is the principle of variation. Keep an open mind. I've been referring to refrigerator soup, but actually I mean the term to imply a much broader range of possibilities. I myself prefer stews to soups. Just one more interval down the thickness scale and we're into hashes. But there are a lot of other ways to go—pot pies, fold-ups, breads, pâtés, even stir-fries.

Which leads to the second principle. Know your food. I mean this two ways. You need to know what lights up what, what flavors work well together. Invention is *not* simply a matter of throwing a bunch of odd ingredients together like a child playing chemistry. Remember the lesson of the cardamom chicken livers. On the other hand, flavor is not a simple matter. Some very sweet desserts make excellent use of fresh-ground green peppercorns, for example. It's best to think of flavor in terms of valences, of many-dimensional collections of possibilities. Nobody can tell you all the combinations, but after a while, after developing some experience, you begin to have a sense for the way *this* might go together with *that.*

The other way I mean know your food is know what you have on hand. My fridge looks as cluttered as anyone's, but I know what's in it down to the tiniest jar of sweet relish. Some might call it obsession, but I call it liking to think about food. And in idle moments or late at night as you're drifting to sleep, your subconscious mind works on the raw material, as a poet's mind works on poetry. And maybe you wake up in the morning knowing what you're going to have for supper that night. Most of the cooking is done in your mind, not in the oven.

The third principle, the principle of differential cooking, follows from knowing your food. This is the principle of *how* it's cooked. You don't necessarily throw everything in a pot and boil it. You want to prepare different ingredients in different ways in order to make the most of their possibilities. You want to combine them at just the proper moment. That's what I was up to with the sautéed turnips. I was altering their flavor and texture, which changed how they blended with the other ingredients. If I'd gone another way, if they had been fresher and I'd been making a salad, for example, I would have peeled and thinly sliced them, for a surprisingly light, sweet crunch. Differential cooking is what you're up to when you save the half cup of chicken gravy, beat it later with sour cream, and fold it into your impromptu variation on risotto.

Fourth and finally, it helps to develop a repertoire of basic strategies. You should know how to make the routine envelopes and fillers—crepes, omelets, tortillas, crusts, popovers, dumplings. Learn how to make a pâté and how to make it either sliceable or spreadable, depending on what you need. Develop a control over gravies, sauces, juices, and puddings. You need to know how to make a good shortbread (and you already do, because biscuits are shortbread). You should know how to make a good yeast-rising bread and how eggs will behave under a wide variety of cooking conditions.

Down the road, we'll get to some of these basic strategies. Just remember that every recipe you read is a formula for a particular case, but it is more—it is also a clue to the general principles that help you make sense of the art of cooking.

EATING EASTER

I'm trying to remember when I first realized I didn't like Easter eggs. I don't mean I didn't like making them and hiding them and finding them. I loved the hexagonal wire dippers and the smell of the vinegar from the cups of hot dye. I loved the little wax pencil you wrote messages with, messages that were invisible until you baptized your egg in color. And hunting for Easter eggs was the essence of spring: rare gems hidden in the fresh grass, in the beds of soft clover.

No, I mean when I realized I didn't like eating them. Jayme says you *don't* eat them, that it's a wonder I didn't die of salmonella. But for me it was completion, follow-through. Your folks hide the ones you made and the secret ones they made, and it's a sunny Sunday afternoon, and maybe you don't find the most, but you've got a nice basket of beauties there, tucked into that shredded green stuff, that Easter straw. What is there left to do but take them home and eat them?

We had ours for Sunday supper. It used to drive me crazy, waiting. The rest of the long drowsy afternoon, and then Training Union, and then preaching service, and then standing around while the grown-ups talked and talked, and then finally, FINALLY, home, and *let me at 'em!*

And that was when the letdown hit. For years I didn't realize that the letdown was connected to eating the eggs. I thought it was just being tired and having to go back to school Monday morning. But it was the eggs. They weren't *bad*. I like a nice cold boiled egg now and then, with salt and pepper. Great with a beer, a tin of sardines, and a couple green onions. No, they weren't bad. Just ordinary, nothing like the feast they had been for the eyes. I would wind up sated but not stimulated, a messy confetti of eggshell on one side of my plate, one last bitten-in-half fingerprinted egg rolling around on the other. Maybe that's why eating and Easter seem so deeply connected to me now, the memory of all those unsatisfactory eggs.

Easter is a ceremony of renewal. We love finding things in the grass. If we could find rebirth there, that would be the greatest find of all, the prize egg. At first glance, the egg seems a proper symbol of that rebirth: a single original gamete, the beginning from which a life will follow.

But the rabbit. I don't know where the confounded rabbit came from. A conflated fertility symbol, probably. I never had any use for the rabbit. I believed in Santa Claus for a while, and the tooth fairy, but the rabbit never fooled me for a second.

Anyway, the egg might be a pretty good symbol, except we take it and drop it in water bubbling at 100°C. A hard-boiled symbol, you might say. We like our symbols dead, you might say. Don't like 'em living and loose, subject to reinterpretation, running around out there where they can actually change our lives.

Which is precisely the disappointment I felt as a child, eating my eggs. The worst of all feelings to a child is the feeling that all this will never change, that there's no way out, that the promise and glory are merely superficial. That what begins as a deep longing will always and only wind up as the mere stifling of a physical appetite. At best.

And which is, to me, the central conundrum of existence. And which is why we need ceremonies and Easters. The basic condition of this earth is that life kills life. You can call it original sin or you can call it survival of the fittest. But whatever you call it, it's a fact, a universal fact. Not one of us escapes it. In the act of living, we cause other creatures to die. This is the lifeless center under all the color, the dry mouthful that chokes me midswallow.

In one way or another all of our religions try to explain this fact, or explain it away.

I know others who worry. They may believe in God, and life after death, and redemption, and they may not, but regardless, they want to do as little damage as possible while they're here. Like the Buddhists, they respect all life and seek to avoid causing harm to the smallest insect.

Some refuse to eat veal, for example, because of the inhumane way in which the calves are raised and slaughtered. Some don't eat beef of any sort, or pork, or mutton. If they eat chicken they ask for free-range chicken. They prefer seafood. It's easy to make fun of that sort of California earnestness, but still. It's one thing to kill in order to eat and it is quite another to disrupt and mechanize the life cycle of an entire species, emptying it of whatever natural dignity and meaning it might have had. I suspect that when our children's children look back at how we made a factory process of birth and growth, they will see us as abysmal savages.

I know people who carry their concern even further: vegetarians, who eat nothing but vegetables, eggs, and milk products; vegans, who avoid all animal protein; and fruitarians, who eat nothing but the fruiting bodies of plants.

I admire them all, but you mistake me if you think I'm preaching against Tyson or Jimmy Dean or red meat. We could correct some of the abuses we visit on other species, but I'm not sure we can correct them all. There are too many humans. We aren't going to raise enough free-range chickens to feed our families, not if we cut down every forest on earth. If we double our arable land and double its productivity, we still will not raise enough grain and beans to stave off protein deficiencies in next century's children. I vote yes for sustainable agriculture, but until we quit birthing so many of our own, we will continue, inevitably, to strip the planet.

Besides, I have problems with vegetarianism. If you argue respect for nature, then you must admit that nature has designed us as omnivores: We don't have vegetarian teeth — twenty of our twenty-eight to thirty-two are for cutting and tearing, not plucking and grinding. There is strong evidence our digestion is not geared for the exclusive consumption of plants. And who says plants have fewer rights than animals, anyway? What's the dividing line? Possession of a nervous system? How provincial of us vertebrates. Watch one of those time-lapse films of flowers growing and tell me you don't see purpose and direction, dance and seduction. The real reason we don't think plants are as vital as we are is that they live at a different speed. We can't *see* what they're doing.

No, for me, life is life. I can't escape the problem of appetite by constructing hierarchies: *This* is less alive than *that,* so it's more OK to eat it. So where does that leave me? I'm not going to confine myself to fruits, grains, nuts, beans, stalks, and tubers, and I'm not going to walk around bowed down by guilt and sorrow at the tragedy of life.

I plan to celebrate anyway, to try to enjoy life's glories and accept my losses.

I hope nothing eats me, I'd fight if something tried, but if I were to lose, how could I cry foul? Manitou, I offer tribute to the soul of this deer. Lord bless this food I eat. Humans say such words. We probably don't really understand them till we hear them floating past our own fading ears.

So in that spirit, let me suggest an Easter brunch, something warm and aromatic to settle down to after the sunrise service. It's just a concession to our tender consciences, but we'll even make the meal meat free. (We'll find a way to make those eggs taste good.)

Let's start with a yard salad, a modified Waldorf. Wash and destem a fresh bunch of spinach and let it drain. Wash and core (but don't peel) a good crisp apple and chop it into bite-size sections. Clean anywhere from half a cup to a cup of pecan halves, depending on how many you want. Now go out and pick a dozen small fresh dandelion leaves, a half cup or so (loosely packed) of pink sorrel leaves, and a good handful of tender, green oniongrass, then wash and drain your harvest. Dandelion leaves are a real tonic, but they're quite bitter so you don't want too many. Sorrel is that tart, green, shamrocky stuff we used to call rabbit clover. It has a lot of vitamin C. The tartness is mostly oxalic acid, which is dangerous in large doses. (Half a cup is just fine, don't worry.) *Don't* go picking anything out of your yard if you or your neighbors use chemicals — we take the Grand Prairie approach to lawn care, ourselves.

I should also say that if you don't have a yard full of dandelion and sorrel, or are not confident in your wild crop identification, it is certainly no cop-out to buzz by the local market and substitute a couple of fresh and likely-looking commercial greens.

Chop the dandelion leaves, tear the spinach, then toss with the sorrel, the apple, and the pecans. Set aside in the refrigerator. I'm using pecans, by the way, because the wild produce gives our salad plenty of edge. We don't need the additional bitterness of walnuts.

Chop the oniongrass but put it aside for later. You're not going to use it in the salad.

For the dressing, blend two-thirds of a cup of olive oil, a third of a cup of white wine vinegar, a teaspoon of minced fresh tarragon, a tablespoon of honey, a pinch of sea salt, and freshly ground pepper to taste. I think salad dressing should always be about two-to-one oil to vinegar. Too much vinegar, and it doesn't have enough body and cling. Too much oil, and you lose flavor.

Never dress your salad ahead of time, the vinegar will cook it. Always dress the salad just before serving.

Our main course will be quiche, aux fines herbes, baked of course in a 10¼" black iron skillet. Wisely, you've made the dough ahead of time and set it in the fridge to relax. I'll tell you how you did it (see the detailed recipe on page 21). You knew that the basic rule for crust is a three-to-one, flour-to-shortening (or butter or margarine) ratio, and that with slight variations in handling, this ratio would produce anything from the hearty foundation of a good pot pie to the flaky membrane of a delectable chocolate meringue. You preferred, just as I do, plain unbleached white flour to the typical bleached and "enriched" stuff, and you used butter or margarine instead of lard. One and a half cups of flour is about right for a skillet-size quiche (plenty of tasty dough bits left over), so you used half a cup of butter or margarine (one stick). You cut the butter or margarine in, with maybe a sprinkle of sea salt. Then carefully, carefully, you mixed in a few tablespoons of ice water, just enough to allow the dough to cling and ball up—probably no more than four at the most—knowing that with so much butter or margarine, you don't need much fluid. You knew better than to knead the dough, and you knew the little trick of wrapping it for the fridge in the wax paper from the butter or margarine. Then you rolled the dough out wide enough to lap over the rim of the skillet, dusting lightly with flour to keep the batch from sticking. You lifted the result and fit it in the skillet, trimming off the excess. You crenellated the edges with the tines of a fork, just like my mother does.

The filling is easy. Beat ten eggs (a dozen if you want to leave out three yolks as a gesture toward cholesterol reduction). Add a half cup of heavy cream, the chopped oniongrass, two teaspoons of dried dill, two teaspoons minced fresh marjoram, a healthy dose of fresh-ground black pepper, and a teaspoon of salt, then beat again till thoroughly mixed. Shred one loosely packed cup of Monterey Jack into the waiting crust, pour the egg mixture over it, place the whole thing in the oven at about 375°F, and get ready to chill the champagne. You're going to top your quiche with more Monterey Jack in about fifteen minutes. You want the cheese to melt and fuse nicely with the rest of the filling, but you don't want it to scorch.

Your champagne—OK, sparkling wine—needn't be expensive. There are a lot of acceptable options in the ten- to twenty-dollar range. Just make sure the label says *Méthode Champenoise* and not *Charmat bulk process*. I favor a dry champagne myself, so I usually pick a *blanc de blancs* rather than a *clasico* or any of the fruity or pinkoid varieties.

By the time you settle your bottle in an ice bucket, twirl it, and drape it with a linen towel—say twenty minutes or so of cooking time—the quiche is probably ready for more cheese. Another cup or so across the top—in thin slices, not grated. Slide the skillet back in for another twenty minutes, more or less.

What for dessert? How about French vanilla ice cream (*not* ice milk) with hot homemade butterscotch topping, and some strong dark coffee?

It would be nice if the weather was pretty. Let's say it is, the sun shining and the small grass waving, and you dine out on your deck or at the picnic table in the backyard. Set the warm savory quiche on its trivet. Say the blessing. Clink a glass of bubbling champers with your friend or *posslq*, and lift a toast: *Here's to appetite. Here's to Easter. Here's to life.*

Yard Salad

1 small bunch fresh spinach
12 dandelion leaves
½ cup pink sorrel leaves, loosely packed

1 apple, cored and cut into bite-size pieces
½ cup pecan halves

For dressing:
Pinch of sea salt
1 tablespoon honey
⅓ cup white wine vinegar

Freshly ground pepper, to taste
1 teaspoon minced fresh tarragon
⅔ cup olive oil

You may substitute appropriate fresh greens for the dandelion and sorrel leaves.

PREPARATION TIME: 30 minutes.

To prepare salad:
1. Wash and destem spinach.
2. Pick dandelion and sorrel leaves and wash them.
3. Coarsely chop dandelion leaves and tear spinach, then toss dandelion, sorrel, and spinach together in a stainless-steel bowl.
4. Put aside in refrigerator to drain and cool.
5. When drained, pour off excess water and add apple and pecans. Toss with salad dressing immediately before serving.

To prepare salad dressing:
1. Dissolve sea salt and honey in white wine vinegar.
2. Add pepper and tarragon and stir, then add to olive oil in a cruet.
3. Shake dressing vigorously to blend before dressing salad. You'll need only 3 to 4 tablespoons for 2 servings of this salad, so save the remaining dressing for later use.

SERVES 2

Here are a few different kinds of quiche you can try. Basic quiche ingredients are listed in the first recipe.

Easter Quiche in a Black Iron Skillet

1 Universal Black Iron Skillet Pie Crust (see page 21)

Basic quiche ingredients:
10 medium eggs
½ cup heavy cream
1 teaspoon salt
Freshly ground pepper, to taste

2 cups Monterey Jack cheese, 1 cup shredded and 1 cup sliced thin

For Easter quiche add:
⅓ cup chopped oniongrass
2 teaspoons dried dill

2 teaspoons minced fresh marjoram

You may substitute other herbs as desired. Green onion tops make a fine substitution for the oniongrass, but the flavor is stronger, so use less. If fresh marjoram is not available, dried will do (but you'll need only about ¼ teaspoon).

TOTAL PREPARATION AND BAKING TIME: 1 to 1½ hours, including 20 to 30 minutes' crust preparation time.

1. Preheat oven to 375°F.
2. Beat eggs with cream until thoroughly blended. Add salt, pepper, oniongrass, and other herbs and beat lightly. Add the shredded cheese and again beat lightly.
3. Pour into prepared skillet pie crust and place in oven.
4. Bake for approximately 20 minutes.
5. Remove quiche from oven and layer top with slices of Monterey Jack cheese, then return to oven for another 20 to 30 minutes, until crust is lightly browned and cheese is bubbling.

SERVES 4 TO 5

Spinach Quiche

1 Universal Black Iron Skillet Pie Crust (see page 21)

In addition to basic quiche ingredients, use:

1 pound frozen or two bunches
  fresh spinach
3 tablespoons butter
1 teaspoon dried dill

1 teaspoon dry mustard
2 tablespoons Parmesan
  cheese, grated

TOTAL PREPARATION AND BAKING TIME: 1 to 1½ hours, including 20 to 30 minutes' crust preparation time.

1. Preheat oven to 375°F.
2. If spinach is fresh, clean and destem it.
3. Sauté spinach in the butter and enough water to keep from sticking, until tender. Add dill and mustard and stir till thoroughly

mixed and water has evaporated. Add Parmesan and half the cream and stir over low heat with a fork or whisk until thoroughly mixed. Set aside.

4. Beat eggs with remaining cream, blending thoroughly. Add salt and pepper to taste. Lightly beat in cooked spinach, leaving swirls. Add the shredded Monterey Jack cheese and again beat lightly.

5. Pour into prepared pie crust. Proceed with baking instructions given in the Easter quiche recipe (page 34).

SERVES 4 TO 5

Ham-and-Scallop Quiche

1 Universal Black Iron Skillet Pie Crust (see page 21)

In addition to basic quiche ingredients, use:
1 pound sea scallops   ¼ pound cured ham
3 tablespoons butter or
  margarine

TOTAL PREPARATION AND BAKING TIME: 1 to 1½ hours, including 20 to 30 minutes' crust preparation time.

1. Preheat oven to 375°F.
2. Drain scallops.
3. Mill fresh pepper into hot butter in skillet. Sauté scallops rapidly in hot butter, tossing to brown evenly—no longer than 3 minutes in all. Set aside.
4. Finely dice the ham, making sure to cut away any fat or gristle. (Ham should be of the finest quality, tender and smoked rather than sugar-cured, and not injected with water.) Set aside.
5. Beat eggs with cream until thoroughly blended. Lightly beat the ham and scallops into the egg mixture. Add salt and pepper to taste. Add the shredded Monterey Jack cheese and again beat lightly.
6. Pour into prepared pie crust. Proceed with baking instructions given in the Easter quiche recipe (page 34).

SERVES 4 TO 5

SEAFOOD AND THE SEA

So I have a fantasy about losing weight to get ready for the beach. I have this other fantasy, that *I will actually lose weight and shape up while I'm there.*

I get this fantasy from television ads, usually for beer. We all know better. Beer makes you fat, not trim. But I see myself loping along the surf line just the same, tan and lean. I tell myself I'll stick to grilled fish and shrimp and oysters, high protein all the way.

The first long run usually shocks me back to reality. *Shock* is the word. The packed sand beats and blasts my legs. Welcome to your summer case of shin-splints, Jack. Time to think about that hip replacement? Isn't it strange how you forgot that the surf line slopes, so running out you feel like you're pounding one leg shorter than the other. And then running back doesn't even matters out but instead leaves you feeling like both legs are shorter than each other.

And the food, yes, the food. Actually, if you were able to stick to fish and shrimp and oysters, you could do OK. No, my problem is the biscuits I have every morning, dreaming how the brisk gulf air will burn off all the extra calories. Or the blue corn chips and homemade salsa, which go so great with the midafternoon margarita. The heaps of tender pumpkin tortellini our New York buddies flew in, freshly cooked and steaming and glistening with oil and heaped with shavings from a hard chunk of genuine Parmesan. The pint of ice cream with the evening brownies, the strawberry shortcake, the blackberry cobbler . . .

Once you relax and accept the fact that you've come to the beach not to look like somebody in an advertisement, but to read yourself into a stupor, sleep, lay out, chase dolphins in the chilling water, come back and lay out some more, have a couple of beers, fly a kite, play computer games for hours, and generally eat, drink, relax, and get fat, things get better. You can quit eating shrimp and oysters because they're good for you and start eating them because they're great.

Is there anything *better* than fresh oysters? I'll admit, I didn't come to them happily. I've always liked them fried, but my first experience with raw oysters occurred during an athletic club initiation in my college days. It involved swallowing a bivalve that had a string tied around it, a string whose other end was attached to the hand of one of the officers of the club. Not enough that I threw up after every track meet, now I had to do it at initiation, too.

Fortunately, I've long since outgrown the trauma. I love shrimp, I love scallops, but I *really* love fresh raw oysters. Best of all is to stand there in the packinghouse slurping from a just-off-the-boat shell that one of the shuckers has cracked open. Second best is to belly up to a good oyster bar, like say the ones in New Orleans, while the guy in the apron, the one with the short sharp knife and the heavy-duty rubber gloves, tries to keep ahead of you.

But I tell you what, standing in the beach house pulling them out of a fresh pint with a fork isn't a bad third. Nearly every day we sent one of our group mainland for fresh seafood. Maybe we'd grill a big beautiful fish for dinner, snapper or mullet or grouper. Maybe fry up a batch of soft shell crab. But for me the appetizers were the highlight. While whoever was cooking that night was beginning to work up the menu, we'd all gather around the kitchen counter. Somebody would have boiled a pound or two of fresh shrimp and put them on ice. Somebody else would have cut lemons into eight wedges each and made dishes of cocktail sauce. And we'd crack a few Bass ales or Coronas and gather around the food like a flock of squawking seagulls.

The very memory makes me happy. I hope your next summer brings you such fine times.

In the event it does, and just so we can compare happiness, let me conclude with my notion of the perfect way to eat a raw oyster. Freshness counts. Oh, oysters that have been flown in on ice can be wonderful. But nothing compares to the taste of a giant bivalve still salty with the bay water it was pulled from early that morning while it was dark and you were sound asleep.

Make sure you have an icy cold beer standing by. You're going to need it. Put your oyster on a wheat cracker—purists prefer saltines, I admit, but try the

OYSTERS AND CRACKERS aren't quite enough. You need some sort of cocktail sauce for the oyster, something with a little sharpness, piquancy, kick. I have known people to put damn near anything on a raw oyster, from Worcestershire sauce to mustard (neither of which I would recommend). I myself have employed condiments as varied as Tabasco sauce, pepper sauce, balsamic vinegar, lemon juice, fresh-milled peppercorns, and Jamaican Pickapeppa Sauce.

Jayme shows a distinct fondness for juice squeezed fresh from a lemon, but I think this is partly because, after she finishes with the oysters, she likes to dump sugar on the remaining fragments of citrus and eat them, rinds and all, for dessert.

In this one area I am, I must confess, something of a purist. I have come to feel that the only appropriate cocktail sauce for raw oysters is the classic mix of two ingredients only—ketchup and horseradish in about a three-to-one ratio (adjusted for your own sensibilities, of course).

wheat cracker. The oyster is so fat it laps over the edges, dripping on your fingers. Put a full teaspoon of cocktail sauce, which also drips on your fingers, on top. Lift the cracker, place the whole thing in your mouth at once, bite, chew, and swallow.

The sweet slide of the good meat, the crunch and salt of the cracker, the kick of the horseradish vaporizing your nose and turning your eyes to hot liquid, and you swallow, and now, now, before you melt down completely, a long cold gulp of beer—

Ahhhhhh. You're there. It's summer, it's the sea, and you're there at last.

GOING WILD WITH BLACKBERRIES

Normally, when I think of idle days on the beach, blackberry cobbler isn't the first thing to spring to mind. But I'm thinking of it now because probably the best blackberry cobbler I ever had I had here on the beach. Really these were dewberries, not blackberries. Close enough. We all went down into the whirling hosts of bay mosquitoes and picked, not two blocks from the house we'd rented, gallons of wild berries. Then came back up and spent the evening making and eating cobbler, all the time talking and laughing and going outside to watch for dolphins or just listen to the surf or, later, to check out the constellations.

June is a good time of year to talk about blackberry cobbler, because this is about the time the wild blackberries are starting to come in. All across the hot and humid South, from June into even maybe sometimes early August, the berries are fattening up and getting darker. I know for a fact they grow all along the San Francisco cliffs as well, overlooking the Pacific, but I can't say what the season is there. San Francisco is such a weird town, never very warm but never very cold either, so everything grows all the time, figs to eucalyptus.

All my life they've been there for the picking, the blackberries. I grew up thinking they were probably mentioned in the Bill of Rights. I remember picking buckets and buckets of them simply from the fencerow, walking down a gravel road in early June.

I know people are growing blackberries commercially now, but I don't really see the point. Picking them wild is just too wonderful. It's true, you pay a price. Along that gravel road, you and the berries both wind up covered in red dust. But hey, it washes off. And of course you're going to get scratched. The little barbs are perfectly curved to allow you to reach in after that one really fat

A LOT OF people don't know the difference between blackberries and dewberries. They're close cousins, both in the rose family. So are, interestingly enough, apples and pears, and indeed almost all five-petaled flowering plants, whether trees, bushes, or vines.

A little terminology: Blackberries and dewberries grow on long thorny stems, which are called canes. The first-year cane, the primocane, doesn't flower or bear fruit. Later canes, because they do flower and bear fruit, are called floricanes. Now for the differences. Dewberries have a smooth round cane, like 'roses, and their barbs are softer and more numerous, almost hairlike at times. The blackberry's cane is quintipartite, like five smaller round canes glued together, and has stiff hard barbs. The fruit of the blackberry is usually smaller and more tart than that of the dewberry, which is a good thing to keep in mind because it will make a big difference in the taste of your cobbler. (Modern cultivated blackberries, however, are an exception— the size of your thumb, they are giant and placid packets of purple saccharine.)

jewel, then snag you as you pull your hand back out. And you're going to get hot and sweaty and itchy, because odds are, you're going to be standing in knee- to waist-high grass and weed and bramble. Speaking of which, you'd better dose up pretty heavily with repellent before you head out or later in the week you'll die the Death of a Thousand Chiggers. Insect life in general will be at a max, giant hoppers rattling away in the stalks, making you jump every time they jump. Flies, gnats, ticks. The mosquitoes I've already mentioned. Those pungent little shield beetles—stinkbugs as we used to call them—they like the blackberries as much as you do. Just hope you don't pop one in your mouth along with a berry like I did once.

No, wild-blackberry picking is not to everyone's taste. You have to develop the fierceness of the artist, one who welcomes the long ordeal if it leads to sublime enlightenment.

Ah, the cobbler. Here's a quick recipe. If you want to serve about six very hungry people and maybe have a bit left over to eat with breakfast coffee, use a 10¼" skillet. You will need roughly four cups of washed berries. First prepare your crust, using any good recipe (like the one I gave you on page 21, the three-to-one, flour-to-shortening ratio, if you remember). For a crust this size, use about two cups of flour—you want plenty of dough left over to cut up into strips for the top.

Jayme likes to cook her berries first, and I prefer not to. In either case, you will need from half a cup to a cup of sugar, depending on the tartness of the fruit. The sugar also helps draw the juice out of the berries. If you cook the berries down, add the sugar and a touch of butter and simmer for a while, thickening with a bit of flour or cornstarch. (You have to dissolve the thickeners in a little cold water first, of course—you can't just stir them right in, you'll get lumps. This is one of those basic principles of cooking, so basic that I almost forgot to mention it. Since the question has arisen, however, let me reiterate—starches and flours will *not* dissolve in hot fluid. They must be predissolved in cold liquid before you heat them to thicken.)

What I prefer to do is layer the fresh berries in on the crust and dust each layer with a flour/sugar/butter mix (half a cup of flour, half a cup of sugar, and a tablespoon of butter does very nicely), then sprinkle more sugar over the top. The juice, mixing with this dry roux, will thicken nicely as the cobbler cooks.

You're almost ready to go—roll out the remaining dough and slice it into strips, then crisscross the strips on top. If you're a perfectionist, you'll interweave them, but I'm usually too hungry to take that much time. It makes a nice effect to sprinkle the top-crust lattice with large-crystal turbinado sugar, but even a sprinkling of regular white granular is pleasant. Pop the dish in the oven and bake it at 350°F to 375°F for forty minutes or so, checking regularly.

You'll have noticed we didn't make our cobbler too overly sweet. This isn't because we're trying to cut down on carbohydrates—cutting down on carbohydrates when you're eating a cobbler is about like cutting down on wine at a wedding. When you celebrate, celebrate.

No, it's because it tastes better that way. And because you'll like the way the tartness contrasts with the buttery richness of the vanilla ice cream. Is there any color on earth more lovely than the royal purple of those berries trickling down over the white cold ice cream, mingling and changing? Eat the cobbler fast, before the ice cream melts.

Wild Blackberry Cobbler

1 Universal Black Iron Skillet Pie Crust (see page 21, but use 2 cups flour and ⅔ cup margarine or butter)

| 1 tablespoon butter or margarine | 1 cup sugar |
| ½ cup unbleached white flour | 4 cups fresh or frozen blackberries |

If you are using frozen berries, you do not have to thaw them first, though you may wish to lower your baking temperature 5 to 10 degrees and add 10 minutes of baking time. This basic cobbler recipe can be used for a wide range of fruits, with changes to allow for variations in sweetness and juiciness. Don't be afraid to experiment with other berries or stoned fruits. (Avoid strawberries, though, since they are best fresh or in jams or syrups—they don't bake well.) Try out one of the variations that follow this recipe. With a little practice, it's practically fail-safe. For what we like to call a black-and-blue cobbler, substitute 2 cups of fresh or frozen blueberries for 2 cups of the blackberries.

TOTAL PREPARATION AND BAKING TIME: 1¼ to 1½ hours, not including picking the berries.

1. Preheat oven to 375°F.
2. In a mixing bowl, cut butter or margarine into flour until mix is consistency of cornmeal. Then thoroughly mix in ¼ cup to ½ cup of the sugar, according to taste.

3. Layer the prepared crust with about a third of the berries.
4. Sprinkle this layer liberally with about a third of the remaining sugar and then sprinkle it with a third of the butter-flour-sugar mix.
5. Roll out dough scraps as thin as you can make them and top the layer of berries. (You don't have to cover the berries completely, as this layer of dough serves to create dumplings.)
6. Repeat this process twice more, so that you have 3 layers of berries and your skillet is full. For the final layer of berries, you may wish to cut your dough into strips for a latticework top crust or into other decorative shapes.
7. Sprinkle the top crust lightly with sugar.
8. Put cobbler in oven. Check it after 40 minutes, although it may need another 10 minutes or so. It is done when the crust is browning lightly and the dark juices are bubbling up through the top crust.

SERVES 8 TO 10

Jayme's Summertime Dream Peach Cobbler

1 Universal Black Iron Skillet Pie Crust (see page 21, but use 2 cups flour and $\frac{2}{3}$ cup margarine or butter)

10 to 12 fresh ripe peaches $\frac{1}{2}$ cup sugar
Juice of $\frac{1}{2}$ lemon or 1 lime

You may use about 3 cups of frozen peaches instead of fresh. With frozen peaches, however, unlike blackberries or blueberries, you should thaw before cooking, since the peach slices need to marinate a bit and produce their sweet liquor. If anything, this cobbler served hot with substantial scoops of French vanilla ice cream is even more delectable than the blackberry cobbler. Which is good enough reason not to oversugar your peaches—the ice cream will provide sweetness aplenty.

TOTAL PREPARATION AND BAKING TIME: $1\frac{1}{2}$ to 2 hours.

1. Peel and slice the peaches into a medium-size mixing bowl. In peeling, waste as little of the meat of the fruit as possible. If the peaches are perfectly ripened, you will often be able to slip a

knife blade just under the skin and pull off a wide strip cleanly, leaving all the meat below.

2. Through a small strainer, squeeze the lemon or lime juice over the sliced peaches and then sprinkle the peaches with a couple of teaspoons of the sugar.

3. Let the peaches sit and brew in their liquor while you prepare the crust.

4. Preheat oven to 375°F.

5. When crust is ready, layer it with about half your peaches.

6. Sprinkle this layer liberally with about half the remaining sugar.

7. Roll out dough scraps as thin as you can make them and top the layer of peaches. (Again you don't have to cover them completely, as this layer of dough serves to create dumplings.)

8. Repeat this process once more, so that you have 2 layers of peaches and your skillet is full. For the final layer, you may wish to cut your dough into strips for a latticework top crust or into other decorative shapes.

9. Sprinkle the top crust lightly with sugar.

10. Proceed with baking instructions in Wild Blackberry Cobbler (page 43).

SERVES 8 TO 10

Crumbly Caketop Cobblers

1 Universal Black Iron Skillet Pie Crust (see page 21)

Fresh or frozen fruit of your
choice (use measurements
given in previous 2 recipes
as a guide)
1/4 cup plus 2 teaspoons butter
or margarine

1 cup unbleached white flour
1/2 cup sugar
1/2 cup buttermilk

I've pieced together this recipe from memories of the cobblers my mother made when I was a child. It substitutes a buttery cake topping for the dumplings and top crust given in the other cobbler recipes.

TOTAL PREPARATION AND BAKING TIME: About 1½ hours, depending on preparation of fruit.

1. Prepare fruit.
2. Preheat oven to 375°F.
3. In a mixing bowl, cut the butter or margarine into the flour until the mix is the consistency of cornmeal. Then thoroughly mix in ½ cup sugar. Set aside ½ cup of the butter-flour-sugar mix for sprinkling the top of the cobbler.
4. Beat buttermilk into the remaining butter-flour-sugar mix until you have a thick but pourable batter.
5. Layer the prepared crust with half the fruit and pour half of your batter over this layer.
6. Add the remaining fruit and again cover with batter.
7. Sprinkle the remaining ½ cup dry butter-flour-sugar mix over the top.
8. Put cobbler in oven. Check it after 40 minutes, although it may need another 10 minutes or so. It is done when the top is lightly brown and developing a slight crunchiness. As with the other cobblers, serve hot with substantial scoops of French vanilla ice cream.

SERVES 8 TO 10

FAMILY SECRETS

It's really a comedown to get back from the beach and resume my life. I mean, I always have a happy little lurch of feeling when we pull up finally at our very own front yard. Home, and look at all the new things blooming that weren't there when we left.

But then it's back to work, back to the routine, back to that old quotidian drag.

These are the times when I need comfort food. I no longer have the romance of exotic mussels or batter-fried arthropods to beguile me. Now I need the old tried-and-true, the stuff that got me through the bewilderment of early childhood, the horrible hundred months of adolescence, the bleak decade of my twenties.

We learn about food, if we're lucky, in the way we learn about life. We begin with the near and dear, the often repeated—the familiar. We develop favorites and we develop antipathies, foods we love to hate, but which show up on our plates despite all our complaints, with the regularity of rainy Mondays. My mother, who is on the whole a fabulous cook, never could get oatmeal right. I love oatmeal cooked with a touch of salt till the kernels are just plump, then laced with brown sugar and butter and real cream. She produced—I'm sorry, Mom, but it's true—an overcooked gruel with the approximate consistency of warm Elmer's Glue.

We develop quirks, too, things we profess to like that nobody else does. My father has always been loud in his praises of what he calls "leathernecks," extremely tough snap beans boiled for roughly a year, and so stringy you flossed yourself automatically as you chewed.

As we mature, we begin to look beyond the family.

We learn that the food we grew up with isn't the only sort of food there is. Your neighbor down the road, Southern to the bone but the daughter of a German mother, serves a thing called hot potato salad, and she puts *mustard* in it. And the farther afield we go, the wilder it gets. Why, there's people who eat vegetables that don't even *grow* in America. There's people who eat worms, and poison blowfish, and bread made from pounded-up palm trees.

At this point people take different paths. Some, intimidated by novelty and strangeness, decide nothing is any good except what they grew up with. A modification of this syndrome is reactionary regionalism. It happens in all cultures, but Southerners are touchier than most.

I cross over the line from time to time. I love to explain to New Yorkers how they don't even know how to *pronounce* "pecan," let alone how to bake a good pecan pie. But I'm as narrow-minded as any Manhattanite, I admit. My producer-friend John Levy introduced me to fish soup in a Thai restaurant once, and I confess I never intend to try it again because I think it's brewed mostly of fish skeletons and plutonium-irradiated cayenne peppers.

All of which is to say, that isn't the spirit in which this book is offered. I want to celebrate the local and the peculiar without encouraging the merely provincial.

I plan to offer you one of our old family secrets just a few sentences down the road. Let me be clear, though: I'm not talking Spam fried in cornmeal batter here, because almost everybody I know grew up on that. What I'm talking about is something that, when I was a kid, I thought everybody had every Wednesday, but that in fact almost nobody made and ate but my own extended clan, unique in our culinary oddity.

Ever heard of pork-and-bean sandwiches? They must have come from one of those meat-sparing wartime recipes in probably *Collier's* or *Pageant* magazine, but I've never met anybody outside my immediate family who's had one. Heartsmart readers, tune out here. Meat-sparing they may have been, but pork-and-bean sandwiches are *not* fat-sparing.

You need a can of pork and beans, four slices of good bread, four to eight slices of bacon, a nice onion (Vidalia if you've got it), and four bread-size slices of mild cheddar. My mother always used store-bought, sliced white bread, it being such a novelty when she was young—a taste of the finer flours previously available only to the wealthy. I myself prefer a good sturdy whole grain loaf for flavor and texture. Toast the bread lightly so it will hold up under the beans. Ladle a quarter of the can of beans onto each slice and top with thin slices of onion.

In the true wartime version, you'd use one strip of bacon per sandwich, cut in half and laid to cover the onion slices. But by the time I was old enough to remember, the war was over, and we were using two slices each, crisscrossed. Mom would put the bacon on raw and let it cook while the sandwiches baked. I prefer the finished product crisper, so I brown the bacon first, lightly. You want to leave it at least partly uncooked, because the juices are going to sizzle and seep down and richen the taste. Bake the sandwiches at 400°F for ten or fifteen minutes, watching carefully to make sure you don't burn the bread (the crust is *supposed* to get a little black). Put the cheese on with just a couple of minutes to go, so it will melt thoroughly but not scorch and blister.

The perfect beverage? A nice glass of milk, chilled to a fare-thee-well. Plain and funky fare, but it made us more than a few satisfying suppers when times were lean.

Postwar Pork-and-Bean Sandwiches

8 strips lean bacon
4 slices whole wheat bread
One 16-ounce can pork and beans

4 to 6 thin slices Vidalia onion
4 bread-size slices cheddar
  cheese

TOTAL PREPARATION AND COOKING TIME: 20 to 25 minutes.

1. Preheat oven to 400°F.
2. Brown the bacon lightly and drain on brown paper.
3. Toast the bread slices very lightly, then arrange on a baking tray.
4. Spoon a quarter of the can of pork and beans onto each slice of bread.

5. Cover the beans with onion slices and then crisscross the onion with 2 strips of bacon for each slice of bread.
6. Put in oven and bake for about 10 minutes, watching carefully.
7. Remove and top bacon with slices of cheddar.
8. Return to oven and bake until cheese just melts.

SERVES 4

THE NOBLEST BEAN OF ALL

As long as I'm going down-home, I might as well talk about the down-homiest vegetable of all. Forget bread as the staff of life. It was butterbeans that kept us going.

We all had gardens back then. Out the front door and hang a right, and there it was, bordering the yard. Enough tall corn for a five-year-old to feel lost in.

When they talked about the Garden of Eden in Sunday school, I saw staked-up tomatoes, rows of turnip greens. Black earth that stuck between the toes of your bare feet. Couldn't understand why Adam and Eve didn't sweat their brows until *after* they got kicked out, since in my experience a garden demanded plenty of sweat from all over your body.

Gardens went with yards very well. They don't go so well with lawns. You sort of have to do more landscaping. Put a little decorative fence around your vegetable plot and keep the rows well manicured so the neighbors understand you're not going totally primitive, you're just making a nostalgic gesture. It's a little unseemly nowadays to raise all your own truck. Next thing you know, you might be plucking chickens and scalding hogs.

It occurs to me that we've lost a social class. It used to be possible to be honorably poor. To be a respected and hardworking member of your community and yet never wear a new suit or drive a new car. You could work hard in your garden and keep your family as well fed as the richest man in the biggest house and not have to bow your head to anyone, not even bankers.

Today you've got the bucks or you get the boot.

Not that gardens are the way to stop riots in the cities. But still, the possibility of self-reliance and the existence of communities that value their citizens in better ways than the merely financial do seem to go together.

Then, too, gardens offer a natural outlet for our aggression. They aren't peaceful places. That corn I was lost in at age five had blades as sharp as swords. It wasn't unusual to surprise a copperhead wiggling away through the squash blossoms. Children were expected to water, hoe, weed, prune, pick, shell, and shuck. *All* of the plants had bristles—you could work your palms raw picking mustard greens. Chinch bugs on the tomatoes, aphids on the peas. Stinkbugs. Wasps. Sweat bees. The air was 75 percent nitrogen, 20 percent oxygen, and 5 percent gnats. Even the *smell* of the garden was violent—the musk of the raw earth, the acrid burst of a stepped-on tomato vine.

Jayme and I have a little garden now. The squash and cantaloupe are blossoming. We had fresh lettuce earlier in the spring. The tall pink-headed garlic leans this way and that. It's nice, but it's not like the gardens I remember. We don't have the space, and we don't have the time.

I think what I miss most is butterbeans. Speckled butterbeans, trained to climb those lashed-together poles, those tripods of rough-cut bamboo that when they were covered with a fabric of leaves invariably reminded me of tepees.

They were the only crop I actually enjoyed shelling, snapping the flat pods open with a thumbnail, reducing rough green bushels to bowls of succulent provender. We had them fresh all the late summer, and we canned what we couldn't eat. When the last few vines went dry in the fall, we kids would sneak out behind the shed and try to smoke the husks. And when you broke the seal on one of those quart jars in the middle of the winter, you swore the canned beans were just as good as the fresh had been. Maybe better.

The butterbean is, to my taste, the very essence of the garden. I can eat crowder peas as long as the next person, and black-eyes deserve a chapter all to themselves. But nothing has ever surpassed the butterbean for richness and flavor.

I shudder when I talk to someone from outside the region and they say, "Oh, you mean limas." I do *not* mean limas. I suppose butterbeans are a species of lima, but to me limas are those huge pale things from tin cans, coarse and pasty and undistinguished. Butterbeans are as closely packed, as silkily textured as anything that ever arrived in a pod. Their flavor is nutty and subtle and clean, no hint of the mustiness you taste in other legumes.

They're easy to cook, too—if you can find them. Some supermarkets carry them in frozen foods, or maybe you can score a mess at the farmer's market. Just drop a strip of bacon in the pot (or a couple of tablespoons of butter or olive oil if you prefer to stay meatless) and simmer the beans till they're ready. You'll know when.

Have them with hot cornbread and green onions and buttermilk, maybe a few slices of fresh tomato. Or do what I used to do (another one of those dark family secrets): Spoon them over slices of store-bought white bread until the bread soaks through. I thought that was the best eating on earth. I used to have that *after* I finished my cake.

Ah, those butterbeans, each as rich and tender as a tiny medallion of the finest beef. Their pot liquor, as savory as the most superior velouté. We were poor, but I didn't feel poor when I ate butterbeans. I felt satisfied. You could grow them yourself, cook them yourself, and eat them yourself. They weren't commercial and they weren't exclusive, but they were the best, the noblest bean of them all. They were—surely you saw this coming—the *human* bean.

Country-Style Speckled Butterbeans

2 ½ cups dry or 6 cups fresh or frozen butterbeans
Salt and freshly ground pepper, to taste

¼ pound fatback, bacon, or fatty ham scraps

Before you start cooking, make sure you have got butterbeans *and not those big nasty limas. This recipe also works for fresh or dried crowder peas, brown peas, speckled peas, black-eyed peas, and pinto beans. It is* not *intended for English peas. If you wish to avoid animal fat, substitute 2 tablespoons of olive oil and 1 clove of garlic, minced, for the fatback. If you are cooking black-eyed peas for New Year's Day, you* must *use hog jowl rather than fatback, unless you don't care about your luck.*

TOTAL PREPARATION AND COOKING TIME: 1 to 3 hours, not including soaking dry beans.

1. Dry beans (or peas) will *never* cook to tenderness if you don't soak them in water overnight. After soaking, drain off the water and rinse the beans a few times.
2. In a stew pot, cover beans to an inch or more with fresh water. Add salt and pepper to taste. Note that the beans will absorb some of the fluid and that the dish will cook down, so be careful not to oversalt them.
3. Bring water to boil, then turn heat to simmer. Add fatback, bacon, or ham scraps and cover. If you don't have a steam-releasing lid, be sure to tilt lid on top of pot to let steam escape.
4. Simmer for at least an hour, then taste. Continue to simmer until beans are done to your satisfaction. But remember, you can cook them for a long time and they just get better. Top with chowchow and serve with hot buttered cornbread and turnip greens (recipe follows).

SERVES 4

Turnip Greens

2 large bunches fresh turnip greens
2 cups water
Salt and freshly ground pepper, to taste

¼ pound fatback, bacon, or fatty ham scraps

This recipe also works for mustard greens, collard greens, or any mix of the 3 greens. You may also add peeled and chopped (or whole small) turnip roots.

TOTAL PREPARATION AND COOKING TIME: 80 minutes to 3 hours.

1. Wash and destem turnip greens, rinsing thoroughly to remove all sand and dirt.
2. Place in a large pot with water, salt and pepper, and fatback, bacon, or ham scraps.

3. Bring to a boil, cover (if you don't have a steam-releasing lid, be sure to tilt lid on top of pot to let steam escape), and simmer until greens are tender, adding water as necessary to keep them from drying out. The longer they cook, the better they get. True Southerners love this dish with pepper sauce, vinegar, or Tabasco sauce. Some add chopped egg, as with spinach.

SERVES 4

EVERYTHING IN APPLE-PIE ORDER

I confess I don't have any resonant affection for apples. Pears, I could tell you about the pear tree in the front yard in Glen Allen, Mississippi: midsummer, midair, munching a dripping honey straight off the branch, listening to Gil Hodges and the Brooklyn Bums. (For you twentysomethings, that was a baseball team, not a band.)

Blackberries. Butterbeans. Catfish. Almost every food calls up a memory, or a whole string of scenes and memories. But apples. One problem is there hasn't been a good grocery-store apple since 1966. They have wonderful names: Winesap, Golden Delicious. They're perfect and shiny as a TV preacher's haircut. But bite into one and you discover they have all the fiber of a politician's moral courage, all the flavor of a CEO's reading habits.

At their best, I admit, apples can be impressive. They have a snapping freshness: You bite, and they bite back. Even so, even then, they're not my favorite. They're too Sincere with a capital *S*. I prefer the voluptuous seductions of a tree-ripened peach.

But they don't say "American as apples," they say "American as apple pie." Apple pie is a whole other thing. Apple pie, as nearly as I can tell, is the main excuse for the existence of apples, aside from maybe the William Tell story or an occasional denture commercial.

Dolly Holl is ninety-five but doesn't look a day over eighty-five. She works her garden, goes to early services, says exactly what's on her mind, and has a good laugh every chance she gets. I once complimented her on her jewelry, and she said, "You know, Jack, a woman always wants something hanging around her neck. If not a necklace, then a man."

Dolly brings us bags of little green apples from the tree we can see over the fence in her backyard. Which is how I got on this subject in the first place.

To make a good pie, rinse, core, and quarter four cups' worth of small apples, leaving the peel on. Then—the country cook's secret—toss them with half the juice of a large fresh lemon, unless you've gotten hold of the very best tart cooking apples. The lemon will also keep them from turning brown when they're exposed to the air, not that it matters, since you're going to bake the heck out of them in just a few minutes anyway.

A crust should be made lovingly, slowly. I've mentioned my three-to-one rule before: three parts flour to one part shortening (by volume).

Put two cups of unbleached white flour in a mixing bowl and add a pinch of salt. Cut in two-thirds of a cup of butter or margarine. After a while, you'll have to work the mix with your fingertips. The way our days go, I tend to wind up with the bowl between my knees watching Vanna turn letters. Why do I root for perfect strangers to win $100,000? Why do I prefer one perfect stranger over another? You got me.

When the mix is the consistency of cornmeal, remove half a cup to a separate bowl and add a teaspoon of baking powder to this portion. Add two to four tablespoons of ice-cold water to the original mixture and *gently* cut it into a silky dough, moist and rich but not tacky. Do *not* knead the dough or use your fingers at any point in this part of the process, except to ball the dough up and remove it from the bowl. Roll it out as thin as you can, dusting each side lightly to keep it from sticking. Fit into a 10" glass pie plate, trim the overlap, and rework the scraps into thin strips. You'll lattice these on top of the filling in just a little while. My mother always crimped the rim of the crust with a fork, so I do, too.

In a skillet, heat a half to three-quarters of a cup of syrup with a pat of butter and just a splash of whiskey. I favor the pecan-flavored syrup we got at Minsky's Market just below Lake Village, but Karo would work fine. Sorghum or blackstrap would be too dark, though.

Now: Quickly sauté the apples in the syrup, just a minute or two, then turn the heat off. With a slotted spoon, ladle the apples into the crust. If you want to sprinkle with allspice, cinnamon, or nutmeg, now's the time. I go light on that stuff myself, but Jayme loves it.

Take the half cup of dough mix you set aside, stir it rapidly into the remaining syrup in the skillet. The dough mix won't dissolve completely, but will make little buttery nuggets that will crisp up while the dish bakes. Spoon the resulting sauce over the apples, patting everything down, then lattice the top with the leftover dough. You might want to drizzle just a tablespoon or so more of syrup over the strips to glaze them. Pop this confection in the oven and bake it at 350°F to 375°F for thirty to forty minutes. The result is more like a tart than a traditional apple pie, but it goes just as well hot from the oven with cheddar cheese or ice cream.

Dolly certainly seemed to enjoy the slices we took her.

Apple Pie

4 cups small apples, cored and
   sliced (but leave peel on)
Juice of $\frac{1}{2}$ lemon
2 cups unbleached white flour
Pinch of salt
$\frac{2}{3}$ cup plus 2 tablespoons
   butter or margarine

1 teaspoon baking powder
$\frac{1}{2}$ cup ice water
1 jigger bourbon
$\frac{1}{2}$ cup syrup
Cinnamon, nutmeg, or allspice,
   to taste

TOTAL PREPARATION AND BAKING TIME: About $1\frac{1}{4}$ hours.

1. Soak the apple slices in the lemon juice while you prepare the crust.
2. Blend the flour and salt, then cut in $\frac{2}{3}$ cup butter or margarine until the mix is the consistency of cornmeal.
3. Reserve $\frac{1}{2}$ cup of the resulting mix and add to it a teaspoon of baking powder. Gradually cut in ice water until dough will ball up.
4. Roll out on a floured board until you have a circle of crust 13" to 14" in diameter.
5. Fit crust into a 10" pie plate and trim the overlap. Crimp the edge of the crust with a fork. Roll out the leftover scraps of dough into thin strips for latticing the top of the pie.
6. Preheat oven to 375°F.

7. Heat bourbon, syrup, and remaining butter in a saucepan or skillet until runny, but be careful not to scorch.
8. Drain off lemon juice from apple slices, then toss apple slices in skillet with syrup mixture and brown for 1 or 2 minutes. Turn heat off. With a slotted spoon, ladle the apples into the pie crust. If you want to sprinkle with cinnamon, nutmeg, or allspice, now's the time. Next, rapidly stir reserved butter-flour mix into remaining syrup in skillet, but do not try to dissolve all lumps.
9. Pour syrup mix over layered apples in crust, then pat everything down to make sure apples are evenly covered.
10. Lattice the top of the pie with the strips of dough.
11. Put pie in oven. Check it after 20 minutes, although it may need another 10 minutes or so. It is done when the latticed top is lightly brown. Serve hot with melted cheese on each slice or with substantial scoops of French vanilla ice cream, or if you are truly decadent, both.

SERVES 8

CATFISH LIGHT

Now I'm not going to hold forth on the only right way to do catfish. Too many people have already done that, and anyhow I get tired of these good-old-boy pieces on the glories of that "GRETTT Southern dish, (fill in the blank)." When I'm not writing them myself, that is. We all know catfish is simply wonderful food. I've never turned it down, not at the greasiest greasy spoon, not in the fanciest Manhattan restaurant, not even at the local Sunday buffet.

I can't remember the last time I ate catfish I *didn't* like.

I do admit to having felt a certain antsiness about the increasing national popularity of catfish, not unlike the antsiness I felt as Bill Clinton approached his first term in office. That is, I was glad all those other citizens of what Pogo used to call the "Newnited States of America" were discovering what Arkansas and the South generally had to offer, I was proud and all that—but when everybody else wants what you got, after a while it isn't exactly and uniquely *yours* anymore. (Incidentally, and in light of all the bad-mouthing the man has received, I want to say that I happen to think Bill Clinton is one of the few politicians I've ever met who has a genuine concern for the people he helps govern.)

But take this business of growing them in ponds. Catfish, I mean, not presidents. Growing up where I did, I can't get used to the idea, it doesn't seem quite right. I mean, that's supposed to be *cotton* out there. OK, aquaculture is ancient and honorable, the Chinese have done it for thousands of years, and some of my best friends are Chinese. And let's be honest, the only catfish I eat anymore are the pond-raised variety, since I get mine from the grocery store just like you do. I may suspect some of the poetry has been lost in translation, but it has been too many years since I caught my own for me to honestly wax eloquent over the marvelous gaminess engendered by the sludge-combing habits of that whiskery and murk-drifting breed.

Still, I do have these memories of taking my cane pole down across the street to Lake Washington after school, to the rickety wooden pier right beside the bait shop, and pulling in three maybe five bream and a catfish or two, all on worms. And taking them home and skinning them. Lord, how I hated skinning them. Because you cleaned other fish, but you by God *skinned* a catfish. I don't know how your family did it, but we spiked the lungers on a big nail on a post and then peeled the gray glistening sharky skin off in strips with a pair of pliers. Usually from a still-living animal, because catfish are primeval and they die hard.

All of which is why it's probably better, or at least easier on our delicate sensibilities, that we get them in the grocery store now. There's probably a catfish-skinning machine that does the dirty work. I hope so. I hope there's not a whole bunch of ex-tenant farmers doing the job for minimum wage now that the cotton's gone. Let it be a machine. Let God figure out whether the machine deserves any punishment for its crimes against a fellow species. That's the great thing about technology. Karma gets more and more bureaucratic. The buck never stops.

But I digress. I say things like that, and you probably think I'm a bleeding-heart type who can't enjoy a good meal. Not so. My relish is not dimmed by the facts. It's a man-eat-fish world, Bubba, and as far as I'm concerned that's better than the other way round.

Catfish can be cooked a lot of fine ways, as anyone who ever had the locally famous mousseline at the now defunct Jacques and Susanne's in Little Rock can tell you. Sometimes Jayme and I simply salt, pepper, and broil them. We don't even add butter because catfish have enough wonderful oil of their own. If you try this, by the way, use a black iron skillet—you can dash a little flour, wine, and cream into the residue and generate a great white sauce.

But the classic way is still the best—fried catfish, with hush puppies and slaw. Myself, I like a chunk of onion on the side, or a garden-fresh stalk or two of green onion. Jayme prefers lemon juice for a dressing, or a white sauce of mayonnaise and horseradish.

The classic way is awfully greasy, though. So what are a latter-day Naylene and Bubba to do when they get that old fried-cat craving?

They could say, "The heck with our hearts and our waistlines, eating fried catfish is a morally superior act and well worth the cost to my health."

Or they could try my version: catfish light. Keep the coleslaw, the onions, lemons, et cetera, but lose the hush puppies. I know, a terrible price to pay. Look at it like this—you can make up the loss by eating another two or three pieces of fish.

I usually wait till the boneless nuggets come on sale, at about half the price of fillets. Instead of using a cornmeal-and-egg batter, I salt the nuggets, grind fresh black pepper on both sides, and shake them in a brown paper sack with a couple of scoops of white flour, until they're evenly coated. If you're lazy or in a hurry, you can use prepared pepper, throwing it and the salt in with the flour before you shake. I like my way better, getting the condiments right up against the meat. And I haven't used already milled pepper in fifteen years.

Drop the nuggets in hot oil (any but olive oil will do). Deep-frying is best, but I don't have a deep fryer, got too much seldom used cookware cluttering my shelves and counters already. And anyhow, it goes against my grain to waste that much cooking oil in one recipe. So I use no more than half an inch of oil in yes, you guessed it, a black iron skillet. Turn the nuggets once with a pair of tongs. It only takes a couple of minutes on each side, just till they're golden brown. You definitely don't want to overcook your catfish. You lose too much texture and flavor if you do. Drain the nuggets on another brown paper sack and congratulate yourself for recycling.

The result may be too modern for some people, too safe and health-conscious to be taken as serious cuisine. But give credit to the beast, whose muskiness triumphs over even aquaculture and the ministrations of yuppie-ish recipes. Ah, those crisp morsels, white and flaky when you break them open, steaming with rich flavor.

A bite of onion now. A swig of Diet Coke. *Come on, wheel.*

Catfish Light

2 pounds catfish fillets

Salt and freshly ground pepper, to taste

¾ cup unbleached white flour

½ cup cooking oil

You'll need a set of tongs and 2 large brown paper grocery sacks.

TOTAL PREPARATION AND FRYING TIME: 30 minutes.

1. Separate the fillets and sprinkle both sides of each with salt and freshly ground pepper to taste.
2. Put the flour in one of the grocery sacks, then add the fillets 2 or 3 at a time, close the sack, and shake vigorously until they are well coated. Set coated fillets aside on the other grocery sack and repeat until all are coated.
3. Heat oil in a black iron skillet until a drop of water sizzles on contact with oil.
4. Add the fillets to the hot oil. In a skillet, you'll be able to fry about half the fillets at a time. Brown fillets lightly on both sides, turning with tongs (no more than 5 minutes to a side).
5. Remove from the oil and drain on the grocery sack.

SERVES 2

You really *have* to have slaw with your catfish (see page 67). A side of green onions is de rigueur. Hush puppies (recipe follows), despite their fat and carbohydrate content, are not optional for true Southerners. Lemon wedges, ketchup, and tartar sauce are. Acceptable beverages include iced tea, beer, and buttermilk. Oh, OK. Coke, Pepsi, RC, or other colas, even the diet varieties.

Hush Puppies

Leftover flour from coating
  catfish fillets
½ cup yellow cornmeal
Salt and freshly ground pepper,
  to taste

1 medium gg
½ cup buttermilk
¼ cup minced onion
1 cup cooking oil

TOTAL PREPARATION AND FRYING TIME: About 15 minutes.

1. In a mixing bowl, blend the leftover flour from coating the fish (as well as any tiny nuggets of fish that have escaped), the cornmeal, and salt and pepper to taste. Beat in the egg and buttermilk to form a stiff batter. Stir in the onion.
2. Heat oil in a black iron skillet until a drop of water sizzles on contact with oil.
3. Using a large metal spoon, scoop spoonfuls of the batter from the bowl and rake them off the large spoon with a smaller spoon, dropping them into the hot oil. They will puff up and float. Brown lightly on all sides (3 to 4 minutes to a side). Remove from oil and drain before serving.

SERVES 2

TWO OF A KIND

I've been trying to figure out why you have to have slaw with catfish. There's not much question you do. You can have slaw with other stuff— barbecue, for example. Hard to imagine a good sloppy barbecued pork sandwich without a pile of slaw on the side.

But you can't *not* have slaw with catfish.

Can't feature anybody I really respect having catfish without slaw. Can see Newt Gingrich, say, eating some catfish in Arkansas at a Republican fund-raiser, just to prove he's a regular guy. But he's the sort of scoundrel would up and ask for English peas on the side, not realizing they only go with fried chicken, cream gravy, and mashed potatoes, or with roast beast, brown gravy, and rice.

Maybe it's because they're both so ugly, cabbages and catfish. A catfish is a ugly animal, nobody argues that. Why would you put whiskers on a fish, for one thing? And then go ahead and give it the kind of a mouth you last saw on the beer-guzzling face of the fella who tried to beat your head in for looking crosswise at Betty Lou Thelma Liz, not that she was all that great-looking to begin with if the truth be told, but you have to look *somewhere.*

What is less well understood is that cabbage is put near the ugliest vegetable ever created, exceeded in nonbeauty only by its close cousin, those little mutant dwarf cabbages known, for reasons that have never been satisfactorily explained to me, as Brussels sprouts.

Maybe it's because they both begin with the letters *C-A,* which is also the medical abbreviation for cancer, and interestingly enough both cabbage and catfish are strong cancer preventatives. Well, anyhow, cabbage has been proven to be anticarcinogenic, which is the kind of seven-syllable word you don't find in your ordinary food book. If you eat a bushel of it a day. And although stud-

I DOUBT ANY two people on the planet make slaw the same way. I've eaten slaw that has *onions* in it, for crying out loud, though why in the world you would want to mix those flavors I can't understand. Seems to me the competition for your taste buds would be too much.

But so far as I know, there aren't any rules. I myself prefer a creamy and sweet slaw, with enough tang to be interesting but not enough to pickle my tongue. My version, which you'll find at the end of this chapter, makes enough for two with plenty left over for those recycled catfish po-boys you'll be eating for breakfast the next two days.

For the life of me, I don't know why they call it *cole*slaw. Which Cole are we talking about, Old King or Nat King? Or maybe it was that Younger boy. He was an outlaw, wasn't he? Be just like him to come up with a dish like coleslaw.

ies have yet to be done, I am firmly assured in my own mind that sooner or later the Hippocratical arts will demonstrate to us that a regular intake of catfish will lower your risk of any given sort of cancer by a full 33 and ⅓ percent.

But my favorite theory, because I have just thought it up, is that they are both bottom-feeders. As I say, almost the only catfish you can get hold of has been pond raised. Lately they have been turning that fact into a selling point. Safe, you know. Don't have that mean old musky flavor. Which for me is about like bragging on a pro linebacker because he went to Exeter. I swear I don't remember ever having a problem eating any of the 2,312 catfish I myself have personally yanked off the river bottom with a worm on a line on a cane pole and taken home and skinned with a pair of pliers.

If I'm going to eat somebody, even if he's just a carrot, I want it to be somebody who has had some experience. Somebody who has swallowed some bad news herself and lived through it. Until now. I belong to an out-of-date school, the one that thinks when you eat somebody you take on elements of that person's soul. I figure if a catfish has eaten bugs hiding in an old tire or some mercury-laden crawdads and lived to tell the tale, then I can handle the catfish.

Cabbages are the same way, I'm sure. Why do you think they help prevent cancer? Look at them—they *are* cancers. Blooming excrescences upon the lovely face of the planet. They can whip the big CA because they understand it, they know where it's coming from, and they get there first. You ever try to kill a cabbage? Short of radiology, it's just about impossible to do. I don't know exactly which chemicals cabbages extract from the soil, but it has to be the chemicals none of the other self-respecting vegetables will have anything to do with. Sulfur compounds. Cabbages must be absolutely crammed to the gills with sulfur compounds.

What I'm saying, catfish and slaw isn't a combination, it's a marriage. We don't of course have to figure all this stuff out every time we sit down to a platter of crisp fillets and a big bowl of sweet coleslaw heavy on the mayonnaise, not any more than we have to understand every word in "Fern Hill" to enjoy the Dylan Thomas masterpiece.

Our bodies know, though. Our taste buds know. Can't have one without the other.

Coleslaw

½ small head white cabbage
1 small carrot
3 teaspoons sugar
Salt and freshly ground pepper,
    to taste

2 tablespoons vinegar
4 tablespoons mayonnaise

TOTAL PREPARATION TIME: 15 minutes.

1. Wash the cabbage and carrot and peel the carrot.
2. Using your food processor fitted with the shredding blade, finely shred the cabbage and carrot.
3. Dump this mixture into a bowl. Toss with sugar, salt, and pepper. Dress with vinegar and toss again.
4. Set aside in refrigerator to marinate. When ready to serve, drain off excess vinegar and beat in the mayonnaise.

SERVES 4

MOSEY FROGHEAD'S
BARBECUE SAUCE

I suppose it's time to talk barbecue. It's a time for sacrifice and feasting, a time for the smoke of cooking meat. I've avoided the subject so far because it's so touchy and because it's such a staple when talking about Southern and Western food.

I'll say right out that I do not intend to join any of the usual debates—which is better, pork or beef; which is better, wet or dry; mustard or no mustard; chile peppers or no chile peppers; who cooks it better, Texans or Arkansawyers; and so on. I like to argue about barbecue, in the same way that I like to argue about baseball and poetry—the argument itself is a sport, no absolute conclusions necessary, and is to be engaged in energetically but without rancor.

And I hasten to point out that I'm only talking about barbecue *sauce,* not about the whole cooking process. I am well aware that barbecuing really means cooking on a grill and that it is technically possible to commit barbecue without the application of any sauce whatsoever. I have friends who are deeply into the craft, who possess those giant smokers that look like 1890 locomotives, and I think it is a fine hobby to have. But I grew up thinking of barbecue as meat cooked with that gooey delicious sauce, whether the meat had been skewered over coals or baked in Momma's oven, and old habits of thought die hard.

I have good credentials for talking about barbecue sauce. A reviewer, some years ago, said that my first novel, *Jujitsu for Christ,* contained "the most terri-

MOSEY MADE IT with gallon jugs of ketchup and blackstrap mixed half and half with honey and sweet pickle juice he had left over from pickles, and the Cokes that people hadn't finished that they hadn't put their cigarettes out in, and whatever seasonings he had on hand that hadn't caked up or gotten weevils. This batch he had also dissolved a couple of licorice whips in. He used a batch a day, two on Saturdays, and cooked each batch on extremely low heat for three days, letting it set up a little overnight, so that he always had at least three big pots simmering. — from *Jujitsu for Christ*

fying recipe" for barbecue sauce that he had ever seen. If that isn't praise, I don't know what is.

In *Jujitsu for Christ*, Mosey Froghead owns a barbecue joint in Jackson, Mississippi. You can find the passage the reviewer was referring to in the sidebar.

Mosey's just a character, but I have to admit he exemplifies my attitude. I'm no purist. I think there are a thousand roads to the royal delight of good barbecue sauce. As with catfish, I can't remember the last time I had barbecue I didn't like. And I myself have made successful sauces that involved elements as wide-ranging as beer, grape jelly, and tamarinds. Barbecue sauce is a synthesis not a factory process. It's one of those convergent recipes, like chili and meatloaf and bread pudding, in which the coming together is what counts.

The secret is to remember the four basic ingredients: tomatoes, sugar, the kick, and sulfurous bulbs. Yes, there are people who prepare barbecue sauce without tomatoes. There are certainly people who prepare it without sugar. But in my opinion, which is really probably not so much an opinion as a genetic predisposition, the classic stuff needs those nightshades, those groundcherries. It needs a solid sweetness. It certainly needs a kick. And it has got to got to got to have garlic and/or onions.

There's a lot of room for variation in the relative proportions. We won't go disputing tastes. But cover those four bases and work from Mosey Froghead's Two Great Principles and you'll have a dynamite sauce every single time. Oh, Mosey's principles:

1. Use anything, so long as it falls into one or more of the four basic categories, and use all four categories.
2. Cook the sauce for a long time. A real long time.

Enough theory. How about some applications, eh? I have a couple in mind, and I owe them both to my once and future spouse. And maybe I'll throw in a bonus.

First, Mosey Froghead's Country-Style Pork Ribs. These are the ribs with which Jayme initially soothed my savage breast, and you may still garner testimonials to their delectability from all over the state of Arkansas. Then a recipe for barbecued chicken that will change your life.

What you do—the thumping you hear next will be the sound of the dropping bodies of a thousand fainting purists—what you do is you get yourself about three pounds of country-style pork ribs and you drop them in a big old pot, and you parboil those babies. With appropriate spices, of course. Peppercorns, sweet basil, and my personal favorite, tarragon. Jayme's prone to toss in a few lemon rinds. She will also sometimes give the stew a healthy dash of cinnamon—one of her few character flaws is her prodigality with cinnamon.

You're boiling the ribs to tenderize them as well as to make the stock that will eventually form the basis for your sauce. The boiling is a good deal of the cooking the ribs will undergo, so that they won't be as prone to dry out as they would with extensive barbecuing. Cover the ribs with water, heat on high until the water comes to a boil, and then simmer for twenty minutes or so (sometimes you have to let the process run a bit longer for bigger or thicker ribs).

When the ribs are ready, fish them out with tongs and set them aside in a baking dish or on a large platter in a safe place. Somewhere the animals can't get to them. In forty-five minutes to an hour, when the sauce is done, you'll finish off the cooking of the ribs by barbecuing them on your outdoor grill. So maybe you want to go out and light the coals now. Good time to take a cocktail break, too.

Now turn the heat way up under your stock and begin to reduce it. I should tell you at this point to remember all this for use with the barbecued chicken recipe (coming up), since the process is almost identical.

As you reduce, add your other ingredients. Sulfurous bulbs first. It's hard to use too much onion or garlic. After many years, I have come to favor garlic, and not just because of Jayme's allergies. Let's see, three pounds of ribs. Say six finely chopped cloves. Maybe eight. If you're using onions, one to one and a half large onions will do. Next, tomatoes. You can use anything from paste to garden-fresh (they take longer, because there's more moisture to reduce) to sun-dried (they take even longer, because they have to reconstitute themselves, but they do help by absorbing fluid). Heck you can even use leftover super-market spaghetti sauce. My preference is ketchup, but I've made this sauce with all of the above and it has worked fine every time. I'm not going to advise you on how much or how little tomato to use because it is a matter of taste, and anyhow I vary it a lot from session to session.

As the sauce begins to cook down, you need to be thinking kick and sugar. Kick is mysterious and subtle. Partly it's a matter of tartness. Tomatoes help, but they can't do it all. I often use wine vinegar, white or dark. Lemon juice is good, too, but a lot more trouble. Vinegar increases your cooking time again, because you have that much more fluid to boil off, so I add it later, in dollops, when physics dictates more rapid evaporation (surface-area-to-volume ratio, if you must know). At this stage, you should be sampling your sauce, the only way to get the kick just right for you. Kick is also a matter of aromatics, herbal pungencies. We've done sulfurous bulbs, but more is wanted. You might go to peppers in their various guises—jalapeños, cayennes, the thousand varieties of Mexi-bells. Some people dash in Tabasco sauce to taste or a few teaspoons of chile powder (see page 152 for more on chile powder versus chili powder). All depends on how high octane you want the stuff to be.

Myself, I go light on the capsicum, preferring freshly milled black pepper-corns. Sometimes I use mustard. It totally changes the character of your sauce, but it does give you a great excuse to clean out those four or five partially used jars of French and German and American yellow sitting around in your fridge. Horseradish is not unthinkable, and neither is ginger or curry, though I wouldn't want curry and mustard in the same sauce.

As you adjust the kick, start adding the sugar. Sugar mitigates tartness, so make allowances, tasting as you go. I have used—if there are any purists still conscious, please, for your own sake, sit down before you read farther—I have used plain sugar, brown sugar, peach juice, applesauce, pecan-flavored syrup, plain syrup, orange juice concentrate, and the aforementioned grape jelly. A nice grape-jelly-and-mustard sauce will really light up your taste buds and also leave the most amazing Tupperware stain you have ever seen in your life.

The classic sweetening ingredient is blackstrap molasses. It gives you a rich, dark sauce, not overly saccharine, and the iron in the blackstrap has a very interesting magnifying effect on the kick. I'd use no more than a cup of blackstrap in this recipe.

Continue reducing until you have a sauce thinner than paste but thicker than weak syrup—you want it to flow but also to cling.

The rest is denouement. Baste the ribs slowly over the coals, brushing on sauce and turning from time to time. You don't want to leave them on the grill too long—most of your cooking has already been done, remember, and the last thing you want is to dry these babies out. All you're really aiming for is that great smoked flavor and a bit of outside crispness. I don't know how hot your fire is or how far off the coals your grill is, so I'll just say to watch the ribs carefully, and be tender with them, and take no chances.

All you need when they're done is slaw (see page 67), huge slabs of garlic toast (page 77), and iced tea or beer. Feeds four hungry people, or myself and Johnny Wink with a bite left over for somebody else.

I am going to tell you how to make Jayme's Amazing Oven-Baked Barbecued Chicken, but I'm beginning to feel a little guilty, so first a word to all vegetarian exiles.

A leading figure in the Virtual Poetry movement once cornered me during a party at our house—appropriately enough, as I was frantically reducing beef patties and hot dogs to their constituent atoms with the aid of a spatula and a charcoal fire that had somehow attained the approximate temperature of the Big Bang—and demanded, "When are you going to write something for us loyal expatriate vegetarians?"

My friend, you are exactly right. I commit to including more vegetable dishes in your literary diet. I think probably the next topic I take up will be my all-time favorite, all-vegetable Southern meal. In the meantime, however, if you'll bear with me, I must follow through on my other promises.

For four people, begin with a large (three pounds or so) package of chicken breasts or leg-and-thigh quarters. Or you can mix and match. I favor thighs and drumsticks myself, as moister and more pleasingly musky in taste, but Jayme prefers the breasts. Leave the skin on—nothing is better than that delicious crusty barbecued skin.

Marinate the chicken overnight in a large dish (the one you'll be cooking in). For marinade, use a decent white table wine—nothing too expensive, but not two-dollars-a-bottle flavored kerosene either. Spice the marinade to your liking with whole black peppercorns, a couple of bay leaves, some dried tarragon, and fresh rosemary, and pour it to cover the chicken completely. Cover the dish with tinfoil, set it in the fridge, make yourself a cup of tea or a dry martini, and relax for the evening, stuck with your melted-cheese-and-leftover-salsa-on-stale-nachos supper, but dreaming of tomorrow.

OK, so with a quick jump-cut it's tomorrow, you've just gotten off work. Pour off the marinade into a large saucepan. It's going to serve as the base stock for your barbecue sauce, much as the pork bouillon did in the previous recipe. In fact, at this point, you should refer to that recipe, because it's what we'll be following the rest of the way.

But wait—I hinted at something different, something amazing that would change your life. Yes, and here it is: mole (pronounced *molay*). What, you may ask, is mole? Mole is a wild and wonderful Mexican concoction of chile powder and chocolate. That's right, chocolate. The stuff is darker than Jesse Helms's attitude toward good art and harder than your average tuff formation. It comes in a little glass jar, and you have to chisel it out in chunks. Be prepared to spend some time crushing these chunks into smaller fragments.

For this size recipe, you want about six to eight tablespoons of mole. Once you've got it, what you do then, you just toss it in the bubbling sauce at about the same stage you add whatever other sweetener you've decided on. Actually, you could use something lighter than the blackstrap molasses I recommended earlier, since the mole will deliver such punch and authority. Once more, be prepared to spend some extra time stirring and further crushing the rubble of mole with your stir spoon. It dissolves without a trace, but not without an effort.

Bake the chicken at 375°F, brushing frequently with the barbecue sauce. Cooking time should be forty-five minutes to an hour, depending on your oven and whether you're cooking breasts or leg quarters (the breasts take a bit longer). You know the rest of the drill—slaw, garlic toast, iced tea or beer. Enjoy.

And what about that bonus recipe? Sure. You may have noticed we made an awful lot of barbecue sauce. That there seems to be a cup or so left over. Not to mention all that rich drizzle in the bottom of the baking dish. Combine it all and let a couple of days go by while it sits in the refrigerator, cold, ruddily gelid, meditating on its future. Also to give you time to crave something barbecueish again. Comes the day. Your stomach is ready. Your mouth is set.

Get yourself a batch of skinless, boneless chicken breasts and slice them into strips. Coat with salt and pepper. You're about to fry up a batch of chicken fingers. But first get out the leftover mole barbecue sauce, heat it to fluidity, add honey and mustard to taste, then heat it some more. You can beat in a little mayonnaise if you want a milder flavor.

Shake the chicken strips in a paper bag with some flour, fry them quickly in hot oil (any kind but olive oil), and drain them. The madeover barbecue sauce is now your hot-and-spicy holy-mole crisp-and-golden chicken-finger dip. No side dishes with this, unless you made french fries (also pretty good with the dip) or went to the trouble of making fresh slaw.

Ok, vegetarians. You're next.

Mosey Froghead's Country-Style Pork Ribs

3 pounds country-style pork ribs
Salt and freshly ground pepper,
   to taste
6 to 8 cloves garlic
1 teaspoon chile powder
1 teaspoon dried tarragon

One 6-ounce can tomato paste
½ cup white wine vinegar
   (more to taste)
½ cup blackstrap molasses
½ cup Karo syrup (more to taste)

TOTAL PREPARATION AND COOKING TIME: 90 to 100 minutes.

1. In a large pot, cover the pork ribs with water and set on high heat. Add salt and pepper to taste. When water begins to boil, turn heat to low, cover, and let ribs simmer for 20 to 25 minutes.
2. Remove ribs from water and set aside to drain, leaving water in pot.
3. Turn heat back up to just below boiling, cover pot again (but leave an escape crack for steam), and reduce pork stock.
4. Set and light coals in grill.
5. While stock is reducing, mince garlic and add to stock. Add chile powder and tarragon. Stir in tomato paste until it is thoroughly dissolved. Pour in vinegar (more to taste after adding molasses and syrup). Next add black-strap molasses and Karo syrup (more to taste if sauce is not sweet enough). Continue to reduce until sauce clings to spoon, stirring frequently to insure sauce does not scorch.
6. When coals are ready, baste ribs thoroughly in sauce and set on barbecue. Leave ribs on grill no more than 20 minutes (depending on heat of coals), turning and basting thoroughly with sauce at least every 5 minutes. You may roast the ribs in the oven instead of barbecuing them on the grill. Allow 30 minutes of cooking time at 375°F, turning and basting regularly.
7. Serve warm with coleslaw (see page 67), garlic-and-dill toast (page 77), and additional sauce as desired.

SERVES 4

Note: You will probably have a good deal of sauce left over. Don't throw it out! Save it for use with other recipes—you can add it, for example, to Jayme's Amazing Oven-Baked Barbecued Chicken (see page 76), or you can turn it into a steak or chicken-finger dipping sauce simply by blending in a little mustard, honey, and mayonnaise.

Jayme's Amazing Oven-Baked Barbecued Chicken

....

3 to 4 pounds chicken quarters
  or breasts
Salt and freshly ground pepper,
  to taste
6 to 8 cloves garlic
One 6-ounce can tomato paste

$\frac{1}{2}$ cup white wine vinegar (more
  to taste)
$\frac{1}{2}$ cup blackstrap molasses
$\frac{1}{2}$ cup Karo syrup (more to taste)
6 to 8 tablespoons mole

Marinade:

White table wine to cover
  (about 2 cups)
1 teaspoon whole black
  peppercorns

2 or 3 bay leaves
1 teaspoon dried tarragon
1 teaspoon minced fresh rosemary

TOTAL PREPARATION AND BAKING TIME: 80 to 100 minutes, not including marination.

1. In a medium-size bowl, mix white wine with the whole peppercorns, bay leaves, tarragon, and rosemary.
2. Arrange the chicken in a 2"-deep baking dish, pour the marinade over the chicken, seal with aluminum foil, and set in refrigerator to marinate (at least 4 hours, but overnight is better).
3. Preheat oven to 375°F.
4. Drain marinade into a pot, sieving peppercorns and bay leaves. Leave chicken in baking dish and set in refrigerator until marinade is done cooking. Cook marinade on high heat until it begins to boil, then turn heat to simmer. Add salt and pepper to taste.
5. While marinade is reducing, mince garlic and add to marinade. Add tomato paste, stirring until thoroughly dissolved. Add vinegar (more to taste after adding molasses and syrup). Next, add blackstrap molasses and Karo syrup (more to taste if sauce is not sweet enough).
6. Crush mole, then blend into marinade, stirring until mole is completely dis-

solved. Continue to reduce until sauce clings to spoon, stirring frequently to insure sauce does not scorch.

7. To shorten preparation and cooking time, you may baste chicken pieces thoroughly before sauce is completely reduced and begin baking them.

8. Bake chicken skin side up for 45 to 60 minutes, until skin is crisp and meat separates easily from bone. Baste regularly and thoroughly with sauce (every 10 to 15 minutes). As with ribs, serve warm with coleslaw (see page 67), garlic-and-dill toast (recipe follows), and additional sauce as desired.

SERVES 4

Garlic-and-Dill Toast

4 to 8 thick slices French or
    Italian bread
Garlic powder

Dill flakes
Softened butter or margarine

TOTAL PREPARATION AND COOKING TIME: 10 minutes.

Dust slices of bread lightly on one side with garlic powder and dill. Spread this side with butter or margarine. Broil or toast until lightly browned, just a few minutes.

SERVES 4

A SOUTHERNER'S FIRST
MEAL IN HEAVEN

I often feel as though I'm writing for people younger than I am—men and women out there working hard in a world that grows more frantic and less rewarding every day. Perhaps this is because of my former students, busily taking over the reins of nearly everything but not always eating that well while they do it. Perhaps it is because our daughters—one finishing high school, two in college, one working on the West Coast—are struggling all the while to recreate, in their own terms, that sense of home and comfort that meals ought to provide, especially at holidays.

I tell you what—if you aren't already squared away with turkey and dressing with giblet gravy, cranberry sauce, sweet peas, oven rolls dripping with butter, mashed sweet potatoes baked with sugar and raisins and with melted marshmallows on top, and that strange greenish cottage cheese and lime Jell-O salad that so far as I know nobody has ever eaten at any other time of the year. (My editor tells me that her family called it Green Goddess Salad and that nobody outside the South will know what I'm talking about, but I can't help that. In my family we just called it lime Jell-O salad, and that is also what it is called by no less an authority than *The Pastors' Wives Cookbook*.) If you haven't already decided to chow down on butterbeans, green-bean-and-cream-of-mushroom-soup casserole (topped with canned onion fritters), sliced baked ham with the fat still on, and hefty slabs of pumpkin and pecan pie. If you don't, I say, already have all this lined up and waiting for you, then maybe I can talk you into a different sort of Thanksgiving feast.

Herewith a paean to the joys of a completely vegetarian but completely tra-

A STANDARD 10¼" INCH skilletful will feed four to eight people depending on how hungry you are and whether you want any left over and if everybody's going to have a piece with their buttermilk for dessert.

I do strongly recommend whole-kernel cornmeal. You may have to look to find it since our idiotic food industry automatically removes most of the nutrition from most items before marketing, but you will be rewarded not only by superior nutrition but by a fuller, nuttier taste and a richer texture, too.

ditional Southern dinner—what I hope my first dinner in Heaven will be, in fact. (I know, I know—you'll be surprised to see me there. What can I say? Mercy droppeth like rain. Anyhow, relax, I'll probably be demoted to the card table in the kitchen.)

The centerpiece of that first meal in Heaven, the organizing principle, as it were, the foundation upon which all must rest—it cannot be else, it must be, it *shall* be none other than buttermilk cornbread. A big black skilletful, hot and fresh from the oven. It has been made with whole-kernel yellow cornmeal and—this is very important—*no sugar at all*. You sever the huge golden wedges, lift them steaming from the skillet, slather them with so much butter that every crumb, every tender morsel is bathed in richness. Born from buttermilk and destined for buttermilk, cornbread is at its finest crumbled in ragged fragments, still warm and buttery, into a tall cold glass of the stuff. You stir once with a long teaspoon, eat with shivers of joy. Every Southerner knows what I mean. But now a problem looms. There are so many *other* ways to enjoy the stuff—hot from the pan by itself, for example, or smeared with strawberry preserves, or smothered in crowder peas and soaked in their liquor. Who has room?

But wait—we're in Heaven, where all things are possible. No problem after all.

Did I say crowder peas? Yes, simmered until they're softer than your first love's kiss, until they have brewed themselves a potful of that velvety, glistening, dove gray pot liquor. The classic recipe includes a chunk of salt pork boiled away almost to nothing, but vegetarians—though it may horrify some to hear me say so—may substitute a generous dollop of olive oil, and the peas will be no less succulent. Get yourself a nice big helping, ladling a pint or so of the juice over your cornbread. Almost perfect but not quite, and this *is* Heaven, so: Open that jar and spoon out a couple of piles of Mom's chowchow for your peas. (Don't worry, I'll tell you about chowchow in the next chapter.)

And now—turnip greens, those raw soldiers of the garden. Stewed for hours, until they're succulent as steamed spinach. Like the peas, usually with salt pork or fatback, but as with the peas, olive oil works fine. (I add one clove of crushed garlic if I'm cooking with oil instead of fatmeat; see my recipe on page 54.) Heaven offers all the right condiments, so you douse your mess of greens with pepper sauce or Tabasco or Louisiana hot sauce. Some might think the dish harsh and metallic, but we know better, don't we? They do have an edge, but they're *supposed* to.

Heaven arranges these things well: Vegetarians will be pleased to note that the whole-kernel cornmeal and the peas yield complementary amino acids (so you get all the protein you would from meat) and that the buttermilk offers not only more protein but also bone-strengthening calcium and a host of friendly and useful bacteria. And while it's true that by omitting red meat from your diet you lose a good source of iron, the greens help make up the deficit: You can literally feel the rush when all those vitamins and minerals hit your bloodstream.

What are the perfect side dishes? Well, you have to have green onions on your plate to crunch on after every three or four bites, and an array of garden-fresh tomato slices is always nice.

Black Iron Skillet Cornbread

4 cups whole-kernel yellow
  cornmeal
1 cup unbleached white flour
6 teaspoons baking powder
$\frac{1}{2}$ teaspoon baking soda

1 teaspoon salt
$\frac{1}{2}$ cup butter or margarine
3 medium eggs
2 cups buttermilk

TOTAL PREPARATION AND BAKING TIME: About 1 hour.

1. Preheat oven to 375°F.
2. Sift dry ingredients together in a large mixing bowl. Cut in all but 2 tablespoons of the butter or margarine thoroughly. Add eggs and buttermilk and beat until a smooth, thick batter forms.
3. Melt reserved 2 tablespoons of butter or margarine in 10$\frac{1}{4}$" black iron skillet (about 2" deep).
4. Turn off heat and pour batter into hot skillet.
5. Put cornbread in oven. Check after half an hour, although it may need to bake for another 10 to 20 minutes. Cornbread is done when it is lightly browned, risen, and slightly split open on top. It will also thump like a ripe melon.
6. Remove from oven and divide into sections of desired size. Butter immediately.

SERVES 6

MOM'S CHOWCHOW

Spice, novelty, piquancy, relish. Why do we crave green onions with our buttermilk and cornbread? Why, within the last decade, has the entire country gone nuts for salsa? Why do I invariably mill fresh black pepper onto my scrambled eggs, my grilled hamburger?

Perhaps it's because even the finest foods, if they grow too familiar, may disappear to the palate. I've already mentioned crowder peas garnished with chowchow, and I've been thinking of that chowchow ever since, how its tartness somehow amplifies and freshens the heartiness of the peas, so that I taste them all over again. I eat what would otherwise be a plain meal with vigor and earnestness, and surely it does me more than the usual good.

I've eaten chowchow all my life, but it dawned on me not long ago that I didn't have the foggiest idea how it was made or what precisely was in it. Of course I called Mom, and of course you, lucky you, get the benefit. This is a batch recipe, so if you don't want this much, cut the ingredients proportionately. But the stuff keeps forever and gets better as it ages.

Wash the veggies I'm about to list and slice to fit into the chute of your food processor fitted with the coarse-chopping blade. You need two medium-size heads of cabbage, ten to twelve medium-size green tomatoes, eight medium onions, and six red peppers (of which one or two should be hot peppers, jalapeños, or chile peppers or some such). You'll also need two tablespoons of mixed whole spices (you can find bags of them already mixed at most groceries), two tablespoons of ground mustard seed, one tablespoon of turmeric (for color), one tablespoon of ground ginger, four tablespoons of whole mustard seed (for texture), three tablespoons of celery seed, four cups of vinegar (Mom prefers cider vinegar), five cups of sugar, and three-quarters of a cup of salt.

Feed the veggies into your food processor, then put them in a large bowl. Add the salt and mix, then let stand overnight in a large bowl or some other adequate container. A stoneware pickling jug would be just about perfect, but almost nobody has 'em anymore. In the morning, drain whatever fluids have accumulated and set aside. Tie up the mixed whole spices in a cheesecloth bag. Combine the sugar and vinegar and simmer for a bit with the bag of spices. Now add the mustard, turmeric, ginger, mustard seed, and celery seed, sipping and adjusting to taste. Remove the spice bag, then add the chopped and brined vegetables. Simmer the vegetables until they are just barely tender, with that edge of translucence.

Now you fill pint or quart Mason jars with the mix and set the open jars in a large cooker of very hot but not quite boiling water. After the jars have reached the temperature of the water, seal them. Those of you my age or older will recognize this as a variation on canning—as the jars cool, a vacuum is created, which helps keep them sealed. It isn't pressure canning, though, which uses superheated steam from an absolutely antiseptic and very tight seal. Pressure canning was always exciting to me, the sense of volatility and risk—all those stories about flawed cookers blowing up in the kitchen. But that's a topic for another day. Another sort of spice, the spice of danger.

Some of you will have noticed this isn't my usual sort of recipe, a one-meal process intended to bring delight and pleasure to the business of our so often too busy days. This recipe implies you're looking down the road, thinking ahead, laying in stores for winter. This one implies you're settling in for the long haul.

A little change keeps everything fresh. It's interesting that the change in flavor brought on by this chowchow has to do with stability, continuity, and heritage. Usually we think of youth as the source of freshness. But hey, what if freshness takes practice? What if change and excitement require a canny head, the patient accumulation of skill and insight?

If chowchow is the essence of dietary dash, zip, fandangle, and pizzazz, it's worth keeping in mind where I found out how to make it: from good old Mom.

Thanks, Mom.

Mom's Chowchow

2 medium-size heads green
  cabbage
10 to 12 medium-size green
  tomatoes
8 onions
1 jalapeño or chile pepper
5 red bell peppers
¾ cup salt
4 cups cider vinegar

5 cups sugar
2 tablespoons mixed whole
  spices
4 tablespoons whole mustard
  seed
2 tablespoons ground mustard
1 tablespoon turmeric
1 tablespoon ground ginger
3 tablespoons celery seed

If you want the chowchow hotter, use 4 bell peppers and 2 jalapeño or chile peppers.

TOTAL PREPARATION AND COOKING TIME: 2 hours, not counting brining and marinating time.

1. Wash vegetables, then slice cabbage, tomatoes, onions, and hot pepper to fit in chute of food processor fitted with coarse-chopping blade.
2. Destem, deseed, and slice bell peppers, then feed through food processor.
3. In a large mixing bowl or stoneware pickling jug, combine the chopped vegetables with the salt and mix thoroughly. Let sit overnight.
4. In the morning, pour off accumulated fluids.
5. Combine vinegar and sugar in large pot and bring to a simmer.
6. Tie up mixed whole spices in cheesecloth and drop into vinegar-sugar mix. Let simmer for 20 minutes. Add remaining spices, then remove spice bag and add vegetables. Let simmer until vegetables are just turning translucent.
7. Fill pint or quart Mason jars with chowchow mix (including fluid).
8. Set open jars in large pan or pressure cooker of very hot but not quite boiling water. Water should come up to the necks of the jars.
9. Bring jars to temperature of water, then seal and keep in pantry until needed.

MAKES 2 QUART JARS

COFFEE TIME

Java, joe, jive, moke, Colombian, kaff, axle-grease, brew, café au lait, cappuccino, espresso, latte, red-eye, wake-up. Coffee is wonderful. It's the only vice they haven't proved anything on yet.

Coffee's a very temporal drink. By which I mean, it changes your perception of time. Maybe it would be more accurate to say that it *creates* your perception of time. You're floating along, cat-sleepy in the boundless Eternal Now. No plans, no thoughts. But gulp a couple of swallows of the magic elixir and zing!

And coffee's temporal in another way for me. It's wound into my personal history, the times of my life. As early as nine or ten years old I was bringing a tray to my parents in the morning—coffee for Dad, hot tea for Mom. As a reward, I could have my own cup. The way I liked it then was thick with sugar and pale with a heavy dollop of condensed milk. I couldn't imagine my father's brew, absolutely black and unsweetened, a dark and wicked cup.

Naturally, over the years, my drink has gotten more and more like his. By the time I went off to college, I was down to two or three spoons of milk, though I was still slurping four or five sugars in six or seven cups a day. I remember vividly the kitchen table in that one-room efficiency on Center Street in Fayetteville my first wife and I shared. Our third place together, the one after the one in which I first made tomato gravy and biscuits. It was a perfect setup for a poet. We were newlyweds with a Murphy bed, a creek behind the duplex, a footbridge across the creek to a hillside graveyard. The table was my desk, and I would make myself cup after cup of syrupy instant coffee and brood on the creek, the bed, or the boneyard, and scribble hot dithyrambs on flux, sex, and decay.

Yes, it's true, at that time I was drinking instant. When I was a child, we brewed drip coffee only, in a tin pot. Usually fresh-ground Eight O'Clock brand from the A&P. This is an age test, by the way. Nowadays fresh-ground has gotten so fashionable that nearly every supermarket has a machine in the coffee aisle. Back then—I ain't saying when, but if you remember it I know just about how old you are—the Atlantic & Pacific store was the only source. Then for several years *nobody* had the machines, and if you wanted fresh-ground you had to buy a cranky expensive German device and do it for yourself at home.

I think my lapse into the bad taste of instant had something to do with being out on my own. You do a lot of stupid things when you first realize that you and only you are responsible for *every single detail of your day-to-day existence.* You rotate your underwear less often than your tires. Your consumption of macaroni and cheese rises to an all-time high. You pull all-nighters to get term papers done and keep yourself awake by drinking gallons of—shudder—instant coffee.

In fact, that was about the last period of my life in which I did drink instant. It's a practice only the young can survive. If you're over thirty and you're drinking coffee out of a jar, *give it up before it rots your brain.* Look at those bozos they put in the ads talking about fresh-roasted flavor from crystals. They're supposedly in a fancy restaurant, only their regular coffee has been replaced with instant, and they're amazed, *they can't tell the difference.* Case in point: Those people are morons.

I got my own tin drip pot when I was twenty-five or twenty-six. At almost the same time, I lost my taste for sugar. It wasn't macrobiotic conviction or anything of the sort, or even my suddenly torpid metabolism, the onset of early middle age. Sugar just didn't taste good anymore. Increasingly, I found myself appreciating the flavor of the coffee itself. Either the bitter brew suits your tongue or it doesn't, and if it doesn't, why disguise the situation?

I have also found myself using less and less cream, until now I'm afraid to let anyone else put the cream in for me because they can't believe I want that little. Why don't I just go all the way and drink it black? I do sometimes, and it's fine. But I like the color, that mahogany gleam, and I like just the hint of a hint of smoothness.

I have to admit that since those instant-slurping days, I have become a coffee snob. I hate to think of myself that way, but it's true. The phenomenon has happened gradually, over the years, as my tastes have clarified. Perhaps it's a function of mortality. Not a matter so much of developing good taste as of deciding what I no longer have time to bother with. With only half a century or so to go, why waste even five minutes on a bad cup of coffee?

The drip method is the best, by far. I've always loved percolators for that rich liquid burbling, the glass knob rattling like the heart of morning—but percolators recycle the brew and overcook it. Coffee should be brewed very hot and taken off the heat right away. The oils are fragile and denature quickly. (I told you it was a temporal drink.)

Which is why you almost never get a good cup of coffee in a restaurant. Not only do they brew it too weak, they let it stand too long. It's sad, but almost the only solution is to have your coffee at a joint that charges so much they can afford to indulge you.

Almost any drip pot or machine, even the tiny prehistoric electric my folks bought a quarter of a century ago, will brew a creditable drink if you treat it right. You can spend hundreds of dollars on gleaming equipment with Teutonic names, and I wouldn't try to stop you, not if you're having fun. But you can also trot a ten-spot down to the cookware aisle and be in business in a matter of minutes.

The main thing is, you need to keep your pot clean. Otherwise, you're drinking old oils. What I recommend for black iron skillets, I do not recommend for coffeepots. You don't cure them—a glass pot antiqued with the varnish of the ages is not a good sign. Scrub that sucker. If you use an electric coffeemaker, every so often you might turn the machine on and run a weak solution of water and baking soda through the coils to clean them and the chamber. (Follow this with a couple of rinses of plain water.) Conversely, if your water is hard and leaves calcium deposits, you can run a vinegar solution through to clean out the lime, following again with several rinses of plain water.

The closer you get to fresh-ground the better. You can make a good cup from canned coffee, but you can make a better cup if you buy the beans whole and grind them at the big machine in the store. Plus which there's that wonderful aroma. You can make an even better cup if you grind them fresh at home for each pot. Plus which there's that wonderful aroma. And here is where I *will* recommend you spend a little moola. A nice solid grinder will run you upwards of fifty dollars, but it's worth every penny.

There are a lot of good choices in beans. We tend to prefer a darker roast, and we like to play around. Sumatran, Hawaiian, Jamaican—I'm drinking Costa Rican this morning. Jayme bought twelve pounds of Italian roast the last time we were in Manhattan.

She and I disagree slightly in one respect, however—flavored coffee. She doesn't do much of it, but in holiday season she sometimes likes a cuppa. Pecan, hazelnut, amaretto, chocolate, cinnamon—pardon me, but it is to gag. Hey, coffee *is* a flavor.

I also differ from a lot of people in that I like my coffee strong. Really really strong. No, stronger than that. If you can see the bottom of your cup, it ain't coffee. I'm getting older, and I will admit to cutting my jive with decaf, especially later in the day, but I want a cup of coffee I can sink my teeth into. So to speak. If you want tea, drink tea.

We use a fairly standard electric dripolator now. American-made, nothing too fancy, probably forty-five dollars on sale. Brews ten cups at a shot. (Which is to say about five real cups. I have the impression that the Japanese are for some reason in charge of cup measurements for all brands of coffeemakers, not merely their own.)

The pot we take camping now is the one I gave Jayme the second time I came to see her.

I had discovered when we first met that all she had in her cupboards was a half jar of congealed instant, which had attained, over a decade or so, the approximate consistency of road tar. So the next time I walked up her sidewalk I was carrying a bright new tin coffeepot from the local Safeway. Looking back, I can see how insulting that might have been.

But she took it well. She's a very very smart woman, and she knew what it meant. She knew it meant that I was serious. She knew it meant I was there to stay.

THE HEALING PROPERTIES OF
CHICKEN POT PIE

We've had a few days of sun at last, and some of the trees are even beginning to bud out. But winter isn't over. Here, as in much of the country, you can count on February to come in with one last round of bad news, one more siege of miserable drippy weather.

It's no wonder more people die in January than in any other month. We need light, and we need fresh air. But it isn't just that, at least not for me.

Let's say somehow you make it through that long Christmas-to-Super-Bowl drag, and you're feeling a little hopeful, and you're congratulating yourself for the moral fiber you showed by just hanging in there, and sure enough the sun comes out again.

You can count on February to slam you back down. Another round of the flu, two weeks of rain, a pay cut because the company has to either reduce expenses or go out of business—it's like losing in overtime after you've made a heroic comeback to tie in the last second of regulation. What can you do then, what can you ever do?

Let me recommend chicken pot pie.

Jayme's relapse of the winter blahs came in the form of the sniffles, a week of increasing mental fuzziness, and general aches and pains—one of those low-level bugs there's no point in going to the doctor for and no way of escaping. I think mine came in the form of realizing I was older than Bill Clinton and I wasn't president of the United States.

It came to me then, in a blinding flash of insight, what was needed. I got out two packs of boneless, skinless chicken breasts, about ten breasts in all. (Boneless, skinless thighs would have done as well.) I cut the chicken into roughly one-inch chunks and sprinkled them with coarsely milled black pepper and a little salt. I heated a couple of tablespoons of olive oil in a black iron skillet. I ground more pepper into the hot olive oil, stirred in the chicken chunks with a spatula. While they were browning—I stopped several times to turn them—I stripped six cloves of garlic. Yes, six. Maybe seven. Garlic is the essential ingredient. It's the philosopher's stone that changes chicken pot pie from mere hot nourishing protein to golden and healing elixir.

The question of what to put in chicken pot pie besides chicken and garlic is a highly rewarding one. Carrots are nice if you have them, but I didn't. I had a few stalks of celery that needed to be used, so I cleaned and chopped them, leaves and all, and stirred them in with the browning chicken. There were some leftover English peas, too, but I held them out for a few minutes, until I was ready to deglaze. Next I got out my garlic crusher, a wonderful device, and crushed my six cloves of garlic into the skillet. I added them at just this moment because I wanted to brown them only lightly. I sprinkled the mixture with about a quarter cup of flour, stirring it in evenly, and then, just as it began to stick, poured in the rest of a bottle of white wine we'd shown no inclination to finish off—a Riesling this time, a bit sweet, but it worked fine—and the leftover peas. I added enough water to almost cover the solid ingredients, stirred to mix the liquid evenly, and turned the heat down to medium-low. Normally at this point I'd add herbs and spices—rosemary, a touch of dill, maybe a lighter touch of basil (fresh herbs are better if you have them on hand, but dried are fine, too). This time, for some reason, I wanted a plainer dish, so I just added salt to taste.

I let the stew simmer and thicken while I made the dough for the crust and dumplings, using about two cups of flour. (Use the recipe for Black Iron Skillet Pie Crust on page 21, but use two-thirds of a cup of butter or margarine with the two cups of flour. Fit the crust into the skillet once you're done browning your chicken, unless you've got an extra skillet.)

I rolled out my dough, decanted my chicken-and-garlic filling into the stainless-steel bowl I mixed my dough in, rinsed and dried my skillet. Then I cut and fit my crust into the skillet, pinching up the edges around the rim with two fingers, a scalloped effect that deepens your dish. I layered half of the chicken mixture in, stripping it with more of the dough, which would double, internally, as dumplings. Another layer of chicken, more strips of dough, this time for a top crust. Forty-five minutes in the oven at that jack-of-all-cooking-temperatures, 375°F.

It was forty-five minutes of increasingly wonderful aroma and increasing hunger. The weather was lousy the next day, which was, wouldn't you know it, a Monday. Believe it or not, we felt great. Believe it or not, chicken pot pie had made us well.

Chicken Pot Pie

1 Universal Black Iron Skillet Pie Crust (see page 21, but use 2 cups flour and ⅔ cup margarine or butter)

2½ pounds boneless, skinless chicken breasts or thighs	6 cloves garlic
1½ teaspoons salt	¼ cup unbleached white flour
Freshly ground pepper, to taste	1 cup white wine
2 or 3 carrots	1 teaspoon fresh rosemary
3 or 4 stalks celery	½ teaspoon dried dill
2 or 3 tablespoons olive oil	1 cup English peas

If you use chicken breasts only, it makes for a drier pie. I suggest you use a combination of breast and thigh meat. I've added mushrooms on occasion. Some people prefer to omit the dumplings completely.

TOTAL PREPARATION AND BAKING TIME: About 3 hours, including about an hour for pie-crust preparation.

1. Prepare the pie crust, reserving the trimmings of the dough for dumplings and top crust. (You won't put this crust in your skillet until you're finished browning chicken, unless you've got an extra skillet.)
2. Dice chicken into bite-size morsels, then sprinkle with salt and pepper, making sure to coat evenly on all sides.
3. Clean and dice carrots and celery.

4. Heat oil in skillet till just before smoking, then add chicken pieces. Brown lightly, turning with spatula. When pieces are brown, reduce heat to medium-low.
5. Crush garlic and add to skillet. Sprinkle flour over the garlic and chicken pieces and stir into mix with spatula, forming a roux.
6. As flour begins to brown, deglaze with wine, stirring constantly with spatula to keep lumps from forming. Add water to desired thinness while continuing to stir.
7. Turn heat to low and add carrots, celery, and spices, simmering for 10 to 15 minutes.
8. Preheat oven to 375°F.
9. Stir in peas, then ladle stew into the pie crust, adding dough strips as desired for dumplings. (Be sure to reserve enough strips for the top crust.)
10. Top with thin strips of dough, completely covering the filling.
11. Place in oven and bake for about 45 minutes. Pie is ready when top crust is lightly browned.

SERVES 6 TO 8

Stewed Chicken with Buttery Dill Dumplings

1 whole chicken
3 cloves garlic, minced
$\frac{1}{2}$ teaspoon fresh rosemary
2 teaspoons salt
Freshly ground pepper, to taste
1 cup unbleached white flour

$\frac{1}{8}$ teaspoon baking soda
4 teaspoons baking powder
$\frac{1}{2}$ teaspoon dried dill
3 tablespoons butter or
   margarine
$\frac{1}{2}$ cup buttermilk

This dish is absolutely wonderful on cold winter evenings—hearty, thick, and invigorating. Mixing town and country, I like it with nothing but a couple of crisp green onions on the side and a nice big glass of chilled Chardonnay.

TOTAL PREPARATION AND COOKING TIME: 90 minutes.

1. Place chicken in large stew pot and fill with water to cover.
2. Turn heat to high and add garlic, rosemary, all but a pinch of the salt, and pepper to taste. Cover until water reaches boiling, then turn to simmer, tilting lid for steam to escape (if you don't have a steam-releasing lid).
3. While the chicken is stewing, prepare the dumplings. In a bowl, mix flour, pinch of salt, baking soda, baking powder, and dill. Cut in butter or margarine until mix is the consistency of cornmeal. Cut in buttermilk until dough forms.
4. Knead dough lightly, folding in half 7 to 10 times and mashing flat.
5. On a floured board, roll out dough to $\frac{1}{2}$" or less thickness. Cut into strips or other desired shapes.
6. When the meat pulls easily away from the bone, remove chicken from pot and debone, removing gristle as well (and skin if so desired).
7. Return chicken to pot, add dumplings, and let simmer until dumplings are done, 15 to 20 minutes.

SERVES 6 TO 8

AVOCADOS ARE MY AVOCATION

Like I say, food is time for me, personal history. Oranges were rare when I was growing up, so rare that, like Hal Phillip Walker in the Robert Altman movie *Nashville,* the odor of oranges being peeled infallibly takes me back to Christmas in the big house, which was about the only time we had any citrus at all. I see stockings filled with oranges, satsumas, peppermints. Brazil nuts still in their shells. But not all foods take me back to childhood. There are some foods I never had until I got older. Another West Coast fruit, the avocado, marked my early adulthood.

Actually, I got a little bit of exposure to avocados when I was a teenager. I suppose they had just come into the local Southern markets, and my mother took to making avocado toast, which, as well as I can remember, was just that — buttered toast with avocado slices on it. I didn't much care for the combination at the time.

It took a few years and a few changes. The period of my life that I associate with avocados is my early-to-mid twenties, and the decade that I associate with avocados is the sixties — by which I mean, really, 1968 through 1971, when I was in Fayetteville, Arkansas, writing poetry and trying as hard as I could to be a part of some latter-day lost generation.

What I see first are avocado pits, like fattened children's jacks, suspended on toothpicks over glasses of water. In our house in Fayetteville there were always from three to six avocado pits perched on the windowsill in the sunlight, brooding over the waters as it were, waiting patiently to sprout. It was the same in all our friends' houses. I think — as well as I can remember those days — that in our good, warm, be-kind-to-the-earth hippie fashion, we simply did not wish to waste a single possibility. I think we felt the urge to let every impetus to life have its term.

The sad thing, if you're inclined to sadness, is that I don't remember any of us ever generating a single avocado tree. (And if we had, what would have been its fate in the relatively harsh Ozark winters?) I remember dozens of pits, like ovoid aliens hovering over their life support, and I even remember a few sprouts. But after that—nothing. Not only do I not remember any avocado trees, I don't remember ever throwing the pits away.

Come to think of it, what ever happened to all those hippies?

No, I'm afraid the earth, to which we were trying to be so kind, is far more nearly in the potential-wasting business than the potential-fulfillment business. The odds are against fulfillment, the deck is stacked. Sorry to have to say so, my fellow Americans, but it's true. You can follow your bliss and still get whacked. We must make the most of our successes, celebrate them with joy and champagne, because they may be few and far between.

Still, those were good and fascinating times, and I admire us as we were then, determined, fuzzy, hopeless, full of good will. And full of avocado sandwiches.

Prices have been good on avocados lately, which is how I got into all this reminiscence. I like diced avocado in an omelet or—my favorite breakfast lately—rolled in a homemade flour tortilla with scrambled eggs, Monterey Jack, and a bit of chili or salsa. Jayme, as I've mentioned, is allergic to onions, so I've devised what is actually a pretty great guacamole that doesn't contain them. What you do is dice a couple of nice ripe avocados in a flat-bottomed bowl, add the juice of half a lemon or lime (or more to taste), mill a bunch of black pepper over the avocado and lemon, crush one small clove of garlic and add it, add a tablespoon of mayonnaise, and mash the ingredients coarsely with a potato masher. Put the result in the fridge for an hour or so, to set up and swap flavors around, and serve with ugly chips. Which is what we learned to call blue corn chips in New Mexico.

But my favorite way to have avocados is the way I first learned to like them. Vegetarian sandwiches were a hot new item back in the sixties in Fayetteville. You could eat and be righteous at the same time. I didn't care for most varieties of those sandwiches, and as far as I'm concerned alfalfa sprouts have all the gustatory charm of chopped dental floss, but with less flavor. And after all, why should we take food out of the mouths of ruminants?

But I loved avocado sandwiches once I learned to leave off the sprouts.

Here's my version of that old favorite: Cut yourself a couple of nice thick slices of some rich and chewy whole grain bread. Slather both slices liberally with Hellmann's Real Mayonnaise. (I don't generally do commercial endorsements, but let's face it, there simply is no comparison.) Now shave off thin slices of Jarlsberg Swiss. You don't want *too* much cheese because that funky nutty Jarlsberg flavor will dominate if you let it. Now a couple or three thin slices of garden-grown tomato.

Finally the avocado. Ripe enough to bruise when you thumb it, firm but ready to collapse to a paste under pressure. It's messy and slippery to cut an avocado in slices, but that's what you need to do, flat surfaces so the green sections won't be so prone to pop out of the sandwich when you bite down. Cover the cheese with a layer of avocado. Sprinkle a little genuine sea salt, in honor of your hippie days. Mill some black pepper.

Eat your creation over the sink with a glass of whole milk or a fresh cup of coffee, looking out the back window at the kids' swingset and remembering how it felt to be lonesome, broke, and full of potential.

Jayme's Onion-Free Guacamole

2 large ripe avocados
Juice of ½ lime or lemon
Freshly ground pepper, to taste
1 clove garlic

1 heaping tablespoon
  mayonnaise
Salt, to taste

Sometimes I stir in a finely diced vine-ripened tomato.

PREPARATION TIME: 15 minutes.

Peel avocados and remove pits, placing meat in a flat-bottomed bowl. Squeeze lime or lemon juice directly into bowl. Mill pepper over avocados to taste (I use a lot). Using a garlic press, crush in the clove of garlic. Mash avocado and seasonings coarsely with a potato masher. Do not reduce to smooth paste. Beat in mayonnaise and salt to taste. Chill and serve with chips, on burritos, in omelets, et cetera.

SERVES 2 TO 3

World's Best Avocado Sandwich

2 slices good whole wheat bread
1 tablespoon mayonnaise
2 or 3 thin slices Jarlsberg Swiss
   cheese
1 vine-ripened tomato

1 small ripe avocado
Salt and freshly ground pepper,
   to taste
Sunflower sprouts (optional)

TOTAL PREPARATION TIME: 10 minutes.

Spread the bread with mayonnaise. Layer one slice with the cheese. Slice the tomato and lay over the cheese. Peel avocado and remove pit, then cut meat into thick slices. Layer the other slice of bread with the avocado. Sprinkle avocado with salt and pepper to taste. Layer with sunflower sprouts, if you're using them. Slap the bread together and eat.

MAKES 1 SANDWICH

JUST ONE OF THOSE THINGS

Every Sunday, after the paper and the first two cups of coffee, when I ask Jayme what she wants for brunch, she says, "One of those things. You know, with the white cheese and avocados." This from a woman who really likes her biscuits and strawberry preserves, her buttermilk pancakes and warm maple syrup. So maybe they're good enough to write about.

I call them creperritos because the batter is like the batter for a crepe, but I handle them like tortillas and fill them the way you would a breakfast burrito. For two people, you'll need four or five eggs, a third of a cup of flour, a pinch of salt, six to eight slices of Monterey Jack, five or so tablespoons of butter, and one ripe avocado. You might also want a few tablespoons of chopped onion, which I like to brown for the filling. But the dish is fine without them.

You'll need a black iron skillet and a stovetop griddle. I use a round aluminum griddle with a handle, some ten or eleven inches across. You could use two skillets, but the griddle makes it easier to turn the creperritos. The handle helps, too, because you can lift the griddle and sort of tilt it toward your spatula as you do the flipping—you can catch your own misses.

Timing is critical for this dish, so you should have all your ingredients prepared and at the ready. Batter first, so it can sit and meditate awhile. You want a happy batter, one that is at peace with its batterness, so to speak. I am batter, hear me pour.

Put your third of a cup of flour (as always I prefer unbleached) into your blender (a regular cheapo blender works just as well as a Cuisinart for this) and add a healthy tablespoon of butter. Blend until you have a coarse yellow meal. Add two eggs and blend once more. A plastic spatula for cleaning the wall of the blending cylinder is helpful in both stages of the process. At this point I usually add two tablespoons or so of water to bring the batter to the right degree of liquidity. Milk works just as well.

I prepare the avocado by cutting it in half along the major axis and removing the pit. Then I use a small dull knife to crosshatch the halves—dull so it will slice down to the peel but not through it down to my fingers. When the time comes, I will scoop the avocado meat directly out of the peel with a soup-spoon, a half avocado for each creperrito.

Chop the onion of course, if you're using onions. Thinly slice Monterey Jack and set it to one side. Beat the remaining two or three eggs in a bowl.

Blend the batter again for a few seconds, just for good measure. Remove the blender cylinder from its base and scrape down the wall once more. Turn heat to high and melt a pat of butter each in the skillet and on the griddle, but take the skillet off the heat as soon as the butter has melted.

Things proceed so rapidly at this point that you'll be making one complete creperrito at a time—only a master chef could manage two simultaneously, though if you have a large griddle you may want to try. Turn the heat from high to medium on the griddle, then pour half the batter, tilting so it runs to cover the entire surface (finish spreading it with the plastic spatula if you need to, but you'll have to be fast). Watch the griddle closely and loosen the creperrito as soon as it sets (though it will tear if you try this too soon). You can tell it's set in the same way you can tell a pancake is set, by the bubbles that begin to appear in the uncooked top. But test it by lifting the edges with the spatula.

As soon as the downside browns in the slightest, turn it.

Put your skillet back on high heat, adding half the chopped onion if you're using it.

Back to the griddle. Cover one side of the creperrito with half the Jack cheese and immediately spoon half an avocado on top of the cheese. (You can turn the heat off under the griddle at this point—the residual temperature will melt the cheese to perfection.)

Back to the skillet. Pour half the beaten eggs into your skillet (with the onions if you're using them) and scramble quickly, turning the heat low after the first stir (don't let your eggs get too dry). Simultaneously, you need to be keeping an eye on the creperrito to make certain it doesn't overcook. Transfer the open creperrito to a waiting plate, spoon the eggs (and onions *in posse*) over the cheese and avocado, mill some black pepper over the lot, sprinkle with salt to taste, and roll the creperrito up like a burrito.

Repeat the process with the rest of the ingredients, starting with the pat of butter each in your skillet and on your griddle. I like to have salsa or red or green sauce on the side with my creperrito—makes it even more like that good New Mexico breakfast.

A good dry white wine makes a perfect accompaniment, or even, if you're in the mood, a nice bottle of icy champagne. And why not? It's Sunday, you're about to have a great meal, and you're alone with your sweetie. How much more reason do you need?

Breakfast Creperritos

⅓ cup unbleached white flour
Pinch of salt
   5 tablespoons butter
5 medium eggs
1 large ripe avocado

¼ cup chopped onion (optional)
6 to 8 thin slices Monterey Jack
   cheese
Salt and freshly ground pepper,
   to taste

I recommend making creperritos one at a time.

TOTAL PREPARATION AND COOKING TIME: 20 to 25 minutes.

1. Combine flour, salt, and 1 generous tablespoon of butter in a blender. Add 2 eggs and blend till smooth, adding water if batter seems too thick to pour well.
2. Cut avocado in half along major axis and remove pit. With a dull knife, crosshatch each half in its skin for easy removal later.
3. Beat remaining eggs in a mixing bowl.
4. On high heat, melt 1 tablespoon of butter each in the skillet and on the

griddle. If you are using onion, turn skillet heat down to medium and sauté till translucent.

5. When butter is sizzling on the griddle, turn heat down to medium. Pour out half of the batter for each creperrito.

6. Pour beaten eggs into skillet with onion and scramble lightly, removing from heat as soon as they are done.

7. Watch creperrito and turn when lightly brown on underside (top will show firmness and bubbles like a pancake).

8. As soon as you turn creperrito, layer it with half the cheese.

9. With a serving spoon, scoop avocado from skin and spread over cheese, half an avocado to each creperrito.

10. Remove creperrito to plate as soon as cheese melts and second side is lightly browned. Top the avocado and melted cheese with half the scrambled eggs. Salt and pepper to taste, then fold creperrito in half. *Very* good with sour cream.

MAKES 2 CREPERRITOS

SNEAKING UP ON MARGARITAVILLE

The cats were trying to figure out what we were doing. They were mewing at our feet, leaning and looking. The pop-eyed calico, Abigail, was up on the counter, cocking her head, dilating her nostrils to test the air. She recognized the gestures we were making. We were putting the green things in our mouths. But when she sniffed the green things, her disbelief was obvious. It was just another monkey trick. We weren't *eating* those things, we couldn't fool her. Those things weren't *food*. They were as bad as the Vicks we put under our flu-ridden noses at night.

We were celebrating is what we were doing. Out of another long gray stupid winter, we were celebrating the possible imminence of sun. Light at the end of the tunnel. Spring.

Spring means ozone to us, in the sense of Commander Cody's "Lost in the Ozone," a little. Even more in the sense of the new perfumes, the ones they call ozonics, which whiff of either the beach or the desert. This time of year we close our eyes and we see Florida or New Mexico. Salt waves or alkali bluffs. Sporting dolphins or petroglyphs on the walls of Chaco Canyon. Long perspectives, and Wide Time, and big weather under a big sky.

And spring, and ozone — that means it's time for the ozoniest of liquors. It's time for tequila. It's time for margaritas. Jayme makes the world's greatest margaritas. You'll find her recipe at the end of the chapter, though it won't do you any good unless you attain her magic touch. But first let's talk tequila.

People take attitudes toward tequila. Some people won't touch it at all. They have an image of it as a sort of low-rent, south-of-the-border busthead. And there are definitely some brands that fit that description. Or they confuse it with mescal, that stuff with the worm at the bottom of the bottle. (It's not

TEQUILAS ARE BECOMING fashionable lately. There are some tequilas being imported now for which you can pay upwards of ninety dollars a bottle. I've always thought it was silly to drink something just because it was fashionable — stay with what you like — and our budget certainly doesn't permit the pretentiousness of the ninety-dollar stuff. But maybe it would be useful to discuss a few worthy brands in the under-fifty-dollar range.

A lot of people swear by Tres Generaciones (Tres for short). Middle range in price, it's entirely adequate for sipping. One of our longtime favorites is Herradura. Herradura comes in three basic varieties (as do most of the finer tequilas): silver, gold, and añejo (or aged). The añejo is pure nectar and costs like it (forty bucks a pop, or more), but the home is not complete that doesn't have at least one bottle nestled back for special occasions.

Used to be Herradura was hard to find (used to be it cost only twenty-some-odd a bottle, too). We first discovered it leaving Big Bend, Texas. We were desolate. We didn't want to go home. We wanted to live in Big Bend forever. A couple of shots of Herradura Silver, though—warm, straight from the bottle—and we felt our spirits restored. All of the West was in that clear fluid: Ethery, peppery, magical, it didn't make up for the loss of Big Bend, but it reminded us that life would have other pleasures, new good moments to look forward to.

I've seen a couple of good swallows of Herradura Gold bring a superdietdoctor friend of mine back from the walking dead on a camping trip, when we'd spent all of a long hot depressing day in the Navajo nation looking for a campground that wasn't called Cottonwoods and wasn't full of RVs from Ohio. I handed him the bottle, and tiredly he sipped, and his eyes lit up—

really a worm, it's a larva—which is much better, right?) But over the years we've come to believe there are some tequilas that rate with the finest whiskeys, tequilas you can sip straight up and murmur over like a gourmet in heat.

I will tell you the secret of good tequila. It is not made from cactus. It is made 100 percent from the blue agave, and nothing else. The blue agave plant, remember that.

I won't tell how Jayme's salty King Kong margaritas were the only thing that got us through one hot horrible summer of remodeling-to-sell in Little Rock. You don't want to know what forty-year-old insulation looks like or how it feels stuck to your skin in the 140° heat of an attic you can't straighten up in.

We weren't actually drinking margaritas in the scene at the beginning of this essay, anyway. We haven't had our first margaritas of the year, actually. I think we're saving them for just the right moment. Just the right celebration. We'll know it when it comes. What we were doing that was causing the cats so much puzzlement was the old salt-tequila-lime drill. Like the T-shirt says, lick it, slam it, suck it. Lick the back of your hand between the base of your circled thumb and forefinger, sprinkle some salt. Then lick the salt off, knock back a half shot or so of tequila, bite into a crescent of lime.

What it was, we were in training for margaritas, sneaking up on them, as it were. You can't just come straight out of the off-season and hit margaritas full stride. You'll hurt something.

So we were working on the main ingredients, all except for the triple sec. Because the real secret of a good margarita is easy. Use fresh lime juice. Only fresh lime juice. That's why there's no such thing, to my taste, as a good bar margarita. They all use mixes.

For one of Jayme's monster margaritas, we squeeze the juice of a whole small lime into a barrel tumbler. (First we've crusted the rims of our tumblers by wiping them with sections of squeezed lime and rotating them in a bed of salt.) To the lime juice add an equal amount of triple sec and about double the amount of tequila, varying according to taste. Last of all, carefully, the ice cubes. Stir the result with a glass swizzle. No fruit, and no frozen blended margaritas, please. I feel that a blended margarita is an abomination in the eyes of the Lord.

Unless of course you happen to be the famous Johnny Wink, in which case there is no point in trying to save you from yourself: Peacharitas away!

One thing I haven't discussed is the quality of the ingredients. I have praised Herradura. Let me now add that El Tesoro del Don Philippe is a most excellent tequila, smoother than silk, and that if you prefer a smoky and thunderous (though absolutely elegant) distillation, you may want to try El Patron, in the hand-blown glass bottle. Assuming you can get these varieties where you live. I had my first swallow of each at 8,100 feet, in the mountain town of Truchas, and I've gotten very familiar with them both since, so I know it wasn't just the charm and grace of our hosts, the poets and artists Barbara and Alvaro Cardona-Hine.

Perhaps you won't mind a bit of travelogue here: If you visit northern New Mexico, you *must* visit the Cardona-Hine gallery. Very out of the way. But if you're lucky, perhaps Alvaro will take you back into his studio and show you his works in progress, and you will realize, as I do each time I go there, that you have seen greatness.

So anyway, all these good tequilas. But here's the thing: You don't *need* a superb tequila, or Cointreau instead of triple sec, in order to make a superb margarita. In the bars in downtown Santa Fe, they'll make you one of those ten-dollar operations, and it may make you feel you're really doing some living now, but it's a waste of money. The margarita is a plebeian drink, a democratic drink, rising synergistically to excellence. The cheapest possible triple sec. Make sure the tequila's 100 percent blue agave and you're relatively safe. We favor Sauza *blanco* (or silver). It's medium priced, and a good serviceable extract.

Actually, on this particular spring afternoon when things suddenly, inexplicably got better, we wound up not even graduating to margaritas. We sat outside and talked and planned the garden and got the first sunburn of the season and drank another wonderful little drink instead, one I hadn't thought of for years. Simplicity itself.

Tequila and tonic. About four to one on the tonic, squeeze and drop in a corner of lime, and you've got something lighter and fresher and more spring-like than even a G&T. Plenty *brio*, to cross linguistic lines. What would you call it, a T&T? Fine drink.

We'll get to the margaritas soon enough.

Jayme's Killer Margaritas

3 or 4 tablespoons large-crystal
  sea salt
3 medium limes

2 ounces triple sec
4 ounces tequila

No substitutes.

PREPARATION TIME: 10 minutes.

1. Put salt in flat saucer or other flat-bottomed container. (Actually, we keep a sealed plastic dish ready at all times, but in wetter climates you may have to prepare salt fresh each time.)
2. Cut limes in half and then slice into each half crosswise $\frac{1}{4}$" or so for easier squeezing. Juice each lime half, saving juice in a cup or bowl. Retain one pulped lime half.
3. Rub the rims of two 12-ounce tumblers with the pulped lime half. Then turn the tumblers in the salt, upside down, to rime the rims with salt. (The juice from the lime half helps the salt stick.)
4. Add ice cubes to glasses, being careful not to disturb the salt around the rim.
5. Pour 1 ounce of lime juice, 1 ounce of triple sec, and 2 ounces of tequila into each tumbler using a 1-ounce jigger. I think it's ridiculous to use Cointreau or other expensive orange liqueurs, and just as ridiculous to use the finest tequilas, since in a blended drink the finer qualities are lost. The cheapest possible triple sec will do, but you don't want use really *bad* tequila. For a totally acceptable drink, I recommend either Sauza Blanco or Two Fingers in the gold or silver.
6. Taste-test your margarita. Limes vary in tartness, and people vary in taste. Don't be afraid to alter these proportions to suit your own palate. When your margaritas are ready, stir, toast each other, and prepare to meet your Maker.

MAKES 2 MARGARITAS

NO SHORTCUTS TO SHORTCAKE

Nothing's better this time of year than strawberry shortcake piled high with whipped cream. The tartness of the berries, the sweet moist crumbly cells of the soaked cake, the smooth heavy luxury of the whipped cream—ah, what a suite of flavors and textures is here, what perfection of desire. Let's talk about the perfect strawberry shortcake, shall we?

Now I make full allowance for idiosyncrasies of taste, for the peculiar effects of all our childhood memories, and for necessity. Jayme loves nothing so much as strawberries and whipped cream on a base of fractured Ritz crackers, and since she is, as so many people are, allergic to milk proteins, her whipped cream is of that variety that always comes prefaced by "Cool" or "Dream" or, in utter contravention of the normal use of language, "Dairy."

I'm sure you enjoy some recipes, some favorite dishes, that are just as frightening.

But I'm talking ideal strawberry shortcake here, *my* ideal strawberry shortcake.

Start with the berries. The berries should be fresh, which means local. They should be right at that peak of ripeness, firm but juicy and red clear through, no green around the tops, no mushiness on the sides. Which probably means you'll have to go out and pick them yourself or sort through the pints from the supermarket or the roadside stands.

Everybody knows the trick of sugaring the sliced berries to draw out the juices—I told you about it on page 42. You need a deep well of red liquor in that bowl or else your shortcake just isn't going to get luscious enough, drenched enough. I confess that we sometimes, in our dietary equivalent of guilty conscience, doctor the sliced berries with artificial sweeteners, but they just don't have the same effect. I also confess I've never quite been able to decide which axis to slice the berries on in order to extract maximum nectar.

Why, Professor Butler, you don't use a axis at all, you use a knife.

Shut up, son, I'm telling this.

In my opinion the berries need to be cold but still crisp. You don't want that refrigerator limpness they get after a few hours. In fact, if you bake your own shortcake, the time it takes to do so will prove to be precisely the right interval.

And please, do bake your own shortcake. I have as big a weakness for junk food as anyone, but honestly, those grocery-store shortcakes, those yellow things in the shape of giant coasters, they just don't do the job. What are they, reshaped Twinkie rejects? No substance, no structure. They collapse under the juice, and you have a sodden mass and not a delectable treat to take apart grain by grain with your delighted tongue.

Do this instead: Add a teaspoon of baking powder to three-quarters of a cup of unbleached white flour, and cut in a quarter cup of butter, until you've got the famous cornmeal consistency that recipes like this always recommend. Now add six tablespoons or so of white sugar, tossing to mix it, and use a plastic spatula to cut in two eggs. Be patient, and do it by hand, and don't beat the batter. Use your wrist and work it until it's stiff and smooth. This batter will be thick enough that you'll have to use your spatula to turn it out into the baking dish—it won't pour. The sort of baking dish I like here is a flat-bottom ceramic dish about two inches deep and five and a half inches across. This will produce a high, rounded, golden shortcake, big enough to feed two greedy, three moderate, or four frugal people—you *were* planning to share, weren't you?

Bake at 375°F for no more than thirty minutes, although you may want to leave the cake in the oven five minutes or so after you turn it off, depending on how done it seems.

Last of all the whipped cream. You really need to whip it yourself, you know—no shortcuts or excuses or wimp-outs here, either. Not even "real" whipped cream from a spray can will do. You need a cup of good heavy whipping cream, cold from the refrigerator, and you should be sure to sprinkle in plenty of sugar in the latter stages, as the cream begins to stiffen. I like my whipped cream whipped until it's just short of butter.

Now, if your timing has been just right, you are in for a few minutes of pure heaven. Turn out the shortcake, still warm, and slice it horizontally, into disks rather than wedges. Situate each disk in a bowl wide enough to handle all the extras and ladle enormous quantities of strawberries over it, making sure you get that golden yellow shortcake rosy and saturated. Slather on piles of cold sweet whipped cream. Let's pretend you got it together enough to make some espresso, the perfect accompaniment, if you don't mind mixing cultures a little, and I know you don't.

It would be nice if you had a big picture window right under the air conditioner, so you could sit slurping happily away, pitying the poor devils wasting forty-five minutes and a gallon of gas to drive through the heat to the grocery store to pick up their frozen strawberries, their processed sponge cakes, their tubs of Styrofoam topping, all in the name of convenience.

Strawberry Shortcake

1 pint fresh ripe strawberries,
   washed, destemmed, and sliced
10 tablespoons sugar
$^3/_4$ cup unbleached white flour
1 teaspoon baking powder
$^1/_4$ cup butter or margarine
2 medium eggs
1 cup heavy cream

TOTAL PREPARATION AND BAKING TIME: 45 minutes.

1. Preheat oven to 375°F.
2. In a medium bowl, sprinkle strawberries with 2 tablespoons sugar and set aside in refrigerator.
3. In another bowl, combine flour, baking powder, 6 tablespoons sugar, and butter. Cut in eggs with plastic spatula. Beat until smooth.
4. Pour batter into $5^1/_2$" circular baking dish (2" to 3" deep).
5. Set pan in oven and bake for 30 minutes, until top is risen and firm.
6. While shortcake is baking, whip cream until it forms smooth peaks, adding remaining 2 tablespoons sugar in later stages.

7. Set whipped cream in refrigerator to cool until cake is finished baking.
8. Remove shortcake from oven, turn out of its pan, and slice horizontally into four disks while it is still warm.
9. On each of 2 dessert plates, layer 2 disks of shortcake with sugared strawberries, making certain to soak each disk with the sweet liquor from the strawberries. Top with whipped cream.

SERVES 2

THE GREEN STUFF

There's nothing like a good farmer's market. I've spent plenty of sticky summer mornings sweating through my T-shirt in downtown Little Rock, but all the same, when I think of going to the farmer's market, I think of cool crisp weather. I think of blue skies with just a few thin clouds racing high, just enough occasional shade to cause a delicious momentary shiver.

There's a good farmer's market here in Santa Fe, Saturday mornings in the Sanbusco parking lot down at the end of Montezuma. I guess the season is just about over here—snowfall can't be more than a month away—but we had a good market visit a couple of Saturdays ago. It was a perfect morning, made to order, just as cool and crisp as I could have wished.

Markets in New Mexico place more of an emphasis on spices. Among my favorite items are the bundles of sage and other savory herbs you can smell almost before you enter, and which you set smoldering, a sort of natural incense stick. Smudge-sticks, they call them.

On this Saturday, they were roasting chiles at one end of the Sanbusco lot. Garlic is a big item, too, buckets and tubs and braids of it. There are huge fields of garlic near here, in Dixon—in the shadow of Los Alamos, the farmer-author claims. Not quite, but it's good garlic.

And flowers. I guess all farmer's markets sell flowers, but I don't remember having seen so many of them as we see here. Lots of purple flowers (whose species name I don't remember). Purple flowers twined into crosses made of dried cholla. Jayme was of the opinion that ten dollars was an awfully good price for purple flowers twined into a cross made of dried cholla. I couldn't tell you. It was pretty. Is pretty. But that seems to be one of those areas in which there is a definite genetic difference between men and women. Understand, I think women and men are at least equal, and maybe even superior to each other. And I *like* flowers. But somehow I never find myself pricing gladiolas at the superstore.

Another thing they have at the market here that I'm not used to seeing at farmer's markets is sheep cheese. Packets of good soft white sheep cheese, about the consistency of cream cheese, but with a slightly sharper flavor. This is especially nice for Jayme, since she's allergic to products made with cow's milk. (She indulges from time to time—nobody can stay away from cream sauce or pizza with cheese forever—but if she overdoes it, she pays.)

YOU MAY BE saying to yourself, Now wait a minute. I thought we were in the middle of Arkansas, and all of a sudden we're talking the Sanbusco market in Sante Fe.

It's true, we've headed out. Eight hundred miles west, and a mile and a quarter up.

Maybe it was all that tequila this spring. Maybe it was fate. Jayme and I have been visiting New Mexico for years. We love Arkansas dearly, that green sweet place. And we miss those slow rich Southern accents, those voices that have been in our ears for half a century. They talk different out there—out *here*.

But we love it out west, too. Out here, they don't have many trees, and they don't have *any* creeks, because they call them all rivers. *Rios*.

Maybe me and Jayme will eventually open that bar I've been dreaming about for years, the one with all the books, the one that caters especially to writers (but you don't get in if we don't like your writing, no matter how big your advance or how many Pulitzers you've won).

Preacher Jack's Liberry, I'm calling the place. Jayme will play honky-tonk piano and sing and whip up the drinks. I'll do all the cooking.

FROM HOMINY TO POSOLE

They had bins of small, dark root vegetables they called blue potatoes, which, by their appearance, seemed to be—well, blue potatoes. It may be a while before I get up my nerve to try those things. I think of blue food—with the two exceptions of blue corn chips and blueberries—as a contradiction in terms. An oxymoron. Some lineal warning from a long-vanished anthropoid ancestor: Don't put the blue stuff in your mouth, little monkey, it'll kill you dead. Besides, if you mashed them, wouldn't they clash with the brown tones of the gravy?

What they don't have here, and a sad loss it is indeed, is black-eyed peas, or butterbeans. Nor do I remember seeing any good-looking tomatoes. Or snap beans.

They did have glorious bunches of carrots, onions, turnips. Jayme had quite a time explaining to the turnip seller, though, that he should leave the green stuff *on* the turnip. That we actually *wanted* the green stuff, that we were planning to cook it and eat it. Yes, there's some educating we can do here. The Lord must have brought us here for a reason.

The green stuff. That's finally what I like most about farmer's markets, I guess. Stay away from the blue stuff, but every now and then you just have to have a shot of the green stuff. It puts some outside in your insides, it clears your mind and puts a tonic in your blood.

We walked away with two especially nice kinds of green stuff that Saturday morning. Two discoveries. The first was sunflower sprouts. I have never really liked alfalfa sprouts, as I believe I have made clear. I wouldn't mulch my garden with alfalfa sprouts. Sunflower sprouts are a different story. Big, tender, crisp double leaves, with a wonderful green-yet-nutty flavor. From now on, it's sunflower sprouts on my avocado sandwiches.

The other discovery was cilantro. OK, I already knew about cilantro. But I'd never cooked with it very much. We bought a great big bunch of it, and I've been playing around ever since. One great thing about it, it's another way to get that nice Western flavor without having to overuse chiles or tomatoes. In fact, I've come up with a few recipes. There's one for chili, a fine stir-fried chicken recipe involving lime juice and pine nuts as well as the cilantro, and let's see, one for meatloaf—

Which gives me a great idea what to write about next.

I'LL DO ANYTHING FOR MEATLOAF
(AND I WILL DO THAT)

You could spend a lot of time arguing over meatloaf. Some people like it loose and crumbly, smothered in sauce; some people like it firm and springy, with most of the flavor in the meat. I lean to the firm and springy, though I've never met a meatloaf I didn't like.

The very name is evocative: meatloaf. The music is spondaic, double-stopped, glottal. Meatloaf, the name says, is throaty and gutsy and basic. Meatloaf is one of those rough-and-ready dishes, one of those melting pot creations, democratic, all embracing. In its incarnation are forgiven the sins of multitudes of leftovers.

And such a creation should be durable, of course. It should improve with age, gain character in the refrigerator. The third-day meatloaf sandwich is not to be belittled as a last dietary resort, a mere stratagem against hunger, but as the culmination and best fate of a superb invention. The true test of a meatloaf is what kind of sandwich it makes.

If you accept that criterion, you ought to love this recipe. It resulted in some of the best sandwiches I've ever eaten.

I began with about three pounds of a four-meat mix—ground turkey, ground pork, ground lamb, and just a little leftover ground beef. I began with that because that's what we had. If we'd had some leftover bacon or roast beef or chicken, I would have probably put that through the blender and incorporated it as well. The moral is, don't worry if you don't have exactly the same ingredients as the ones I list. Use your common sense and substitute what you have. It'll come out good and surprisingly like my dish anyway. The process is, I am sure, what physicists refer to as the "renormalization" of meatloaf.

I also had a cup and a half of those leftover blue corn chips — the ones that gather at the bottom of the bag, too small for salsa — one old cold biscuit, and a slice of stale bread. I threw in a half cup of wheat thins because I didn't think I had enough filler. I blended all this coarsely with a couple of tablespoons of chopped fresh cilantro, and a little salt and freshly milled black pepper.

Next I took down my venerable black iron skillet, heated up a tablespoon of olive oil, and dropped four large cloves of crushed garlic into the oil. Be careful here: You want only to soften the garlic, not to caramelize it — after your oil is hot enough, turn the eye off and wait a moment, then add the garlic, stirring lightly with a thin spatula.

I've been playing with pine nuts lately since New Mexico is pine nut country, and this time was no exception. I tossed a half cup or so in the skillet just as the garlic was turning translucent, and stirred them around till they had browned just the tiniest bit. Then I took the skillet off the eye and added the blended breadstuff and cilantro, turning until the oil had been evenly absorbed and the garlic and pine nuts were evenly mixed in. I let this mélange cool a bit, then added eggs. I only use about one egg per pound of meat, since, as I say, I like meatloaf relatively firm. In this case, three eggs. Four probably wouldn't have hurt.

I just cracked in the eggs whole, stirred until they were evenly mixed, and then added my meat mixture. You have to do this part with your hands. Think mud puddles, playing in mud puddles when you were a kid. Squeezing the cool soft stuff between your fingers.

You could just cook the dish in the skillet you used for mixing, but I prefer meatloaf to be more loaflike. It fits in sandwiches better that way. So I packed my recipe into a loaf-shaped glass baking dish and popped it in the oven. (Another advantage of the glass is you can see the meatloaf all the way round when it's done.)

Bake at 350°F to 400°F for an hour to seventy-five minutes, depending. Serve with a salad and some basmati rice, maybe. Trickle the juice from the loaf over the rice. Whatever.

The real treat comes later. When you're packing sandwiches for a hike in the fall woods. Take that leftover of leftovers out, slice off some big fat slabs. Get yourself slices of a really good bread, sheepherder's bread toasted with garlic and butter or maybe some seven-grain from Sylvek's, or a nice baguette. Slather the bread with mayonnaise. Mustard and ketchup if you like, though I prefer to keep my meatloaf sandwiches free of such overwhelming condiments. Throw on a few of those aforementioned fresh sunflower sprouts, chilled overnight in the fridge.

Then go climb a mountain.

Nothing will ever taste better than that meatloaf sandwich, high in the fresh air, washed down by nothing more sophisticated than the water from your canteen.

Four-Meat Piñon Country Meatloaf

1 cup loosely packed cracker or chip crumbs
1½ cups loosely packed bread crumbs
2 tablespoons chopped fresh cilantro
1½ teaspoons salt
Freshly ground pepper, to taste
1 tablespoon olive oil
4 cloves garlic
½ cup piñon (pine) nuts
3 medium eggs
¾ pound each of ground pork, lamb, turkey, and beef

You may vary the kinds and amounts of ground meat to taste or according to availability.

TOTAL PREPARATION AND BAKING TIME: 1½ hours.

1. Preheat oven to 400°F.
2. In blender, combine crumbs, cilantro, salt, and pepper; blend coarsely but evenly, 2 or 3 bursts.
3. Heat olive oil in black iron skillet. Reduce heat to medium and crush garlic into hot oil. Sauté lightly, stirring with spatula. As garlic becomes translu-

cent, add pine nuts and sauté for 1 to 2 minutes. Turn heat off and add crumb mixture, stirring with spatula until oil is completely absorbed. Add eggs and mix well with spatula. Cutting in roughly with spatula, add meat until thoroughly blended. (You can complete thorough mixing with hands or by some other method if preferred.)

4. Transfer meatloaf mixture to glass baking dish (I use a standard bread loaf pan) and place in oven until done, about an hour.

5. Remove from oven and loosen sides with table knife before slicing to serve. The juice will make an excellent gravy for rice or mashed potatoes. Cold, the leftover meatloaf will slice into sections for superb sandwiches.

SERVES 6

MEATLESS LOAF

I'm still thinking about meatloaf, only without the meat. Meatless loaf, Jayme calls it, which I think is a pretty good name, suggesting as it does the origin of the dish while simultaneously denying its original main ingredient. I would have probably come up with something like "tofu loaf." Which, let us admit it, sounds terrible.

I am on record as being less than passionate about tofu generally, I know. It has always struck me as the sort of food that does more for your sense of virtue than it does for your senses. No matter how you work on it, it's still tofu, tofu to the core, invisible, tasteless, inert, the kapok of the proteins, the argon of the elementary foods.

But why should our vegetarian friends be denied the pleasures of loaf? Why should they have to do without the rich sustenance of a well-aged loaf sandwich, dripping with mayonnaise? They shouldn't. In spite of my current views, I understand and respect vegetarianism, having practiced it for a while myself, back in my, *ah, hrm, hrm,* salad days.

A disclaimer: Vegetarians who refuse not only meat but all animal protein can't expect much from this recipe, unfortunately. It is simply impossible without the eggs.

Anyhow. Back to the recipe. Thinking of my vegetarian friends, I tinkered around and came up with a tofu recipe that surprised even me. Here's how you do it.

To some extent, you follow the pattern of the meatloaf recipe I gave you in the last chapter. Because of Jayme's allergies, I did without tomatoes, peppers, and onion. I'm sure you could come up with some great variations that include these ingredients, so don't be afraid to tinker. The way I cook, nothing ever turns out the same way twice, but on the other hand, it very seldom turns out badly.

First, sauté finely chopped celery (including a few leafy tops) in plenty of olive oil with generous showers of freshly milled black pepper. Toward the end, as the celery becomes relatively tender, add three cloves of crushed garlic, being careful, as before, not to overcook.

Next, mince something like a quarter of a cup of fresh cilantro. I had several handfuls of sunflower sprouts in the fridge that were about to get too old and that we weren't going to get to in the next few days, so I blended them in the Cuisinart (very briefly) with the cilantro.

I chopped one pound of *firm* tofu and put it in to sauté with the garlic and celery, stirring frequently and giving it a few minutes to absorb the flavors. Next I added the cilantro-sprout mix, then flavored to taste with a little dried rosemary and dill, some cumin, plus just a teaspoon or so of curry. (Curry is my secret Western-recipe ingredient. In very small amounts, it adds a great mysterious nuttiness, but you want to be careful not to make the dish *taste* like curry.)

I deglazed with wine and the tofu water I had held back (so as not to waste the calcium in the water). I added soy sauce to taste, being careful not to make my concoction too salty, since it would get saltier as it cooked down.

(At this point you have the mix for a fine vegetarian chili, if you'd rather go in that direction. Add tomato sauce, chile powder, and simmer for a couple of hours.)

When the mix has cooked down, it's ready for the bread crumbs. I run my bread crumbs through a burst or two in the blender to make something a little more like a very coarse meal than like a collection of croutons. (This time I used a high proportion of cornbread in my bread crumbs — it adds a nice texture.) It's also a good idea to run a half cup or so of pine nuts through the blender first, then put the bread crumbs in on top. The hint of smokiness from the pine nuts does a wonderful job of offsetting the blandness of the tofu.

All that remains is to mix the bread crumbs with the stuff in your skillet, mix in four eggs very thoroughly, pack into a glass baking dish, and bake until done (no more than forty-five minutes at 375°F, though you might let it stay in the oven a bit after you turn the heat off).

As for the sandwich question: Jayme and I have performed extensive field tests, and carnivores that we are, we are ready to declare the meatless loaf an unqualified success.

Meatless Loaf

½ cup piñon (pine) nuts
1½ cups loosely packed bread and/or cornbread crumbs
1 cup loosely packed cracker or chip crumbs
1 pound firm tofu
4 tablespoons olive oil
Freshly ground pepper, to taste
2 stalks celery, including tops, finely chopped
3 cloves garlic
2 tablespoons chopped fresh cilantro

3 to 4 tablespoons chopped sunflower sprouts
1 teaspoon minced fresh rosemary, or the equivalent dried
1 teaspoon dried dill
2 teaspoons cumin
1 teaspoon curry powder
½ cup red wine
2 tablespoons soy sauce
4 medium eggs

TOTAL PREPARATION AND BAKING TIME: 1¾ hours.

1. In blender, coarsely chop pine nuts, then add crumbs and blend with 2 or 3 bursts to form a coarsely chopped mixture.
2. Finely dice tofu, reserving packing water if any.
3. In black iron skillet, heat olive oil over high heat. Mill in pepper to taste. Reduce heat to medium and add celery. Sauté 3 to 5 minutes, until slightly tender. Crush garlic into hot oil and sauté lightly with celery, stirring with spatula. As garlic becomes translucent, add tofu and sauté on low heat for 3 to 5 minutes. Add cilantro and sunflower sprouts and continue sautéing for 1 to 2 minutes. Add remaining spices and stir. Deglaze with wine and re-

served tofu packing water or fresh water as necessary. Add soy sauce and let simmer 3 to 5 minutes.

4. Turn heat off and let cool 15 minutes or more.

5. Preheat oven to 375°F.

6. When sauté has cooled, add crumb mixture, stirring with spatula until fluids are completely absorbed. Add eggs and mix well with spatula. (You can complete thorough mixing with hands or by some other method if preferred.)

7. Transfer meatless loaf mixture to glass baking dish.

8. Place in oven and bake until done, about 45 minutes.

9. Remove from oven and loosen sides with table knife before slicing to serve. Cold, the leftovers will slice into sections for superb vegetarian sandwiches.

SERVES 6

SHEPHERD'S WINTER BISCUITS

I like to experiment, but I don't believe in doing too much tinkering with a good thing. Take biscuits, for example. I've delivered a good basic buttermilk biscuit recipe earlier in these pages (see page 13). Whether you use it or one handed down from your old great-granny, there's no real need to try out variations.

I especially abhor the addition of cute seasonal ingredients. Pumpkin biscuits for Hallowe'en or Thanksgiving, say. Or green biscuits for St. Paddy's Day.

About as far as I'm willing to go in that regard—and it isn't seasonal—is cheese biscuits. I have been known, on occasion, to prepare a platterful of hot, golden, cheddar savories. Even so, I don't think cheese biscuits are an improvement on the original. Worth a fling from time to time, but on the whole, why mess with perfection?

All of this is of course preamble to telling you about a new biscuit recipe I've come up with. I can explain. This recipe began as an accident, sort of.

What happened was, we were out of buttermilk. And seeing as how we had a good pint of this soft creamy sheep cheese from the farmer's market. So anyway, I decided to substitute the sheep cheese, with the addition of a little water and vinegar, for the buttermilk.

Then what happened, I forgot to add baking powder and baking soda until I'd already mixed the dough. And that, as Robert Frost had one of his voices say, has made all the difference.

Here's how you go: two cups of unbleached white flour, a pinch of salt, five or six tablespoons of butter or margarine, five teaspoons of baking powder, a quarter teaspoon of baking soda, a half cup of soft goat cheese, a half cup of water, and a teaspoon of white wine vinegar.

Mix the salt and flour and cut in the butter or margarine to the approximate consistency of coarse cornmeal. In a separate container (do I really have to tell you that?) blend the goat cheese, water, and vinegar into a smooth fluid.

Now begin cutting the fluid into the flour, reserving a little until you see how wet your dough will be. You want a nice moist dough, soft and easy to handle, but not so wet that it clings. Conditions vary, so you may not need all of the fluid.

When the dough balls up and the consistency seems right, add the baking powder and baking soda to the mixing bowl, pressing and turning the dough until it has picked up all the leavening. Normally you wouldn't knead biscuit dough, but these aren't normal biscuits. Knead the dough thoroughly in order to make sure the rising ingredients are evenly distributed and to give the biscuits a unique, chewy texture.

When you've finished kneading, pat or roll the dough out one-half to three-quarters of an inch in thickness, depending on how high-rise you want the results to be, and cut the biscuits out with a biscuit cutter. (This amount of dough will produce five or six huge, high biscuits.)

Place them on a baking sheet or in a pan so that they touch (that way, there'll be those wonderful rough pull-away patches on the sides). Bake at 375°F for twenty minutes or so, until they are lightly browned on top. At this point, I turn the oven off and let the biscuits sit in the fading heat another four or five minutes.

Take them out and immediately slather them all with liberal doses of oleaginous, high-cholesterol milk or vegetable by-products. They will be both crusty and chewy, with a hearty flavor and robust texture. They're great eaten by themselves, but they respond equally well to gravy, preserves, or blackstrap molasses.

I call them Shepherd's Winter Biscuits even though I don't know any sheep-herders and even though I made the first batch of them before winter set in. But I imagine they'd cook up pretty nicely in a Dutch oven. I imagine a sheep-herder would eat them right up.

Jayme certainly did.

Shepherd's Winter Biscuits

2 cups unbleached white flour
Pinch of salt
5 tablespoons butter or
  margarine
½ cup soft sheep or goat cheese

½ cup water
1 teaspoon white wine vinegar
5 teaspoons baking powder
¼ teaspoon baking soda

TOTAL PREPARATION AND BAKING TIME: 35 to 45 minutes.

1. Preheat oven to 375°F.
2. Mix flour and salt in a bowl. Cut in butter or margarine until mix is consistency of cornmeal.
3. In separate container, thoroughly blend sheep cheese, water, and vinegar. Add this fluid gradually to the flour and salt, blending with spatula or large metal spoon. When dough balls up, add baking powder and baking soda and knead dough till thoroughly incorporated.
4. Turn dough out on floured board, dust both sides with flour, and roll out lightly to a finger's thickness.
5. Cut into individual biscuits with a 3" biscuit cutter. Roll out remaining dough as above and cut into biscuits, repeating until all the dough is used.
6. Place biscuits on cookie sheet and put in oven, baking until just golden brown on top, 20 to 25 minutes. Remove from oven, cut open, and butter immediately.

MAKES 6 TO 9 BISCUITS

HOMING IN ON THE RANGE

Why is simplicity so expensive? The more simply and efficiently something does its job, the more beautiful it tends to be, which is fine, and the more it costs, which isn't.

We finally bought a house in Santa Fe. By the time we finish remodeling, it will cost us just under what we sold our house for in Little Rock five years ago. It's two-thirds the size of that house and in a much less upscale neighborhood. All of which, in Santa Fe, makes it a bargain.

But it doesn't feel like a bargain. Remodeling sucks you in. Dino is a good contractor, a man with imagination and a keen sense of design, and his men, Xoribio and Jesús, do fine work. We keep coming up with ideas, sleek little design touches, or extras like a one-bottle-wide wine rack using those four otherwise wasted inches between the refrigerator and the door. And they keep helping us along and the money just keeps flowing out.

But it's fun, it's exhilarating to get things exactly the way you want them. It dawned on me that for all our mutual love of food and the preparation of food, neither Jayme nor I had ever enjoyed a kitchen suited precisely to our specifications and preferences. Oh, we've done some repainting and we've improved the lighting and so on, but both of us have always simply accepted what was there and made the best of it. It's the same with my writing—for all the words I've cranked out over the years, I've never had an honest-to-goodness study. Which we are also about to provide ourselves, but that's another story.

There are limits to our improvements, of course, mainly financial. But also limits imposed by our needs and by our tastes. Our kitchen is going to be clean and beautiful and open and highly functional and full of light, but it isn't going to be one of those kitchens you see pictured in *Architectural Digest*.

We couldn't afford one of those, but that's OK, because we don't need the scale and we don't need the glitz.

In the early stages of our planning, we went shopping for a new range. The one that was here had a defunct oven and was small and ugly, enameled in one of those horrible colors that decorators were foisting off on their hapless victims twenty-five years ago—harvest bronze, they probably called it, or maybe, out here, desert copper.

The search was an eye-opener and was what first brought home to me the simplicity = money equation we would be dealing with from then on out. It was clear enough we weren't going to buy the $10,000 red enamel AGA. It was beautiful, but it was the approximate size and weight of a tank. I understand they're all the rage in this trendy town, but you'd have to have one of those huge trendy houses and a full-time cooking staff to justify the purchase.

Still, there were lots of possibilities. Stainless-steel commercial ranges, appealing not only in that they were made to work well and handle volume cooking, but also in the way that I suppose "official" major league or NBA gear must appeal to the armchair athlete. Still—did we need that much stove? $2,500 worth? Not really.

What we wanted was what we considered the perfect cooking combination, gas burners and an electric oven. As it developed, we couldn't find anything we really liked that had that combination and all the other features we wanted. Jayme was adamant that we have a self-cleaning oven, and I was all for the idea. Once I found out what sealed burners were—a continuous stovetop so that no food can drop down inside and there aren't any chrome plates to lift out, scrub, and which get irrevocably stained and discolored and cruddy—I was willing to settle for nothing less. The salesman made a great pitch for the aluminum gas vents as opposed to the heavy cast steel ones—a finer flame, especially on low and especially in these high altitudes.

True, we could have gone to a separate cooktop and oven, a sleek modernish sort of look. But the cooktop we really liked was well over a thousand in its cheapest version, and by the time we put a good oven with it, we would have been back in the cost vicinity of the commercial ranges. And on the affordable cooktops, the knobs were on the top, directly in front of the burners, which struck me as awkward. And anyway, our kitchen is small, and the separate hookups would cost us a lot of under-the-counter space.

The range I fell in love with was black-on-black. I'd never even considered black before. Aren't all stoves supposed to be white enamel? But once I saw it—well, we decided black was a really nice look and would go really well with the antique hardwood of the floor and countertops. It had great, heavy, black enamel hobs, and I liked that. No flimsy hobs for me.

The last thing we did was waver a little. The range we wanted was over $800—with taxes and delivery and the like, nearly $900. Not all that much to some, but a lot to us. There was a range down at one of the malls, last year's discontinued model, white, for half the price, that was almost as good. But it wasn't black. And finally we took the plunge.

As it turns out, we were right about the way the black would look—and now we've bought a dishwasher and microwave to match. (The black tile backsplash we decided to add does a lot to tie the look together.)

And along the way, it has become obvious why simplicity costs so much. Because it's only simple on the using end, of course. It takes a lot of thought and effort on the design end to make things simple on the using end. Quality of life, we keep telling ourselves. The quality of our lives, that intangible benefit, will make it worth the cost.

A HISTORY OF KITCHENS

As you probably gathered from the previous chapter, I'm a kitchen man. Always have been. In my father's traveling life as a Baptist preacher, and in my own peripatetic existence, I've lived in a lot of houses. I form a powerful attachment to any place I call home, but the room that I usually remember most clearly is not my own room, the one I slept in and dreamed in and played in. The room I remember most is the kitchen.

The first kitchen I remember was in a little clapboard house near the big house in Alligator, Mississippi. I remember high cabinets, my mother's sadness, learning to read at the vinyl-topped table. Peering at *Compton's Pictured Encyclopedia*.

I remember standing on a stool to wash dishes in the kitchen of the right half of a duplex in Newton, Mississippi. My mother got me started early, and to this day, I like washing dishes, hands in the hot soapy water. We've had one for years, but I've never warmed up to the dishwasher. The duplex was student preacher housing for Clark College, and I was eight years old. Later we made a jump up the social scale, into an actual house. It couldn't have been more than seven or eight hundred square feet, but it felt huge. The kitchen must not have impressed me, though, because I don't remember it. Sure enough, I feel less nostalgia for that little house than for any other dwelling in my history.

In Clinton, Mississippi, the first time, we lived in a little green house that provides an exception. I loved that house, but what I remember about it most is not the kitchen but the silver submarine (or, as occasion demanded, horse)— the side yard's butane tank. I remember also the wild brambly fifty-two-acre gully out back, taken away by I-20 in a few years, as the new Mississippi College basketball gym took away the house itself. I suppose the butane tank and the gully represented two of my other great loves—playful imagination and the natural world.

In New Orleans, in the cement-block housing project, while Dad went to seminary, I looked out a tiny open window over the sink and heard the cries of the vendors in the street below—shrimp, fish, vegetables, bananas fresh off the boat—and smelled my mother's pudding, made with vanilla wafers and batches of those same bananas, baking in the oven.

In Isabel, Louisiana, in the pastorium of Dad's first full-time church, the kitchen window looked out on a tumbledown barn and beyond it, on the piney woods that were my playground and second home. This is the kitchen I saw in my mind when I wrote "Preserves," the poem about my mother canning food for winter, which you may read in the sidebar if you like.

We had a nice kitchen in Glen Allen, Mississippi, looking out on a clothes-line and a chicken run. It was a clean kitchen, well lighted, the freezer stocked with catfish from Lake Washington across the street. I've told how mornings I would make coffee for Dad and tea for Mom, and carry in their tray. How I was allowed to have a cup myself for the service, and how it was there, in that kitchen, at the age of thirteen or fourteen, that I got hooked on coffee.

In Clinton, Mississippi, the second time around, where Dad pastored his one and only huge brick church and where I began and finished high school, we lived for the first time in a suburban house, small, tight, comfortable, and impersonal. The kitchen window looked out up a hill toward the home of the girl who would become my first wife (I was her first husband, too). All I knew at the time, though, was that my first girlfriend, Barbara Lambert, had left me, and so I wept for love in that kitchen. I do believe it was there that I began a lifelong habit—writing poetry at the kitchen table. Kitchens not only have been sources of nourishment, centers of family life, and the places where you sit and talk when friends visit, but they have also seemed, to me, the truest arena for creativity and intellectual excitement.

The kitchen in Sedalia, Missouri, where the former Lynnice McDonald and I put up as newlyweds was the only one not to have a window over the sink, though it had windows on two other walls. It was, as I described earlier, the kitchen in which I began to reteach myself, out of necessity, the recipes of my childhood.

On Center Street in Fayetteville, Arkansas, Lynnice and I had a hillside one-

PRESERVES

Great love goes mad to be spoken: You went out
to the ranked tentpoles of the butterbean patch,
picked beans in the sun. You bent, and dug
the black ground for fat, purple turnips.
You suffered the cornstalk's blades, to emerge
triumphant with grain. You spent all day in a coat
of dust, to pluck the difficult word
of a berry, plunk in a can. You brought home
voluminous tribute, cucumbers, peaches,
five-gallon buckets packed tightly with peas,
cords of sugar-cane, and were not content.
You had not yet done the pure, the completed,
the absolute deed. Out of that vegetable ore,
you wrought miracles: snapbeans broke
into speech, peas spilled from the long slit pod
like pearls, and the magical snap of your nail
filled bowls with the fat, white coinage of beans.
Still you were unfinished. Now fog swelled
in the kitchen, your hair wilted like vines.
These days drove you half-wild—you cried,
sometimes, for invisible reasons. In the yard,
out of your way, we played in the leaves, and heard
the pressure-cooker blow out its musical shriek.
Then it was done: You had us stack up the jars
like ingots, or books. In the dark of the shelves,
quarts of squash gave off a glow like late sun.
That was the last we thought of your summer
till the day that even the johnson grass died.
Then, bent over sweet relish and black-eyed peas,
over huckleberry pie, seeing the dog outside
shiver with cold, we would shiver, and eat.

—from *The Kid Who Wanted to Be a Spaceman*

room efficiency, the one in which I poured down all that syrupy instant coffee. What they meant by "efficiency" was apparently that the same area could either be a miniature living room or a miniature bedroom, depending on whether we let the Murphy bed down. The kitchen window opened onto the flat rooftop of the apartment below, however, and that de facto deck looked out over a wonderful little creek and the wooded cemetery on the hill beyond it. Evenings the lightning bugs swooped and soared and flashed like so many luminous souls in infinite space.

The poetry flowed and the sugary coffee flowed—that was where I wrote "Preserves," matter of fact—as I sat in one kitchen, writing about another. I was alive with hope, despair, and visions of immortal beauty. When I'd finish a poem, I'd run down the street and show it to my friend, the famous Johnny Wink. When we finished playing a summer game of touch football or little red rubber ball baseball, we'd all go back and sit around the table sweaty and cooling and happy, knocking back ice-cold gin and tonics.

And that would have been a good place to end, maybe, writing kitchen poems and death poems, happy in the immortality of my youth. But way leads on to way, and kitchen led on to kitchen, and life leads on to life. What did the kitchen in Fayetteville lead on to? To a rent house in the woods in southeast Texas. The house had been built by a deaf man named Smith, though he wasn't related to the original Deaf Smith. It was catty-cornered and anti-goggling and all out of plumb, rooms added on crazy-quilt, and I loved it.

Its kitchen looked out into pine and magnolia, the darkness of trees, and not of trees only. It was in that kitchen that I first tried my hand at sangria and tried and gave up on lentil burgers and other vegetarian approximations. We were living off the slender proceeds of a fried-pie route I had set up, and it was in the oven of that kitchen that we slowly and painfully, tray by tray, over the course of a whole night, dried out the accidentally rain-soaked pies of the batch for my first run, a batch that represented the investment of our total capital. It worked, sort of. Most of them didn't go bad, though the coconut seemed to turn pretty quickly.

It was in that kitchen that my wife and I prepared and fed our first daughter her first solid meals, our daughter who will be graduated from college this spring.

I didn't write poetry in that kitchen, though. As friendly as it was, it was too cramped and narrow, no good place to sit. I wrote poetry in the orange morris chair in the tilted living room. I wrote poetry *about* the kitchen, of course.

The next rent house we took, in the Ouachita river bottoms near Arkadelphia, was smaller and chintzier, the approximate size and shape of a boxcar, just four rooms in a row, but the kitchen was good for poetry and stories. Lynnice nursed our second daughter there, and it was there that a small circle of local poets gathered to read their work to each other. It was in that kitchen that I learned not to mix cardamom and chicken livers and from whose door I stepped out to feed the landlord's cows. It was there that I once tried to boil a dead owl in order to get the skeleton, and got instead a character named Christian Bean in a book called *Hawk Gumbo and Other Stories.*

From there we moved to a cabin I'd built, a cabin in the Arkansas woods west of Hollywood (and I hope that phrase, which became the title of my first published book, a collection of poems, sounds familiar to at least some of you). I'm not quite sure how we fed ourselves in that cabin, though actually we ate pretty well. There was really nothing there you could call a kitchen, just a sink in a small countertop right under the sleeping loft. No running water or electricity. We cooked our meals on a campstove and ate supper, often as not, by moonlight.

There was poetry there, but what we learned, mostly, was how very complicated and difficult the simple life is. The meal that brought all that home to me was an oyster stew. We'd splurged—it definitely seemed a splurge at the time—on one of those plastic ten-ounce containers of supposedly fresh oysters, and I concocted the stew in order to stretch the meal. The stew was good, but somehow, in the cooking, the oysters completely disappeared.

"The Mysterious Case of the Disappearing Oysters," I called it, and began, at long last, a search for easier kitchens and better ways.

I'm going to skip over the sad kitchens, the succession of extremely temporary habitations, less than a year each, in which my first marriage came apart. I'm going to start right in with the kitchen in the red-barn house. Actually, another marriage, ill advised on both our parts, began and ended there, but you don't need to know about that. Read the book if you want the juicy details.

The red-barn house was in Fayetteville, or actually, at the time, sort of just outside it, out Old Wire Road just across 286. It was a great location, a creek nearby, huge patches of blackberries in the pasture across the fence. I picked gallons and gallons of those berries, and made cobblers and tarts and wine and syrup. I once made Buddy Nordan, the great novelist and short-story writer, sick as a dog. I persuaded him to come pick blackberries with me, not realizing how deadly his allergies were.

But what I mainly remember about that kitchen is the people I fed there, the friends who came to visit. It was a big kitchen, with a sort of a breakfast counter separating it from a dining area, and although it was too dark—no windows except in the dining area—it was a very friendly kitchen. I fed Johnny and Susan Wink there, I fed the poet Larry Johnson. I fed my hero, Ben Kimpel, there. Ben came out more than once for breakfast, mainly because breakfast featured the biscuits I was, and am, so proud of. Nothing made me happier than serving that wise old gourmet something he really really enjoyed.

Well, almost nothing. That kitchen is also where I cooked Jayme Tull the first of many meals. It seems to me that allergies were involved there, too. I don't remember the menu for that first visit of hers, but I seem to recall that it featured onions pretty strongly—I loved cooking with onions—and that we were at that stage of the romance in which you don't mention such difficulties. In the same way, I hadn't said anything about the instant coffee she had served me on my first visit to her place. We got over that shyness pretty quickly, though—she let me know about the onions, and as you know, I brought a coffeepot with me the next time I came to her place. If you mean business, you don't waste time getting these things straight.

Within months, we were sharing a spacious kitchen in the Heights in Little Rock, a fine little brick two-story on a street full of rainbows. The kitchen looked out into a green backyard, where the huge Gray Dog roamed and raved. We remodeled, track lighting and light gray Formica countertops and lots of white paint, and it wound up feeling very light and airy and pleasant.

That kitchen had one dark secret, though. Cockroaches. Roosterroaches, as Don Harington's Stay Morons phrase it. The Heights is mightily infested with these beasts. You see them scurrying through the grass, hustling black bugs the size of a three-wheeler. They hide in the walls, behind framed paintings, in the crack behind the bookcase. The only way you can rid yourself of them is to massively poison your entire house, and how healthy can that be?

There were no cockroaches in the house we took in Conway. It was a great little house, but little is the operative word. We did minuets around each other and the chopping block. At parties, if you opened the refrigerator door, two people had to leave the room.

It was a good party kitchen in spite of that, looking out onto a sunporch and through it into a tree-shaded backyard with a beautiful blue kidney-shaped pool and patio. Maybe the best party we ever had there was the three-day party in October of 1992, when two dozen poets came into town for a conference and our house became the hospitality suite for the lot of them, with the kitchen at its center. The poets helped with the cooking and cleaning and serving, and we all ate, drank, talked, and laughed, and had a wonderful time.

And that brings me to our latest. As I mentioned a while back, we've done more to design this one the way we want than we've ever done in a kitchen before. So I'm sitting here, here with the wraparound hardwood countertops and the wraparound black tile backsplash, here with the new black-on-black range and the view of the Sangre de Cristos, and I'm wondering.

I'm wondering if this is the last kitchen, if this is home for good. I'm wondering who's going to sit at our table—when we have a table—and eat our cooking. I'm wondering what memories we're going to be making here. And I'm looking forward to it all.

ELENA LESTER'S AUTHENTIC
ORIGINAL GREEK MEATBALLS

You know what a premium I place on authenticity. I'll have you know I drove 240 miles through the frozen wastes of upper Massachusetts in the aftermath of the worst blizzard to hit the East in a century, and all just to get this recipe for you.

Well, no, actually, I was driving up to visit my daughter Lynnika at college, and they fed me the leftovers from their last meal, and the leftovers were Greek meatballs cooked by Lynnika's roommate Elena Lester and they were so good I insisted on the recipe. But it *was* a blizzard, and I *was* thinking of you.

What I'm trying not to think of is the kitchen the meatballs were cooked in. The house is co-ed, and somehow that seems to create the worst disorder of all, even worse than the residences of those other Greeks, those other meatballs, the frat rats. It's as if when men and women live together their individual messinesses somehow amplify each other. It wasn't the scattered bottles of beer and schnapps, the fragments of pizza on the floor, the dirty clothes in the hallway, the encrusted logjam of what I took to be cookpots and plates and utensils filling the sink and flowing over onto the counters. That wasn't what worried me, the hygiene of it all. What worried me was these people's futures.

I mean, living together like this, seeing all of this, what are they saving for marriage? What happens to the mystery and surprise my generation felt when we each individually discovered the truth about the way our new mate kept house?

Anyway, the meatballs. You need a pound of ground beef and a third of a pound of ground pork or ground lamb. (Elena's recipe calls for pork, but I didn't have any handy so I substituted the lamb, and listen, Elena, the meat-balls turned out wonderful. Try it.) You need three medium onions, chopped fine. You need enough butter to sauté the onions, which you may as well go ahead and start doing. You need some cooking oil. You need three table-spoons each of chopped fresh parsley and chopped fresh mint. You need an egg. You need three slices of wet white bread, squeezed out. (Elena didn't say what to wet the bread with, so I suppose you can play around. I used white wine.) You need a supply of flour to dust the meatballs with.

Mix the meat, egg, bread, parsley, mint, and sautéed onions in a bowl. Form medium-large meatballs, Elena says, and roll them in the flour. I wasn't sure what medium-large was, so I made mine about the size of the ones Lynnika and Elena fed me—palm-size, slightly larger than golf balls. They were easier to control at that size, too. I wound up with sixteen to twenty of them.

Fry the flour-dusted meatballs in the cooking oil, just lightly, turning them until they're browned all over. Drain them and then bake them in a baking dish covered with aluminum foil at 375°F for thirty to forty-five minutes.

And I decided, hating to waste anything, to make a sort of sauce. Pouring off most of the cooking oil, I browned the rest of the flour with the crusty leavings in the skillet, deglazed with more white wine and water, and added the juices cooked off from the baking when the meatballs were done. I sim-mered and tinkered till it thickened properly, and then I turned the heat off, returned the meatballs to the skillet, and let them soak while I finished my other preparations.

You see how authentic this all is, so don't write me those huffy letters set-ting me straight on what the *real* recipe for Greek meatballs is. It's true that Elena is an American citizen, but she was raised in Italy and that's close enough. Besides, she got the recipe from her mother and her mother may be Greek for all I know.

One other authentic touch: We had one of those long skinny jars of grape leaves. The kind of gourmet food you give people at Christmas, you know, that sits on their shelves until their children dispose of it after the funeral. But I thought to myself, *Greek, Greek, don't the Greeks have something to do with grapes, seems I remember something about they use grape leaves in something or other.* So I got the jar down.

What you have to do is slide the whole wad of leaves out—they're rolled up like the skin of a cigar and you tear them trying to pull them out one at a time. Then you unroll however many you want and arrange them on a platter to be filled.

I had cooked a pot of rice to go with the meatballs, so I decided that was how I was going to fill the grape leaves. I put a good couple of sticky tablespoons on each of the big star-shaped leaves I had extracted, folded the points of the star back over the rice, and then set the six or seven little olive green packets I'd made in a steamer for fifteen minutes or so while I finished the meatballs.

And that was our meal — rice wrapped in grape leaves, Elena Lester's Greek meatballs, my sauce, and a little wine. I know it wasn't *really* all that authentic. But it sure was good.

Elena Lester's Authentic Original Greek Meatballs

3 medium onions, finely chopped
2 tablespoons butter
3 slices white bread
4 tablespoons white wine
1 pound ground beef
⅓ pound ground pork
3 tablespoons chopped fresh parsley
3 tablespoons chopped fresh mint
1½ teaspoons salt
1 medium egg
Flour to coat
4 tablespoons cooking oil

Substitute ground lamb for the pork for a fine variation.

TOTAL PREPARATION AND COOKING TIME: 1 to 1½ hours.

1. Sauté onions in the butter till translucent.
2. In a shallow bowl or baking dish, soak bread in wine. Squeeze out excess liquid from bread.

3. In a medium bowl, thoroughly mix beef, pork, sautéed onions, parsley, mint, salt, soaked bread, and egg.
4. Form mixture into 16 to 20 palm-size balls (golf-ball size) and roll them in the flour to coat.
5. Preheat oven to 375°F.
6. Heat cooking oil in skillet (the same skillet you sautéed the onions in will be fine) and lightly brown meatballs evenly all over.
7. Drain meatballs, then place them in a baking dish and cover with foil.
8. Place in oven and bake for 30 to 45 minutes.

SERVES 2 TO 4

OYSTERFELLERS ROCK 'N' ROLL

In the spring, an aging man's fancy turns to thoughts of oysters. Normally, this time of year, we'd all be down on the beach on an island off the Gulf Coast, getting an early sunburn and sporting with the dolphins. Getting into freedom and wind and big water. About the late middle of the afternoon, we'd go back up to the house and find that some one of us, that day's volunteer, would have gone across the causeway into town and fetched back fresh shrimp and oysters from one of the fish houses lining the bay. So then it would be time for a feast.

Only now, this year, here we are in the north half of one of the drier and more landlocked states in the country, too broke and busy to find our way down to the big salt water.

That's the bad news. The good news is that there's a lot of obnoxious rich people in the area who insist on having exactly what they want when they want it. You'd think the Tesuque Village Market was a typical quikstop, for example, until you noticed all the Range Rovers parked out front, or passed Gene Hackman eating lunch on the patio, or went on inside and saw the chilled Dom Pérignon lying in the cooler beside the quarts and six-packs.

So you *can* get good seafood here. I had a wonderful sea bass with Thai-style sauce at the Brett House up in Taos last week. And this week—

The writer Larry Brown was in town, and he came in hungry, and what he was hungry for was oysters. We debated going out but finally decided we'd rather just kick back at the house, where the drinks were the right size and the right price. So he and Jayme and I went by the big Furr's grocery on Pacheco and headed straight back to the seafood section. Furr's is just a supermarket, one of a chain of them all over the state. There's three or four of them in town.

The one on Pacheco is the best, but it's still just a supermarket. But here's where you have to be grateful for all those rich people, because even the supermarket stocks good seafood.

I like the guy at the seafood counter. A long skinny drink of water he is, aw-shucks friendly, and he really seems to enjoy his job. He can sell you anything. He comes on the store PA announcing specials—they've been featuring salmon fillets at $4.99 a pound lately—and I'm a gone gosling, a cooked goose. He had talked me into trying the jars of supposedly fresh-shucked Washington State oysters the other day, and now I was bringing my friends.

The Washington State oysters *are* good, though very different from the Florida oysters I'm accustomed to. Huge things, spilling over the cracker on all sides. Take a lot of ketchup and horseradish. You have to eat them over the sink. *In* the sink would be better, because you need a good hosing down when you're through.

Anyway, we enjoyed them, but our eyes had been too big in the store, and we'd bought a couple jars more than we needed. Larry left the next day, and how were Jayme and I going to eat all those oysters ourselves? Well, at the beach, at least one evening of each vacation, Jayme always winds up baking her version of oysters Rockefeller. Thinking of that, I thought maybe an oyster casserole would be a good idea. I had two ten-ounce jars of oysters (five giant oysters in each), and I thought a loaf-size glass baking dish would be just about right.

I chopped three pieces of what Jayme calls bird bread (whole grain with lots of seeds in it) in the blender, together with perhaps a dozen club crackers and four ounces of grated cheddar and a nice handful of fresh parsley. Sliced and diced a couple of sticks of celery and stirred that in. Cooked up some chopped spinach (frozen, half a bag). Preheated my oven to 375°F.

I made a bottom layer of half the bread-cracker-cheese-parsley-celery mix, topped it with one jar of oysters, juice and all, salted and peppered the oysters, then covered them with a layer of the cooked spinach, and finally grated Parmesan over the top of the spinach. I repeated this layering one more time and my baking dish was full.

I happened to have some leftover dough from the previous night's pot-pie crust, so I rolled that out very thin and topped everything else with it. But I'd imagine the crust is optional.

I call the dish Oysterfellers Rock 'n' Roll because it sort of takes its original inspiration from oysters Rockefeller, but then I did some rocking and rolling with the recipe. I baked it for a good hour and served it steaming hot, no side dishes. We thought it was pretty good.

Not as good as being on the beach, but pretty good.

Oysterfellers Rock 'n' Roll

1 large bunch fresh or 1 package frozen spinach
3 tablespoons butter or margarine
3 slices whole grain bread, shredded
1 dozen club crackers, crumbled
3 tablespoons fresh parsley, chopped
3 stalks celery, chopped
1 cup cheddar cheese, grated
Two 10-ounce jars or 1¼ pounds fresh shucked oysters
Salt and freshly ground pepper, to taste
¾ cup Parmesan cheese, grated

TOTAL PREPARATION AND BAKING TIME: 80 minutes.

1. Preheat oven to 375°F.
2. If spinach is fresh, clean and destem.
3. Sauté spinach in butter and just enough water to keep from sticking until tender and water has mostly evaporated. (If spinach is frozen, you will not need to add much water.)
4. In blender, combine bread, club crackers, parsley, celery, and cheddar with 2 or 3 bursts.
5. Put half the mixture from the blender in a loaf-size glass baking dish.
6. Layer bread mixture with half the oysters, juice and all. Salt and pepper the oyster layer to taste and layer it with half of the spinach. Sprinkle evenly with half the Parmesan. Repeat until all ingredients are used.
7. Place in oven and bake for 1 hour. Serve with ketchup and horseradish or other condiments as desired.

SERVES 2

WHEN IT RAINS, IT POURS

I cut my finger a while back making supper. I was chopping carrots and the tip of my left forefinger strayed into the chopping zone. Bled like a stuck pig but wasn't too deep, really. Just about all healed up by now.

Went to put a Band-Aid on it. You know that little red thread? The one where it says on the packet, *Tear off end/Pull thread down?* I'm here to tell you, it actually worked. For the first time in my natural life I didn't have to tear into the thing with teeth and claws like a badly inflamed weasel. A week and a half short of fifty, probably my 3,000th Band-Aid, and I had finally successfully torn off end and pulled thread down. What a rush.

It worked because I finally noticed something. The *Tear off end/Pull thread down* message is on the *opposite* side of the packet from the thread. For half a century, I've been trying to pull the confounded thread through the confounded bandage. Now this is the sort of thing Jayme noticed when she was two, but Jayme is an unusual human. If in fact she is human. Is it fair of the company to expect the rest of us to notice? Especially when they put a red line symbolizing the thread between the *Tear off end* and the *Pull thread down*.

I ask you, friends, is this intelligent packaging?

Which is the subject of this chapter. Packaging. Food packaging in particular. Somehow, perhaps because I had been busy with supper, the Band-Aid incident triggered all my latent discontent with the ways in which food is commercially packaged.

Cheese, for example. Most of the cheese I buy is shaped like a brick, only with slightly more coloring added. Now why is all such cheese wrapped in a completely inflexible plasticized binding that *cannot* be opened neatly, that can only be torn open, and that *cannot* be resealed? Isn't there some mass manufacturer out there, some cheesy giant who cares enough to help me keep the edges of my dairy-based food product from turning hard and dark?

Or chips. Similar irritations pertain. Have you ever crumpled an empty potato- or corn-chip bag into a palm-size ball and then watched in awe as it resumed, with a slow steady ominous crackling reminiscent of *Terminator 2*, its full original volume and shape? Clearly the material was developed from the wreckage found near Roswell in 1947. How are we supposed to close such a container, oh how guarantee snapping-fresh *gnosh* to our guests?

Yes, we use the big yellow clips, but the point is, we shouldn't *have* to.

Spaghetti. OK, OK, pasta. I know the yups instantly transfer it to large crockery jars on their well-designed counters, where it becomes an article of decoration. Most people don't. When my life is over and heaven prints out the manifest, I expect to see that I have spent at least three full days of my time on this planet bending over to pick up scattered spaghetti from the kitchen floor. Would it be so difficult to design a nice rigid container with a flip-up spout sized to deliver a serving at a time?

I love mayonnaise. Hellmann's Real is the choice of choices, but I never met a mayonnaise I didn't like. What I don't like is mayonnaise jars. I have licked a lot of mayonnaise off my knuckles in my time. Is there any particular reason the mouth of every mayonnaise jar ever made has to be narrower than the body, in just such a bell-shaped fashion that no instrument is capable of scooping up the last three tablespoons of the stuff? The peanut butter people can design a cylindrical jar. The technology involved doesn't appear to be a matter of national security. Attention, Hellmann's—how about it?

There are other issues besides convenience. Jayme's pet peeve is the packaging of air and water. Not only is it a matter of greed—Contents May Have Settled in Shipping; Net Weight Sixteen Ounces, Fluid Content Thirteen Ounces —it is also a matter of environmental concern. Such packaging attacks the environment on several fronts, from wasteful use of raw materials to increased consumption of fuel for processing and shipping.

I could multiply examples, but I'm running out of room, and for some reason I am beginning to hear, in the back of my mind, the annoying nasalities of Andy Rooney.

AND IF YOU use an ulu, you'll love your ulu, too.

What is an ulu? Well, it's a kind of Eskimo knife. Or perhaps I should say Athabascan, that family of Northwestern seacoast tribes. Which gives a bit of a cultural connection to our present locale, because there is some evidence that the Navajo and their first cousins, the Apache, are of Athabascan lineage. But as far as I know there are no Navajo ulus.

Not that our ulu is all that fancy or anything. And the materials are certainly not exotic. It is made, as nearly as I can tell, from an old circular sawblade, a quarter section of it set, radius point first, into a slightly larger than palm-size wooden handle and fastened with a brass screw whose shaft has been milled flush with the handle. A simple device, ready and comfortable in the hand. The lineal descendant of tools that were probably made of bone or, on occasion, stone. And contrary to the general theme of this chapter, an example of superb design.

I've always envied those cooks who could speed-julienne a carrot or slice mushrooms instantly into paper-thin sections. My hands are very steady, but I've never developed the fingering to feel safe with a fast-moving knife. The ulu helps, because the edge of the blade is the arc of a perfect circle. You hold it in perfect balance from the top, and you can rock the blade back and forth, more or less feeding the innocent vegetable through with the other hand.

Years ago I hated the chopping, the slicing, the dicing, the mincing, all the tedious business of preparation. Gradually it has come to be one of my favorite

To be fair and in the spirit of offering constructive criticism, I will close with what Jayme considers an example of highly successful packaging: It's durable, it's round and fits a hand perfectly, it keeps the product dry and in good shape, the spout is sized perfectly for filling smaller service containers, and it has become the industry standard.

It's the Morton Salt container, of course.

parts of the process. I love good tools, the exactly right tools. I have come to abhor the salad shooter, and I am discovering in myself a growing reluctance even to use the food processor.

It is true that my way takes more time. Or it's sort of true. What's time to a hog, as the old joke goes. And really, if you think about it, isn't there a whole lot of assembling and disassembling and washing and drying and reassembly and storage involved when you use one of those multiple-attachment gadgets? More good old American overkill. Substitute a technology for a tedium and then spend all your time maintaining the technology or making the money to pay for the upkeep. No, you can choose the form of your drudgery, but you can't escape a certain amount of it. And I prefer that variety of busywork that offers the smells of fresh bell peppers or mint or minced garlic, the textures of the blade and the chopping block, the rhythm of the moment.

I admit I make an exception for coleslaw because cabbage goes everywhere when you chop it by hand. And sure, if I need a batter beaten really fine, I'm not going to sit there and whip a whisk back and forth for half an hour.

Otherwise, it's manual labor for me. Do the thing yourself, do it with your hands, do it slowly as you need to, and do it right: Do it with pleasure.

And if you come across one on your next trip to Alaska, you can do it with an ulu.

THE REAL CEREMONY

Williams College is old, rich, and more ceremonious than a fund-raising parson at a Daughters of the American Revolution tea party. I was in northwest Massachusetts once again, this time for my daughter Lynnika's graduation.

At Williams, they figure that if something is worth doing once, it's even better to do it three or four times. So we had Ivy Exercises, two and a half hours of sitting in the sun. Baccalaureate that evening (which we all skipped). And commencement, three hours of sitting in the sun. Not one Olmstead Award for excellence in secondary education, but four awards, with long speeches for each presentation. Not one, but two class poems. Not one or two, but four honorary doctorates, with long speeches for each presentation. Not one but three senior-class student speakers. The commencement address was excellent, almost had me cheering, set forth a hell of a humane vision for the future. Went on awhile, though.

But what about the food? Any good do ought to involve food.

In this area, we were on our own. Excluding the sugar-cookie, tepid-lemonade, melon-and-strawberry-on-a-toothpick, mill-around-under-the-awning president's reception, I mean.

Fortunately, some weeks ago, Lynnika had conceived a notion that her significant other, Luke, and I should put our heads together and whip up a Saturday night, pre-commencement meal for her, her best friend, Elena (she of the Greek meatballs), Elena's fellow, Blake, and the families of all the aforesaid. I have already described the kitchen of the house Lynnika and Elena lived in, so you understand the challenge involved.

Luke and I went shopping for booze. My first wife had contributed a bottle of Iron Horse, which for inexpensive champers is not bad stuff at all. I had the feeling we were going to need at least two more bottles for the eleven people in attendance, and I think I just about drove Luke crazy ransacking the store for acceptable bubbly. I finally came up with Paul Cheneau and one other whose name I forget, but which was the real stuff, not bulk process.

Next, we had to loop back, pick Lynnika up, and do the grocery shopping. We had about settled our menu—Lynnika and Elena would make their famous yeast-rising cheese bread and their famous fruit-flavored yogurt-and-Cool-Whip frozen pies. Luke would make his famous coconut-batter tempura shrimp. And I would make a couple of my famous quiches. The question was what sort of quiche? I was leaning toward one each of spinach and ham, but you never settle questions like that till you see what the grocery has in stock. I went with the spinach for one, but saw some nice-looking scallops, so decided what we needed was a scallop-and-mushroom quiche flavored by just a few tangy shreds of Virginia ham.

By now it was after five and time to get cooking. The kitchen became the scene of a wonderful chaos. We worked all at once everywhere at once, the long-board table down the middle of the kitchen covered in clutter. Was there a mixing bowl? Of course not. Then cut the butter into the flour in a huge plastic thing that might have once covered a light fixture. Who's going to help peel the shrimp? Somebody needs to be cleaning and destemming the spinach. Thank you, Blake. Go ahead and sauté it in some butter when you're done. Where's the cream? Is that glass clean? Somebody brought down a player and we had rock and roll. Elena, who craves my body, as well she might, helped me out by lifting my bourbon-and-rocks to my lips from time to time so I wouldn't get flour all over the glass.

I realized it was time for martinis, the parents were getting restless. I had of course forgotten to get vermouth at the liquor store, though I had bought gin. We swapped with some students who were having a cocktail party on the front lawn, limes for vermouth.

It all came together—recipes, accidents, people. Too much crust, so I turned the leftovers into a sort of focaccia, and that and Elena's folks' pâté made appetizers. Later on Lynnika tried her hand at a recipe for whiskey sours she had gotten from her friend Andreas, a recipe that seemed to involve brown sugar, barrels of oranges and lemons, and unknown other substances, a recipe for which she had received a last-minute coaching, having run into Andreas in the grocery store, and a recipe that in fact produced the best whiskey sours I've ever had.

By nine o'clock, we were feasting. Luke's shrimp were superb, the bread was hot and chewy and delicious, the quiches disappeared rapidly, the music went on and on, we brought out the chilled champagne and toasted the seniors, and we were raucous and having fun.

It had all been fortuitous, it had all been lucky. There had been depression and problems before, there would be depression and problems to follow. But for the moment, we were all happy together. My daughter, I saw, is a wise woman, and I congratulate her on her wisdom. It was a night to remember. It was the real ceremony.

THE WAY TO A WOMAN'S HEART

Whoever said that the way to a man's heart is through his stomach (besides being ignorant of the *real* hierarchy of male anatomy) made an egregious oversight: As a woman who has been swept off her feet in no small part by the culinary genius of a man, I can testify that our tummies are every bit as open to seduction as theirs.

I suppose I should back up a little and give you some explanation. If the gender thing has confused you because you were pretty sure Jack Butler was a guy, you can rest easy: I am merely his daughter, fresh out of college (as you have doubtless heard).

Anyway, it all started at the end of my junior year with some homemade guacamole fed to me at a party by a devastatingly handsome stranger. The avocados were fresh and ripe, there were chunks of onion and maybe a hint of garlic, some tomato if I remember correctly, and the balance of lemon juice and Tabasco was brilliant. Already I was impressed, and I could tell by the suave confidence of the chef that this was not a man to be intimidated by the unprepackaged, instructionless, *fresh* foods shunned by so many of his fellow creatures.

In fact, through a series of events too coincidental and scandalous to relate, I found myself the very next night eating a tomato, basil, and Brie pizza I had watched him make from scratch, and a simple dessert of strawberries and champagne. I was beginning to realize that Luke (by this time I had learned his name) had an almost instinctive feel for flavors and spices.

Believe me when I tell you that it would have taken a strong woman indeed to withstand such an onslaught: His friends saw me succumbing to his culinary charms and tried to warn me about the darker side of his character. But all my girlfriends, who got the romantic play-by-play from me on a daily basis, were just as floored as I had been by the sophistication of a man who was better in the kitchen than any of us.

In the whirlwind of the next weeks and months, Luke kept me entranced with one amazing creation after another. Just before his graduation, he showed his Sensitive Nineties-Man side by treating his fellow skiers and me to a spinach and wild mushroom lasagna inspired by the menu of a local restaurant (secret ingredients: Feta and lots of nutmeg).

Since then, several modifications of that recipe have awed friends and housemates. A version with three kinds of mushrooms, less cheese, no cream, and more pureed tofu made Jayme (of the legendary allergies) very happy indeed.

The next summer, he charmed his way into my mother's heart with gazpacho made from scratch, then lured me off to Lake Michigan, where we ate refrigerator omelets for breakfast and picnicked on the beach for lunch with beer and the ultimate bagel sandwiches: Grey Poupon, cream cheese, Vermont cheddar, fresh lettuce, homemade hummus, onions, tomatoes, ham or turkey or whatever there was, and salsa if we were feeling a little crazy (on a *toasted* bakery bagel, of course). For dinner one night there was even blue chicken: a stir-fry made with chicken marinated in, among other things, the leftover wild blueberries we had picked that morning for pancakes.

That fall I began my senior year at Williams. The months since have had their share of new concoctions, but space prevents my giving you all the details. Suffice it to say that, as Luke will happily tell you, after fourteen months of eating his food, I'm in love like you read about.

The message in all this is as follows: Women, find yourselves men who can cook better than you and aren't embarrassed about it, and you will probably spend months or years discovering a wealth of other fascinating talents; and men, a little culinary finesse can make an otherwise bland personality seem infinitely mysterious and intriguing.

MUTTON CHEF

If you go to any of the Indian markets around here—and if you visit New Mexico at the right time of year, which is right about this time of year, high summer, you *should* go to some of them—be prepared for food that's a little different. That is to say, it's different from what you might get at War Eagle or Riverfest or any typical Arkansas fair. Certainly it's not different to the people who conduct the markets, or to most of their regular customers.

There are points of similarity. You can often find snow cones, and some booths at some markets produce that most dangerous of carnival treats, funnel cake. I suppose tamales are not that unusual in other parts of the country. But there are no Junior Leaguers selling cornbread and black-eyed peas, and there are no Greek booths selling gyros. New Mexico Indian market cuisine is distinguished by the prevalence of two things: mutton and fry bread.

You can buy all sorts of other comestibles: whisper-thin, stone-baked piki bread, roasted ears of corn, tortillas filled with chile sauces and beans or meat or cheese, half-spherical loaves of bread baked in *hornos* (those outdoor adobe ovens you still see everywhere across the state).

But sooner or later, you'll get around to mutton and fry bread.

Fry bread is a chewy, flour-based, deep-fried favorite, full of air pockets, leathery when it gets cold, but irresistible fresh from the cooker. You can wrap it around chile and cheese (the famous Navajo taco), use it as the packaging for slices of roasted mutton or an otherwise perfectly ordinary cheeseburger, or simply sop your posole or mutton stew with it. It is, naturally enough, extremely greasy. In a harsh dry climate, that fact is not all to the bad. You do save money on skin conditioners: The classic way to munch fry

SOME OF YOU may have noticed that I refer variously to chile or chiles, and then again to something I call chili. This isn't a matter of careless spelling—there's method in my madness. To the Hispanic populations that have made these plants an indispensable element of their cuisine, the volatile peppers are chiles, with an *e* in the final syllable. The ubiquitous modern spelling, *chili*, is a corruption, which we might as well blame on Texas.

Throughout this book I use the spelling *chile* to refer to the plant or to any pure derivatives of the plant. I use the spelling *chili* only in reference to that concoction of tomato sauce and ground beef, which was probably invented in Texas not all that long ago, and is not at all a historical Mexican dish. So, when I call for chile powder in the paragraph on seasoning my mutton stew, I mean pure ground-up chile peppers and *not* the supermarket chili powder with an *i*. That powder is a mix with comino (or cumin) already in it, meant specifically for creating its namesake dish. I disdain it because the proportions of chile and comino are predetermined, and you can't roll your own.

As long as we're on the subject: I'm no chile-head, but I have picked up one or two other useful bits of information. As for example the difference between red and green chiles. The essential difference is when they are picked. When you visit a Santa Fe restaurant and you get some of that "authentic" Southwestern cuisine, you may be asked whether you want red chile or green chile with it. Some people think there's a difference in heat levels, but there isn't. Or at least, not a *predictable* difference. Red chile is made from fully ripened chiles. Green chile is made from the same fruit, but picked while it is still green. Any variations in flammability are a result of local variations in the batch, or of other treatments or ingredients.

bread is to wander from booth to booth in the August sun, juices dripping over your hands and an oily sweat beginning to film your sunburnt *belagana* brow.

Mutton appears at the markets in many forms—this is sheep-raising country, after all—but the two most common are the ones I've mentioned, roast mutton and mutton stew. Mutton is not a lean meat, and often as not the mutton served up at the markets is tough and stringy. The locals are not going to be eating the fancier cuts of meat, not any more than I do at home. Rest

To my palate, there *is* a variation in taste—green chile tastes, well, greener. Red chile is fuller bodied, especially if it has been roasted. There are thousands of kinds of salsa made from red and green chiles, and your only reliable guide to the heat factor of any given batch is your own tongue. I have never yet met a waiter who told the truth in this area. I myself prefer salsas that have not been junked up with onion, tomato, cilantro, et cetera, which pretty much eliminates most of the mass-market brands.

If you come to New Mexico for a visit, you may see people selling braids and wreaths of chile peppers beside the road. These are known as *ristras*. Extravagantly priced, for the most part—a medium-size ristra, in season, can easily run you thirty bucks—they are attractive and do make nice gifts. If you are visiting earlier than the last half of August, though, the ristras you see are likely to be from last year's crop. In any case, ask.

One of my favorite dishes is chiles rellenos. Rellenos, by the way, means "stuffed," so that you can have sopapilla rellenos—or, after finishing one, you yourself may be rellenos. I've found that the chiles used in rellenos around here are usually fairly mild, and most of the heat comes from whatever toppings have been applied.

One last warning: *Carne adovada* is pork that has been simmered in a chile powder sauce for a long time. A lot of sauce, for a real long time. You think you want a carne adovada burrito for breakfast. You don't. Not that it isn't good. It is good.

It's just that your screaming will disturb all the other diners.

easy, though—the same phenomenon that makes fry bread taste so good at the market makes this gristly meat seem a mouth-watering delicacy.

I wish I could tell you I was going to give you authentic recipes for mutton stew and fry bread, but I haven't learned them yet. Still, I was thinking about them the other day, and the thought inspired me to create a meal I *will* give you the blueprints for.

I bought a couple of bone-in mutton chops, the cheaper cuts, enough to provide me with about a pound of cubed meat after cleaning. It took thirty or forty minutes to debone and defat the chops, but then I enjoy taking my time preparing meals. It's the way I relax after work: laying out all my instruments, choosing my spices, premixing ingredients, peeling and washing and slicing and dicing. I fix myself a whiskey or a potato vodka martini, and the setting sun makes the snow on the Sangres a rosy effulgence, and the houses of the neighborhood begin to glow in the last light, and things begin to bubble and simmer and smell good . . .

So anyway, I set the bones and fat and trimmings to boiling with a little salt and pepper. I threw one whole carrot and celery stalk into the pot, then chopped up three carrots and three celery stalks and set them aside to add to the stew later. Then I salted and peppered and floured the cubed mutton and browned the morsels in hot oil, draining them on heavy paper afterwards. I deglazed the skillet with just a little wine and added the wine to the boil. I turned the heat down and left matters at that stage for a while, until my lamb trimmings had cooked enough, an hour or so.

Then I drained the broth into a kettle, removing the fat, gristle, bone, celery, and carrot, cleaned what meat there was off the bones, and returned the meat to the broth. I chopped three cloves of garlic very fine, added them and the rest of the celery and carrots, and returned the broth to the fire.

Finally, I added the browned mutton and half a tablespoon each of comino—which is what they call cumin here—and chile powder. I thickened the mix just a little with flour dissolved in cold water—not much, because you don't want it sticking—and let things simmer a couple of hours, until the mutton was tender.

This approach yielded a stew of almost Biblical savoriness, warm and hearty and heartwarming. I served it with golden brown Southern-style corncakes, my own personal fry bread equivalent. They made a superb match of flavor and texture. Tell you what—why don't I give you my corncake recipe (see page 158), and you can try the whole shebang out for yourself.

Mutton Stew

2 bone-in mutton chops (about
¾ pound each)
4 medium carrots
4 stalks celery
3 cloves garlic
Salt and freshly ground pepper,
to taste

Flour for coating and thickening
2 tablespoons cooking oil
½ cup red wine
¼ cup sun-dried cherries
½ teaspoon chile powder
½ teaspoon cumin

This recipe also makes an excellent pork stew.

TOTAL PREPARATION AND COOKING TIME: 2½ hours.

1. Defat and debone chops and cube meat.
2. Throw fat and bones into a pot with 1 whole carrot and 1 whole celery stalk and cover with water.
3. Bring to a boil, then simmer for 1 hour or until remaining meat easily pulls away from bones.
4. Chop remaining 3 carrots and celery stalks. Mince garlic. Set aside.
5. While broth is simmering, salt and pepper meat cubes to taste and coat with flour.
6. In skillet, brown meat cubes in hot oil, then set aside to drain.
7. Pour remaining oil out of skillet, then deglaze skillet with wine.
8. Pour wine from skillet into broth and simmer for about an hour.
9. When broth is ready, sieve out the bones, gristle, fat, and vegetables.
10. Remove meat that clings to bones and return meat to broth. Add chopped carrots and celery, garlic, sun-dried cherries, chile powder, cumin, and browned mutton cubes to broth. Bring to a boil again and simmer for an hour or until meat is tender.
11. In the last stages of cooking, thicken the stew with 2 tablespoons or so of flour dissolved in a little cold water. Serve piping hot with corncakes (page 158) or Shepherd's Winter Biscuits (page 124).

SERVES 4

CORN TAKES THE CAKE

Actually, I assume all Southerners know how to make cornbread. I assume they have recipes somewhat different from mine, which they are willing to defend to their sadly mistaken deaths. So I ought to assume most Southerners know all about corncakes, too. But assumptions are tricky things. There's a whole generation coming up for whom the hometraining in cooking for yourself has been sadly lacking.

I won't call them Generation X because trendiness has an adverse effect on my psyche. Anyway, there's nothing new about the idea. It's just an updated version of the Lost Generation, as if there were any generations that weren't lost, eventually. We've had the Lost Generation concept around for — well, generations.

I'm not worried about their angst, if that's still a usable term, or the supposed drift in their moral compass, or the fact that they're highly educated and underemployed. I'm worried they're not going to be able to eat well if they don't learn how to cook for themselves.

You can't solve every problem all at once. You have to start with single simple things and do what you can. So I'm starting with corncakes.

I've talked about cornbread before, and I won't re-cover all that ground. But when I was growing up, cornbread came in three basic varieties. You had your big round skillet cornbread, suitable for slicing into big butter-slathered wedges and drowning in pea juice or crumbling into a big glass of buttermilk and eating with a spoon. Which, when you think about it, is not that different, nutritionally speaking, from eating granola crumbled into yogurt. Although with cornbread and buttermilk you somehow don't tend to envision a well-muscled shirtless fellow in loose-fitting jeans leaning against a sun-drenched wall in southern California.

You had your cornbread sticks, baked in those rectangular, cast-iron, corn-bread-stick makers. The sticks were great for picking up and munching, hot from the oven or cold from the fridge. They also went well with soup—you could soak one end of a stick in the broth then bite it off—delicious. Let's be clear about this, by the way—you want just the plain cornbread-stick pan. You do *not* want some cute little thing intaglioed to make the sticks look like ears of corn.

And you had your skillet-fried corncakes. Corncakes are made of cornmeal batter just like skillet cornbread and cornbread sticks, but you pour them out and cook them like pancakes. They're for when you need cornbread bad, but there's none left over and you're in a hurry. Or for when you just want corncakes instead of the other two kinds.

I make my corncakes with two cups of cornmeal to one cup of flour, which is more flour than I would use for regular cornbread. You're going to be flipping these suckers, and you want them to have enough gluten to hold together. I put in a pinch and a half of baking soda, three teaspoons of baking powder, a bit of salt, and mix my dry ingredients. Then I add three tablespoons of vegetable oil or butter, and cut it in. Next I make a hollow in the mix, crack a couple of eggs into it, and begin adding buttermilk. I beat the mix into the liquid until it begins to get too thick, add more buttermilk, and continue beating. You can't really go wrong, except by adding too much buttermilk. You want a thick batter that will just barely pour. Beat it a long time to loosen up the gluten in the flour.

I cook my corncakes in melted butter in a black iron skillet on medium heat, two at a time, something like a half cup of batter per cake. (Actually, I use a gravy ladle at about two ladles per cake.) A cast-iron griddle would probably work just as well or better, but you know me and skillets. As with pancakes, flip them when they begin to bubble on top, though you might test them early, lifting up the edges gently to make sure they're not sticking or burning.

Butter them as you take them off the heat, and they're ready for a thousand wonderful combinations. They do just fine as a quick companion to a heated-up can of black-eyed peas, especially if you have some green onions handy. Jayme likes them with jelly or syrup. And as I say, they're absolutely wonderful with that mutton stew (see page 155). In fact, they're great with stews and soups generally—we used to have them with beef-and-vegetable soup all the time when I was growing up. You can crumble them into the soup, dip them like cornbread sticks and bite off a sopping chunk, or just have them on the side.

And here's a new one: Jayme has taken to crumbling a leftover corncake into her scrambled eggs, just as the eggs are beginning to skin up. She folds the crumbles gently in, and keeps everything nice and moist. Sounds weird, but I tried it, and it's a pretty good breakfast. Especially if you grate yellow cheese over the top and then spoon some chili or salsa over the whole kit and caboodle. Huevos rancheros con corncakes — Olé!

Skillet Corncakes

2 cups whole-kernel yellow
   cornmeal
1 cup unbleached white flour
3 teaspoons baking powder
$\frac{1}{8}$ teaspoon baking soda

1 teaspoon salt
5 tablespoons butter or margarine
2 medium eggs
$1\frac{1}{2}$ cups buttermilk

TOTAL PREPARATION AND COOKING TIME: 20 to 25 minutes.

1. Sift dry ingredients together in a large mixing bowl. Cut in 3 tablespoons butter or margarine thoroughly. Form a hollow in dry mix, then crack in eggs and begin adding buttermilk, beating until a smooth, thick batter forms.
2. On high heat, melt 2 tablespoons of butter or margarine in skillet. Then turn heat down to medium and pour batter into skillet (two 4" cakes at a time, about $\frac{1}{2}$ cup batter each). Brown, then flip like a pancake when bubbles begin forming on top. Brown other side. Repeat until all batter is used.
3. Brush with butter and serve with stew, soup, or buttermilk.

SERVES 4 TO 6

A SIMPLE LITTLE MASTERPIECE

That's what Jayme called it. It was good, and it wasn't very hard to make.

I can't really take credit for the basic trick, though. I learned it better than thirty years ago from the poet John Wood, back in the glory/horror days in Fayetteville. When I knew him, John was a great big round golden-haired exotic fellow, a gourmet, a gourmand, an antique collector, a man with a host of interesting bits of knowledge. It has been years since John and I have spoken, I'm not sure why. Time and distance, maybe. Maybe also because he thinks I have that piece of toilet paper on which Ezra Pound drafted one of the Pisan cantos. I think he thinks Ben Kimpel left it to me in his will. I think he wanted it, and he thinks I have it. I don't.

I know who does, though.

So enough of this history, what's the basic trick? I'll get to it in the sidebar.

Your experience with pasta has probably been a lot like mine. We didn't have pasta when I was growing up, we had spaghetti. Dad made a big vat of tomato-and-ground-beef sauce and spooned it over the hot spaghetti. If he was being really exotic, really Continental, maybe he made meatballs instead of cooking the ground beef loose. That was all I knew of pasta, that and macaroni and cheese, and I didn't associate the two dishes in any way.

But I have belatedly come to an appreciation of all those other lengths and thicknesses and wiggles and curlicues. I have even taken to referring to them generically as pasta, which will cause them to check your ID at the Good Old Boys Club. (I hasten to add that I began doing this *before* we moved to Santa Fe, lest you mistakenly conclude that Sunbelt trendiness is to blame.)

Since we try to avoid an excess of carbohydrates in our diet, pasta is dangerous. You can't really afford to load up on it, not unless you do marathons.

THE TRICK I'VE been hinting at, this trick that I learned from a writer, is a good trick for writers to know. It's a good trick for writers to know because it's quick, simple, cheap, and fortifying. I was a starving writer when I learned it, and it helped.

You apply the trick almost at the very end of your preparations, just before you grate the hard cheese all over everything. It works like this.

Drain your pasta quickly, return it to the pot you cooked it in (or to whatever skillet or other dish you have cooked your sauce in), toss the pasta with your sauce, and then, while the noodles are still hot, rapidly stir in a raw egg (or two, depending on the amount of pasta you have). The remaining heat cooks the egg quite thoroughly, and coats each strand or sliver or tube with a creamy richness. Not only have you thickened your sauce, making the dish seem more substantial, but you've also just added a nice little dollop of protein to your diet.

It works for almost any sauce or type of pasta—can be used in carbonara and many another dish, for example. Actually, it works for soup, too. When I've been sick and unable to take in any sort of nourishment except fluids, I have sometimes dropped an egg into a hot bowl of, say, chicken soup, beaten it rapidly, and let the heat of the serving cook it. The result is a whole lot like cream of chicken, except that you've got more protein and fewer carbohydrates.

But pasta has so much to recommend it. It's easy, for one thing. You can nearly always throw together a good sauce in a matter of minutes from whatever leftovers you have in the fridge. The sauce that occasioned the title for this chapter involved bits of grilled kielbasa and diced broccoli—broccoli!—from the night before.

In one of my favorite pasta sauces, the ingredients are simply olive oil, crushed garlic, and fresh oyster mushrooms. Last night I made a sauce with standard grocery-store mushrooms, olive oil, crushed garlic, diced firm tofu, and a handful of washed basil leaves and rosemary. You get the idea. In the matter of pasta sauces, begin with a little (a very little) olive oil and a lot (a very lot) of garlic, and you can hardly go wrong. I often deglaze with white wine, and, like the mushrooms, many ingredients will generate their own liquor. But I prefer my sauces thick, so that they'll cling to the pasta. So I usually cook them down a bit, removing my solid ingredients first if there's a danger of overcooking and returning them when I toss everything together. As for the pasta itself, I'm no connoisseur—I like it soft and tender, not al dente. Jayme prefers it a little more to the tooth, but then she has more teeth. As often as not I don't really *toss* my pasta, either. I'll drain it, let it sit a half a minute to steam itself completely dry, then tump it all over into the skillet and stir the mess around with a spatula.

I know, I know. Not fooling anybody with these country confessions. First he's saying "pasta" out loud, and now he's cooking with tofu. Keep up like that, and he ain't gone hardly have no image left a-tall. What can I tell you, Bubba? I still wash it all down with Wild Turkey.

So anyway, pasta is simple, quick, filling, and good.

Especially if you crown the steaming noodles with a mound of fresh-grated Parmesan or Romano or Reggiano. I urge you to get hold of a chunk of genuine hard cheese. It will change your life. If you can't get it locally, go to St. Louis or New York. It will keep long enough to make the trip economically feasible. We just finished up a piece we got in Washington, D.C. That one piece got us most of the way through five years in Conway, Arkansas, traveled cross-country again, and got us through yet another year in Santa Fe, New Mexico. The stuff is immortal and delicious, and besides—with no more extra effort than a little elbow grease, you, too, can feel like a master chef from the showplace restaurants of northern Italy.

Basil Pasta with Egg Dressing

3 tablespoons olive oil
Freshly ground pepper, to taste
1 clove garlic, minced
2 medium leaves fresh basil,
  minced

½ pound dry spaghetti or
  fettucini
2 medium eggs
3 to 4 tablespoons Parmesan
  cheese, grated

You can make this quick and easy dish with an almost infinite variety of fresh herbs, or you can add chopped mushrooms or other vegetables to the sauce.

TOTAL PREPARATION AND COOKING TIME: 20 to 25 minutes.

1. Heat 2 tablespoons olive oil in skillet. Mill in fresh pepper to taste, add garlic and basil, and sauté lightly until garlic is just translucent but not brown.
2. Turn heat off.
3. In a large pot, bring water to boil for pasta. Add remaining tablespoon of olive oil and a pinch of salt, then add pasta.
4. Reduce heat to medium and cook pasta to desired tenderness, no longer than 10 minutes if you like it al dente. (Test a strand or two to be certain.)
5. Drain pasta in colander and immediately, while still hot and steaming, turn pasta into skillet and toss with olive oil sauce. Immediately crack eggs into skillet and continue to toss pasta until thoroughly coated with egg (the heat of the pasta cooks the egg). Top with Parmesan and serve with sliced fresh tomatoes or a salad.

SERVES 2

THE SAME OLD GRIND

I get sick of food sometimes.

I hope this isn't a shocking confession, me being a food author and all.

Normally my evening's entertainment is preparing dinner. Normally I eat too much and love it. But every now and then I just get, well, fed up with the whole shebang.

I get sick and tired of shopping for food. I get sick of cleaning and chopping and slicing and marinating and parboiling and batterfrying. I get tired of washing the dishes, stowing the leftovers, throwing out the old stuff, sweeping the floor where the crumbs fell, securing the garbage so the cats won't eat the chicken skins or the shrink-wrap the hamburger came in.

I get sick and tired of even thinking about food sometimes.

Heck, I get tired of *eating* it.

It doesn't happen often, but it happens. One day it all just seems too much trouble. I begrudge the cost in time and energy and imagination. I begrudge the very drudgery of chewing: grinding my chops, reducing the complex to the simple, the exquisite to slurry. Mastication, that's what it is. An abstract mechanical act. It's like being a robot. Several times a day, no matter how elevated I think my thoughts are, no matter how noble my dreams, I'm going to sit stupefied and ruminating like Bevo on Darvon. Keep the fuel coming, keep the engine running.

Really, this shouldn't be too surprising a confession. I think it must happen in every love affair. The normal values of your life suffer a polar reversal, like the Earth every few thousand years, and for immediate reasons that are at least as mysterious. Whatever it is you love, whether it's a person, a place, or a life's work, you sometimes get too close. You get absorbed in it, in far too literal a sense. There's no *you* anymore. You have to get away.

I get sick of food when I start feeling like the *food* is swallowing *me*.

When that happens, I don't cook, and I don't eat until I start feeling weak or the pain in my stomach gets too distracting. Then I throw down a few spoons of yogurt, half a chocolate cookie, a handful of stale potato chips. I may lick peanut butter from a table knife or chew on the edge of a cold hamburger patty, too bored to bother with onion, lettuce, and mayonnaise. Milk is handy because you can pour down a half a cup in no time at all and shut your belly up.

Sometimes I fast. Even though I'm not doing it for penance or to attain a visionary state, I'd call it a semireligious act, because it is an act of abandonment: Weary of one part of the world of illusion and desire, for a while, for a brief little while, I live on a different plane.

But even then, I take my vitamins. I'm not *that* tired of the world of illusion and desire.

The longest I've ever fasted was four days, when I was much younger. That time I quit when my chest started hurting during my daily run. Nowadays twenty-four hours is a max. It wouldn't hurt me to abstain on, say, Fridays and to donate the unspent money to help allay world hunger. But the one time I tried it, everybody I'm married to looked at me real funny.

What breaks down, I think, is my sense of play.

Humans have turned every single basic activity into play. Eating is not for us what it is for the animals—it is far more elaborate and artificial. It's game, it's ritual. The same with communication. What is this chapter but an extended riff, an extrapolation from the cat's purr, the wolf's howl? And certainly the same with sex.

I don't mean that we take things less seriously by making games of them. Precisely the opposite, in fact. Eating and talking and sex are life-and-death matters, and that is why we devote so much of this new cerebral cortex, this still-nowhere-near-capacity gray matter, to them. That is why we invent our rules and counter-rules, our ceviches and celebrations.

But it doesn't hurt to step outside the dance every now and then. Appetite is like a muscle. You can't flex it all the time because it will lose all its resilience and quit working.

So I've learned to relax when the disinclination comes on. I know that sooner or later I'll be sneaking glances at that last piece of apple pie in the refrigerator, imagining it toasted up hot and steaming and then smothered in Ben & Jerry's Cherry Garcia.

THE DAY THE BISCUITS WENT BAD

As you already know, I'm proud of my biscuits. I know how to make them tall and light. I know how to make them crusty on the outside but steaming and tender to bite into. I make them so they're good with gravy, good with jelly, good with blackstrap molasses, or good just drenched with melted butter and washed down with a cold glass of milk.

I'm proud of my cooking generally. Hard not to be when the person you mostly cook for keeps telling you, morning after morning and night after night, how good the stuff is.

And it is a fact that I've gone up a level lately. Made a couple of crusts for fruit tarts recently that absolutely *defined* flakiness. Last week's bread pudding was baked crisp on the outside and was moist but crunchy with walnuts on the inside—hot out of the oven, a few dabs of lemon hard sauce sizzling away to pools of golden liquid—good eating, no doubt about it.

And before that there had been golden-fried pork chops, there had been the all-time great three-meat meatloaf, there had been pasta salad with crabmeat.

Heck, even the corn dogs came out wonderful.

So I guess I was suffering from food hubris. I guess I was about due for a comeuppance.

Things started out normally enough. We were laughing and joking, sipping our cocktails. I was cutting butter into leavened flour. Jayme, who may like the dough better than the end product, was pretending impatience: "Isn't it ready yet? When will the dough be ready?"

I finished mixing in the buttermilk, floured the board and rolled the mass out, pinched off a tithe for Jayme, cut out the biscuits with my stainless-steel biscuit cutter, what a joy to use, and popped the plump suckers in the oven.

Only twenty or so minutes now. We could relax and enjoy the evening, knowing what pleasures lay in store.

When I took them out, I noticed they looked a little flat. And when I buttered them, I noticed they seemed a little hard and smelled a little funny. Then, when we tried to eat them, we noticed that they were a whole lot horrible.

They were completely inedible. My biscuits are usually a pale golden color, but these had turned out a rather violent gall-yellow. They had a bitter metallic taste that was so foul and strong as to seem almost poisonous.

I found myself in a curious frame of mind. I didn't feel silly or like a failure. I felt more like you feel when you step out the front door to get the paper and find out someone has removed the front step during the night. A severe, unexpected jolt on familiar ground. I was just baffled, couldn't figure out what had gone wrong. Jayme thought I must have, in the midst of our kidding around, accidentally doubled the dose of baking soda or baking powder. But I knew that wasn't so because the dough had passed muster, and if the problem was too much in the way of sodium bicarb, why had the biscuits come out so flat?

What happened on the night of the Frankenstein biscuits remains a mystery. The only thing I can do now is try to figure out what to make of such a sudden, inexplicable failure.

And what can I make of it?

Just this, I think. Why be afraid to try? I know people who won't learn anything new, because they're afraid of looking bad. Fear of failure paralyzes them.

Bad enough when you're talking mathematics or skiing or learning to play a musical instrument. It seems a *really* sad condition when you're talking about something as fundamental and warm and domestic as learning to cook. And yet I know plenty of people who are completely intimidated by the thought of learning how.

The message is this: You're going to fail. Everybody's going to fail. No matter how good you get, you're going to screw up some of the time.

So why not try? Start whipping up those recipes. And when the cake falls, when the eggs turn out rubbery, when the chili is inedible, just remember me and my horrible biscuits.

Just tell yourself, Jack's biscuits died for my sins.

A CHICKEN OF A DIFFERENT COLOR

Like I say, I think of myself as an improvisational not a formal cook. Rock 'n' roll, not Beethoven. Though I love to have Beethoven roll over me while I'm rolling out something for the bake-oven. I base whatever I do on an understanding of the qualities of the ingredients I'm working with.

Zen cookery? Nah, nothing so high-flown. Probably more like messing around with the chemistry set when I was a kid. Fewer messes, though. Chemistry is very unforgiving.

So you'd think, being improvisational and all, that my cooking would offer continual surprises. That we'd hardly ever get bored having the same old thing.

Not true. A message for all the artists out there hung up on creating their own original isolated vision, which is nearly all the artists in the country, since after all we're Americans and originality is our birthright and eleven of our first ten commandments: The dirty little secret of nonstop improvisation is that it tends to get awfully same.

What the self can produce, caught in a continual feedback loop, working always only with its own input, tends to zero in toward a steady state of ultimate boredom. If you *really* want to be different, best go to school and learn classical structure. Best study hard and learn how to imitate others.

It had been several weeks of running through the variations for the evening meal. Chicken, pork, beef. Chicken, beef, pork. Lamb? No, not quite. Porky-beefychickenthingy. Biscuits, rice, fries. Salad broccoli peas. Peas carrots salad salad salad yecchhh.

It was chicken's turn again. I was staring into the freezer. What could I do with chicken to add a little zip to our lives? A little tangy zip, as the Mirkle

Wipe people put it so redundantly in their annoying ads. Or maybe they mean zippy tang.

Mirkle Wipe because that's what daughter Catherine used to call Miracle Whip when she was a baby child and zipping so tangily about the house.

See what I mean? Even now, I'm bored with the thought of that chicken. Keep digressing. So anyhow, there I was, standing at the fridge, studying what to do to a package of frozen fowl.

What do I usually do with chicken? I'm good with it, but I realized I had been working basically with five versions: I did crisp and succulent chicken fingers, I did a savory chicken pot pie, I did old-fashioned chicken and dumplings, I did high-garlic chicken soup, and I sometimes did a light and refreshing chicken salad. All involved a certain related palette of spices, usually rosemary, marjoram, freshly milled pepper, and maybe a touch of dill.

None of which appealed to me at the moment.

And then the lightning hit.

Now it is true that I didn't go to a cookbook, that in fact this dish was as improvisational as any of my others. But I did nevertheless take a cue from others, in this case from vague memories of chicken Kiev and from Jayme's style of cooking, which I won't go into since it deserves a book all its own, except to say that she will color code her spices, cooking with say all green spices one meal and all yellow ones the next, and that lately she has been talking about size coding, which seems to mean cooking things together that are all the same size.

What I did was thaw out some chicken tenders. I think boneless, skinless breasts would have worked better, but tenders was what I had. I sprinkled them with salt and pepper and rosemary and floured them with the good old paper-sack method. So far no big differences.

But then I put breast-size clumps—three tenders together—of the floured chicken between sheets of wax paper and hammered those suckers flat. And then I grated part-skim mozzarella over the surface of the flattened pieces. And then I rolled them up into sticky tubes. They stayed in tubes because they were so sticky. And then I chopped, finely, several cloves of garlic and several leaves of fresh basil. And then I heated some good-for-your-heart canola oil in the skillet. And then I refloured my chicken roll-ups, and then I cooked them wonderful golden brown all over and set them to one side to drain. And then

I poured off most of the oil but left enough to brown the minced garlic a few seconds, and then I stirred in a bit of flour and browned it and deglazed with a healthy dash of dry vermouth and plenty of water, and then I added the chopped basil and put the browned chicken roll-ups back in to simmer.

And then—get this—I added capers. That's right, capers.

I covered the skillet and let this agglomerate simmer for a good thirty or forty minutes. Then I removed the chicken, finished thickening the sauce, and served the sauce over piping-hot fettucini topped with a grating of Parmesan, and the chicken on the side.

The chicken was not only good, it was good cold the next day in a sandwich. And it was good chopped in a green salad dressed with mayonnaise for Jayme's lunch later. And it was different. It was really different. It wasn't my usual dish. I copied someone else.

I've been feeling freer and more creative ever since.

Capered Chicken Kiev

2 pounds boneless, skinless
   chicken breasts
Salt and freshly ground pepper,
   to taste
1 tablespoon dried rosemary
Flour for coating and thickening
1½ to 2 cups grated part-skim
   mozzarella
4 to 5 tablespoons cooking oil

¼ cup dry vermouth
½ cup water
2 cloves garlic, minced
2 medium fresh basil leaves,
   minced
½ cup capers
3 tablespoons Parmesan cheese,
   grated

TOTAL PREPARATION AND COOKING TIME: About an hour.

1. Salt and pepper each breast to taste on both sides. Lightly sprinkle each piece with rosemary. Coat with flour by dredging or shaking in a paper bag.
2. Place each breast between sheets of wax paper on butcher board and, using a meat mallet, flatten.

3. Remove from wax paper and sprinkle mozzarella on each breast, then roll up into a tube. Pin chicken breasts with toothpicks if they won't stay rolled up.
4. Coat with flour again.
5. Heat oil in skillet and fry rolled-up breasts, turning till golden brown all over.
6. Set aside to drain.
7. Pour oil from skillet and deglaze with vermouth and $\frac{1}{4}$ cup water. Add garlic and basil and return chicken breasts to skillet. Add capers. Cover and simmer on low heat until breasts are tender, about 30 minutes, adding water if needed.
8. Remove breasts to a dish and keep warm in oven. Thicken fluid in skillet into a sauce with 2 tablespoons of flour dissolved in remaining $\frac{1}{4}$ cup water.
9. Remove toothpicks and serve chicken on the side. Pour the sauce over the chicken and a bed of pasta. Top the pasta with Parmesan. Good with a salad, fresh vegetables, or fresh bread.

SERVES 4

HOW TO GET RID OF BEER

I'm not a heavy-duty beer drinker. I like stout, and I like Alaskan amber. Which, incidentally, as I found out on my last trip to Alaska, is what they now call the beer formerly known as Chinook. I spent half a week in Fairbanks asking after Chinook and not finding it before anybody bothered to straighten me out. Seems somebody decided that reminding the thirsty customer of the smell of dead fish just at the point of purchase wasn't all that grand a marketing strategy. Maybe not. The beer's just as good, either way.

I do like a snappingly cold brewski or two after a long hike or a hot game in the summertime, but I will never park in front of the tube and start in on a six-pack.

Nevertheless, we always seem to have extra beer around the house, lots of extra beer. Usually several different brands. Lately it's been Pearl Light and Miller Ice Draft. I can, by the way, recommend Pearl Light as an excellent swimming-pool beer for those 100° Arkansas or Carolina or even Connecticut July days. Only seventy calories a can, and it tastes pretty good. I mean really, I'm not kidding, it tastes pretty good. For American beer.

Anyway, what happens is that we have a party or have some people over, so we go out and buy some beer, and then the people bring their own beer, and then everybody winds up drinking white wine or gets into my Wild Turkey while I'm not looking.

So then we have a refrigerator full of beer. It stays full for months and months while I try to figure out ways to get rid of it. And that's our situation right now.

I can manage a can or two a month myself, if I decide to have boilermakers for a change, but that's about all, especially during the winter. Clearly, then, I am in need of alternatives. Lately I've been experimenting with beer batter. I like batter-fried things. The greasier the better. Grease is good for you, after all. And it's fun to play around with different sorts of batter. I grew up on cornmeal batter and egg batter, though mostly when I do steak fingers or catfish or fried chicken nowadays, as I've told you, I just salt, pepper, flour, and fry.

Beer batter is completely different.

The recipe I use is simplicity itself. (I want to caution you that there's nothing official about this recipe. This is not, repeat not, *authentic* beer batter.) I put white flour in a bowl, the amount depending on how much batter I think I'm going to need. I sprinkle in some salt according to how salty I think I'm going to want the batter to taste. I cut in some butter or margarine in the ratio of roughly a tablespoon to a cup of flour. I add cold beer, stirring until I have a nice thick batter—liquid, but dense and clinging. I drink the rest of the beer.

Beer batter comes out a lot like tempura, which means it isn't suitable for just anything. I've tried it out on all sorts of things recently, even catfish and chicken livers. On the whole, I don't think I'd recommend it for most meats, though the chicken livers were just fine hot from the skillet. Jayme liked the catfish, but I had some reservations. My thought is that it would work better for extremely firm-fleshed seafoods, like shrimp and, *hm, ah,* shrimp.

And vegetables. Beer batter is really great for those deep-fried happy-hour veggie-type gnoshes. It works great for mushrooms, which are almost impossible to get any other sort of batter to stick to. It would, I am sure, if you can bear the concept, work great for nuggets of cauliflower or broccoli, or for dill pickles. It is supreme for onion rings, which I dearly love, and of which good ones are mighty hard to get.

What I do is flour my fryees—the rings, the mushrooms, whatever. Just shake them in a bag with flour, dip them in the batter, drop them in hot oil in a deep fryer, get them golden brown all over, and drain them (beer batter holds a *lot* of oil).

Then you can sit down with your crunchy munchies and tune in to see what the score of the game is, and whether Mike Piazza has hit any more home runs.

And what the hey, maybe even have a cold beer with your meal. It would be appropriate, and you'd be getting rid of two of the cotton-picking things in one evening.

Beer-Batter Onion Rings

1 cup unbleached white flour	1 tablespoon butter or
1 teaspoon salt	margarine
1 small onion, cut into $\frac{1}{4}$"-thick	6 to 8 ounces beer
rings	Cooking oil for deep-frying

This batter will also serve as a fine tempura-style batter for a wide range of vegetables.

TOTAL PREPARATION AND FRYING TIME: 30 to 35 minutes.

1. Mix flour and salt.
2. Put flour mixture into a paper bag.
3. Throw in onion rings and shake, then set aside. They should be only lightly coated.
4. Transfer flour to a mixing bowl and cut in butter. Add beer gradually, stirring until batter thickens.
5. Heat cooking oil in a deep fryer (a high-walled skillet will do). The oil is hot enough for frying when water dripped onto the oil pops and sizzles.
6. Coat onion rings thoroughly with batter and drop into oil. Fry until golden brown all over, then remove to paper and drain.

SERVES 2

THE HIGH YEAST EXPERIENCE

I'm thinking about yeast because I've been thinking about beer. Me and yeast used to be good friends. Back in Fayetteville in the late sixties and early seventies, and for years afterward, I brewed beer. I baked whole wheat bread, dinner rolls, French bread, sourdough loaves, and I frittered up sourdough flapjacks. I've even done a few vintages, most notably the crazy autumn wine that originated in a grove of wild plums west of Hollywood.

Whether brewing or making bread, I don't work with recipes unless I'm trying to reproduce some very specific item with very precise requirements (filled challah, for example). I work by touch and by sampling. Or as some might say, by guess and by golly.

Still, some of you may remember how easily that amber homebrew used to go down at parties (it *never* gave me a headache). And most of my attempts at bread have turned out well—crusty and dripping with butter, that warm aroma filling the kitchen, maybe the best smell on earth.

My point is that the yeast deserves most of the credit. The wonderful thing about working with yeast is that it's alive. When you make bread or brew beer, you're not a director, you're a partner in a process. You're not a factory hand stamping out products, you're the creator of small ecologies, and you encourage them to follow their own natures.

All of which implies that if you work with yeast, you have to be patient. You can't rush the process, force the changes. You have to think about what the yeast wants, the conditions that make it happy and comfortable.

At the risk of being overly mystical, I've always assumed that was why I had good luck with yeast, that I was *simpatico,* that I understood it as a host of fellow creatures.

Another thing I like about yeast is the sense of continuity. Every loaf of bread, every bottle of homebrew is lineally connected to all of the others, even if you buy your yeast in little packets from the grocery store. Yeast reproduces, and it is that reproduction whose by-products — carbon dioxide and alcohol — help us to the stuff of life and sacrament, our bread and our wine.

I have saved and reused the yeast from one batch of beer to make the next, generation unto generation. But perhaps my favorite reminder of this rhythm, this heritage, is sourdough. Once you whip up a starter, it will keep you in business for years and years. Use half of it to activate your current batch of bread, recharge the rest, and keep it in a jar in your refrigerator.

Sourdough is yeast, basically, but yeast in a medium. What happens with all yeast is that when conditions are not favorable, when the environment is too cold or too dry or there's not enough available nutrition, it hibernates. The cells form walls around themselves — they encyst, like frogs in dried mud — and wait for a change in the weather. Then when you come along supplying heat, moisture, and sugar or starch, those cells wake up, break out, look around, see that spring has come, and start doing what comes naturally.

Like I say, me and yeast used to be good friends, but in recent years we've gotten out of touch. One thing and another. Life got terribly busy, or busily terrible, and all those good things that require time and tact and patience — bread, brew, poetry, love — all those things suffered.

We don't have *lives* anymore, we have lifestyles.

But I've been doing a little bit of sourdough lately, and I think it's time for some more. Time to put up the first batch of northern New Mexico beer, break it out on a sunny day this October up on the trail overlooking Holy Ghost Creek, overlooking sheer mountainsides of glowing aspen. Hold the bottle up to the same sun that's lighting up the golden leaves. Spread a little country pâté on a slice of sourdough bread. Thank the good Lord I'm still here to love it all.

Yep, it's time. Time to renew old acquaintances.

What I'm recommending overall is a mountain excursion with a menu. The menu will require some advance planning — a minimum of three weeks' worth, for reasons that will become clear. So use the time to your advantage, try these recipes out first, practice them a couple of times, see if they work for you. Then, just when the fall is at its peak, you'll be ready.

I recommend a mountain picnic, a jaunt to the Smokies or the Bostons or Ouachitas or the Berkshires or the Sierra Nevadas, just when the air is crisp and cool and the leaves are in total and brilliant change. You pick the final destination, but it should culminate in a bluff view, so that you can sit among moss-covered rocks and watch the hawks wheel and hear them cry over the valley below. You know where I'll be—in the Sangre de Cristos, missing the full riot of color from a good Arkansas fall, but happy with sweeps of sun and golden aspen.

Our menu? Homemade beer, homebaked sourdough bread, and country pâté. We're starting with the rough-and-ready homebrew here.

Rough-and-ready is the operative phrase: I caution you, this stuff is really good, but my methods are not the methods of the connoisseur. So no long letters setting me straight, please. I know what I'm doing, and I know what I'm *not* doing.

You'll need a packet or two of yeast, a three-pound can of malt extract (already hopped), a five-pound bag of sugar, a large, never-before-used plastic garbage pail or equivalent container, fifty or sixty longneck bottles (not screw caps), a box of bottlecaps, a bottle capper, a funnel, a large measuring cup for dipping and pouring, and a Mason jar (to use for your sourdough starter). You should be able to find the malt extract at your local supermarket. If not, check a brewery supplies store. If you haven't been wisely storing up longnecks, see if you can buy some from your local distributor.

Any good hardware store will have bottlecaps and a manual bottle capper (which is a tall, lever-action piece of steel standing on a flat base).

Step one: Dissolve a packet or two of yeast in very warm but not scalding water, a half cup or so. Stir in a teaspoon of sugar to activate the yeast. Yeast grows exponentially, so you really aren't saving much time by using two packets instead of one. Step two: In a large pot, dissolve the malt extract in a gallon of boiling water. Malt extract is very thick and gluey, so this takes a while. Toward the end, I usually drop the stripped can in the water to let the last of the malt dissolve. Pour this solution into the garbage pail. Step three: Dissolve five pounds of sugar in a gallon or so of boiling water and pour this solution in the pail as well. Step four: Bring the total fluid in the pail to five gallons by adding more warm water. Step five: By now your yeast should be foaming happily. Pour it into the garbage pail and stir vigorously. I should have told you before you filled it up and made it too heavy to move easily to put your garbage pail in a warm, protected corner, but I thought you had brains enough to figure that out. The yeast won't brew if it gets too cold. The brew needs to breathe, but you want to keep flies, gnats, and fruit flies out of it, so cover the top of the pail with cheesecloth or some other fine mesh, and secure this screen so that it won't slip off.

You're done with the beer for a week to ten days. The yeast will be doing all the work. Changing dextrose into alcohol and carbon dioxide, making more yeast. If you let it sit until all the new yeast settled out, you'd have a quart of sediment.

But we're not going to wait that long. Let's say your ten days are up, it's time to bottle your beer. Be prepared for a spell of spills and disorder. Bottling is a messy business. Your kitchen will smell like yeast and will need a good mopping. You'll struggle with the capper until you get the hang of it. But it's all *worth* it, remember.

Line up your scrubbed and rinsed bottles, your box of caps, your capper, your funnel, your measuring cup, and a quart of sugar water (half a cup of sugar to a quart of water). Put a teaspoon of sugar water in each bottle. This will create a slight additional fermentation after you've sealed the bottles, just enough to create a good head when you pour it. (And no, I've never had a bottle explode—that happens if you use too much sugar or cap your brew too soon.) Using the funnel and measuring cup, fill each bottle to an inch above the collar of the neck and cap it.

Rinse the bottles off and store them in a warm place. All that's left is to wait for the brew in the bottles to clear—it'll take longer for the last bottles you filled because they were from the bottom of the pail, where the sediment was thicker. But two weeks at a maximum should do it.

Chill your beer, crack it, and drink it. But a word of caution: Since we're doing this rough-and-ready, the individual bottles have sediment. So when you move or pour the beer, be careful not to stir the sediment up. Have a glass handy, and pour all the beer off in one smooth flow, stopping before the sediment pours.

Do it right, and you have a fine amber clarity to hand, hearty and friendly and just right for the season. Wait'll you taste it with bread and pâté. Which we're going to get to right now.

OK, go back a few days. Your beer is brewing, you can't do anything but wait, so it's time to practice that sourdough. Sourdough is basically just another yeast vehicle, so named because of the slight tanginess of the yeast-digested flour. It has dozens of uses, which I won't go into here. But you should seek out recipes for such things as dinner rolls, flapjacks, and even doughnuts.

To make a good sourdough starter, activate a packet of yeast just as you did for the beer—no more than half a cup of warm water and a teaspoon of sugar. When the yeast is frothing, add a half cup of buttermilk and mix in flour until the mixture is just too thick to pour. Set it aside in a Mason jar in a warm place and let it seethe for a couple of hours.

Then, whenever I make sourdough bread, I use about half the starter. (Be sure to add enough flour, water, and buttermilk to bring the seed back to its original level. Let it sit and brew again, of course, before you store it in the fridge. You don't *have* to store it in the fridge—that was the whole point of sourdough for those famous Alaskan prospectors.)

We're going to be working on dill-garlic sourdough bread. Add enough very warm water to half of your starter to liquefy it completely, and let it sit a few minutes to wake up the yeast. Then add enough very warm water to bring the liquid to just a little over two cups. Throw in a teaspoon of salt, beat in a couple of tablespoons of oil, and blend the liquid into six and a half cups of unbleached white flour. You may need more, but add it cautiously. Your dough should be moist and easy to work, but shouldn't cling. Knead it lightly, place it in a large bowl, cover the bowl with a damp cloth, and set it in a warm place to rise.

When the dough has roughly doubled in volume (about an hour, though the time varies wildly for rising bread), take it out and knead lightly again. By the way: Doubling in volume doesn't mean doubling in every direction. That would be *eight* times the volume. Doubling in volume means getting roughly 25 percent larger in every direction.

Shape the dough into an oblong loaf and place it on a flat clean ungreased cookie sheet. Slash the top deeply with a serrated knife, sprinkle it with dried dill and garlic powder (making sure to get plenty down in the slash), and pack the slash with softened margarine or butter. Put the loaf back and let it continue rising. When it has again roughly doubled, pop the loaf in the oven and set the temperature to 375°F. Do not preheat. Once the oven temperature is

375°F, bake for thirty-five to forty-five minutes. When it's ready, the slash will have stretched, making beautiful crusty tears and ligaments, and the top will be a light golden brown, and the loaf will thump like a ripe melon.

Now for your hearty pâté, the final element of our picnic. Actually, pâté is easy, and there are a thousand variations. You can make a good version by simmering chicken livers in butter with salt and pepper, blending the result, and letting it chill until it sets up. Many people find this recipe a little too strongly flavored, though, so I'll tell you about my last batch, which was robust but not too musky or dark. This is just to give you the idea—feel free to improvise.

I sautéed about a pound (total) of boneless pork and chicken nuggets (straight from the supermarket) in half a stick of butter with chopped garlic and plenty of chopped red and green bell pepper. When they were done, I put the whole mess in the blender, deglazed the skillet with a little wine, and poured this juice over the stuff in the blender. Then I sautéed a carton of fresh chicken livers in the other half of the stick of butter. (I sautéed the livers separately because they cook much more rapidly and tend to stick.) Don't overcook the livers—they should be soft and pink inside (but not red). Into the blender, deglaze again, into the blender with this juice. Grind a bunch of fresh pepper in, blend, taste, add salt if desired, blend again until you get the consistency you want, coarse or smooth. Decant the compound into a glass loaf dish, let it chill and set up, and you've got a spreadable feast.

Pâté means "paste," and one of the tricks is getting it to the right stiffness. I like mine sliceable while cold, but not gelatinous to the point of being chewy, like head cheese (a kind of redneck pâté). Which is why I use butter or hard margarine. (No matter what you do, pâté is going to be rich and fatty, so if you are that sort of a worrier, stay away.) If you prefer a little more gelatin, you can use stock made from simmered rather than sautéed meat (a kettle of chicken backs, skin on, cooked down and bones removed, makes a wonderful base).

Now it's time to head for the woods. I'm sorry we're going to be driving instead of walking, but you don't want to shake up that beer, and anyhow this is too much food to carry and after you eat and wake up from your nap you aren't going to want to walk out.

Pop about three of your homebrews per capita in an ice chest—believe me, that will be plenty—and store your loaf and your pâté in a big linen-covered basket. If you don't have a convertible either, get somebody to drive while you and your sweetie ride in the back of the pickup. The world is beautiful this time of year, isn't it? Enjoy.

Dill-Garlic Sourdough Bread

For sourdough starter:
1 teaspoon sugar
½ cup warm water
1 packet yeast

½ cup buttermilk
1½ cups unbleached white
   flour

For bread:
½ starter (about 1 to 1½ cups)
1 cup warm water
1 teaspoon salt
2 tablespoons olive oil
6½ cups unbleached white
   flour

Dried dill, to taste
Garlic powder, to taste
Butter or margarine for top
   crust

This bread can be made without the dill and garlic, for plain sourdough, or with other herbs for other flavors.

TOTAL PREPARATION AND BAKING TIME: 6 hours, including starter preparation and rising time.

For sourdough starter:

1. Dissolve the sugar in the warm water in a mixing bowl, then dissolve the yeast in the sugar water.
2. When yeast is foaming, stir in buttermilk, then beat in flour until mixture is just barely too thick to pour.
3. Store in a Mason jar in a warm, dry place for at least 3 hours. Make sure jar has twice the volume of the starter, because the starter will ferment and rise. When starter has fermented, it may be used immediately or stored open in the refrigerator for later use.

For bread:

1. In mixing bowl dissolve half the starter in enough warm water to bring total liquid volume to 2 cups. Stir in salt and oil. Beat in flour gradually until too thick to beat, then continue mixing with hands until dough is springy and does not cling (but it should not be too dry).
2. Knead dough lightly and return to bowl. Cover bowl with a wet cloth and put in a warm place to rise.
3. When dough has doubled in volume, turn out and knead again. I use a doubling technique for kneading, folding the dough in half, pressing it flat, then folding it in half again. For this bread, 10 folds is enough.
4. Shape the dough into an oblong loaf and place on a clean ungreased cookie sheet.
5. Slash the loaf once lengthwise, to a depth of not more than an inch, and sprinkle dried dill and garlic powder in the slash. Pack the slash with butter or margarine and put loaf in warm place to rise again.
6. When dough has doubled in volume, place in oven and turn heat to 375°F. Do not preheat oven. The loaf will rise just a bit more while oven warms.
7. Bake for 35 to 45 minutes after oven reaches 375°F, until light golden brown on top. Slice or tear and serve hot and buttered with soup, pâté, or wine and cheese.

SERVES 4

French Bread

1 teaspoon sugar	1 teaspoon salt
1½ cups warm water	4 cups unbleached white flour
1 packet yeast	(more if needed)

TOTAL PREPARATION AND BAKING TIME: 1½ hours, including rising time.

1. In a mixing bowl, dissolve sugar in $\frac{1}{2}$ cup warm water. Dissolve yeast in warm sugar water to activate. When yeast is foaming, add remaining 1 cup water and stir in salt. Add flour gradually, beating until too thick to beat. Continue adding flour, working with hands as necessary, until dough is firm and springy, but not dry or tough.

2. Knead dough lightly and return to bowl. Cover bowl with wet cloth and set in warm place to rise.

3. When dough has doubled in volume, turn out and knead again.

4. Shape into desired loaf, place on ungreased cookie sheet, and return to warm place to rise again.

5. When dough has doubled in volume again, place in oven and turn heat to 375°F. Do not preheat oven. Loaf will rise just a bit more while oven warms.

6. After oven reaches 375°F, bake for 35 to 45 minutes until light golden brown on top. This bread is quite crusty and delicious.

SERVES 6

Chicken Liver and Pork Pâté

$\frac{1}{2}$ red bell pepper
$\frac{1}{2}$ green bell pepper
1 clove garlic, minced
$\frac{1}{2}$ pound boneless pork nuggets
$\frac{1}{2}$ pound boneless chicken nuggets

1 stick butter or margarine
$\frac{1}{4}$ cup white wine
Freshly ground pepper, to taste
1 pint fresh chicken livers
2 teaspoons salt

TOTAL PREPARATION TIME: 25 minutes, not including chilling time.

1. Clean, deseed, and chop red and green peppers.

2. Sauté bell peppers, garlic, and pork and chicken nuggets in $\frac{1}{2}$ stick butter or margarine.

3. When just done through but still very tender, transfer sauté mix to blender.

4. Deglaze skillet with half the wine and pour resulting fluid over pork-and-chicken mixture in blender. Mill in fresh pepper to taste.
5. Sauté chicken livers in remaining butter till just done through but still lightly pink in middle. Transfer to blender with pork-and-chicken mixture.
6. Deglaze skillet with remaining wine and pour the resulting juice into the blender. Add salt and more pepper to taste.
7. Blend until desired consistency, coarse or smooth, cleaning sides of blender with rubber spatula as necessary.
8. Turn pâté into a glass loaf dish and place in refrigerator to chill and set up. When loaf is completely cold to the touch and spreads firmly, it is ready to serve.

SERVES 12

THE GHOST MOUNTAINS

Jayme and I want you guys to know that you have us to thank.

As much as we love the South, we told ourselves, we were not going to miss the 100° summers and the 100 percent humidity. And in fact, the week we packed to move—late July of 1993—the whole of central Arkansas sweltered in the kind of weather that makes you feel like you have all the strength and willpower of wax running down the side of a candle.

But it would be better when we got to Santa Fe, we told ourselves. Let others think we were moving out to the frying-pan desert. We knew how temperate the summers were at seven thousand feet. We knew how much difference the absence of humidity made.

So of course we haven't had normal weather since we got here. Last winter was, according to the locals, abnormally dry of snow, and this winter appears to have begun a month early, with temperatures twenty degrees below normal and heavy snows in the mountains. This summer a high-pressure front locked itself into place over us, and we set all-time temperature records.

Meanwhile, of course, people in the rest of the country were having the coolest, mildest, most pleasant summer on record. Apparently we're under a weather jinx. We wander around with little black clouds over our heads, like that character who used to appear in *Dogpatch,* Joe Bftlspk (or some similar spelling). We took the bad weather with us, and left you the good.

So if you're having a grand fall, and if you enjoy the most amazing and pleasant winter ever seen in your neck of the woods, just remember that you have us to thank.

But even the weather-cursed have their good days. We've had a few fine rambles among the glowing aspen. Then one day after work a couple of weeks ago

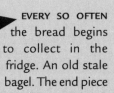

EVERY SO OFTEN the bread begins to collect in the fridge. An old stale bagel. The end piece from a loaf of high-fiber sandwich bread. A biscuit that somehow survived the fresh-from-the-oven massacre but has now lingered too long to toast up well. Two or three unused hamburger buns from the last time you grilled, a couple of weeks ago.

It is, of course, time for bread pudding.

Bread pudding is a wonderful dish, practical as all get-out, and just about as good as a sweet soft thing can be. With a grasp of basic procedures, you can produce any number of delicious variations (see the recipe at the end of this chapter). Our latest came about be-cause Jayme was having one of her seasonal things. The cold weather had hit, and it was time for cinnamon and nutmeg and allspice. And apples. Home from the market with five shiny green Granny Smiths, she was talking apple tart at first. But we had all this leftover bread. What was needed was some sort of creative synthesis. As usual, she had the idea, and as usual, I put it into operation.

So if the weather has changed where you are, give it a try. Bread pudding is perfect for those dark chilly winter months, warm and rich and comforting. And you can warm it up and have it any time of day—it makes a fine dessert, obviously, but with all those eggs, and the fruit, and the bread, it is sub-stantial enough to make a grand Sunday brunch all by itself.

we dashed up into the mountains to watch the first snow falling. Something about that was really moving.

Then there was the farmer's market a week and a half ago.

When the weather changes, you want to change what you eat a little. Different seasons seem to call for different diets. We felt a drive that was almost biologically intense, an urge to get out to the farmer's market and see what was being offered this time around.

It was the last market of the year, and it was cold and drizzling. Doesn't sound promising, but it turned out to be the most satisfying of all. The weather hadn't discouraged anybody, so there we were meandering from stall to stall under our tattered umbrellas, colliding like bumper cars at a fair, getting our ankles soaked, and generally having a great time.

We bought the last turnip greens of the season—a pretty discouraged-looking clump of sandy greenery, but you have to be loyal—and then got a clump of healthier-looking mustard to add to the pot. Later that day I cleaned and cooked the greens, throwing in a few chunks of bone and fatback from the Petit Jean ham some good friends had sent Jayme for what was it, her eightieth birthday or so? I put the greens in the freezer, and some day soon, when it's really cold and gray and huge flakes are blowing in the violent spillover from the Sangres, I'll heat them up, and along with some buttermilk and green onions and hot cornbread, they'll warm our Arkie hearts.

We bought some goat's milk yogurt, a loose concoction more like buttermilk than grocery-store yogurt, with which I later made a variation of Shepherd's Winter Biscuits (see page 124) and into which, in fact, Jayme later crumbled some hot cornbread and had what she said was a fine equivalent to the Southern dish of buttermilk and cornbread.

For me the star of the show was the hot lamb sausage. We bought two pounds of the gut-cased meat, and it has been keeping me happy ever since. It's dry, not at all fatty, and heavily chile-powdered, so that it cooks up a wonderful dark peppery red. I haven't had good pork sausage since we used to make it on the farm—the sour, fatty trash you can get commercially nowadays isn't fit to put a fork to. But this lamb sausage is wonderful, and I know where to get more.

After the farmer's market, we came home and had hot biscuits and tender scrambled eggs, with Petit Jean ham for Jayme and lamb sausage for me. So even if our weather curse continues, we're fixed for food to chase away the blues.

Oh, the ghost mountains? Well, right after the farmer's market we dashed out to Trader Jack's flea market (on the top of the hill just past the opera). It was just about the last weekend of the season for the flea market, too. We love going to the flea market, even when we don't buy anything. Love watching the tourists, you know. Us insiders, us locals.

I love it also because from the hill you can see all the mountains all around.

Sometimes while Jayme's pricing Nigerian beads or antique carpenter's tools, I just stand there and watch the mountains. I will look up into the hills, from whence cometh my help.

And on this particular day, over eastward, in the direction of Arkansas and Mississippi and all the earlier stages of our lives, over the Sangres, veils and smokes of cloud ranged and drifted. And the way the slopes of the mountains in the foreground lined up with the slopes of the mountains in the background made the farther mountains look closer and grayly transparent. Mountains you could see through. Ghost mountains on a cold chilly wonderful day.

A day when the weather changed. Good weather for lamb sausage.

Good eating weather.

Apple Bread Pudding

5 tart apples, cored, peeled, and sliced
½ cup brown sugar
1 tablespoon cinnamon
1 teaspoon allspice
1 teaspoon freshly grated nutmeg
½ cup plus 2 tablespoons butter or margarine
5 to 6 cups bread crumbs
1 tablespoon vanilla extract
½ cup bourbon, rum, or brandy (optional)
1½ cups white sugar
1 cup milk
1 dozen medium eggs

You may substitute raisins or sun-dried cherries for the spiced apples, with excellent results (if you are using dried fruits, you should reconstitute them first, perhaps by soaking them in a flavorful spirit such as rum, bourbon, or brandy). You may add chopped walnuts or pecans just before cooking, either as a substitute for the fruit or in combination with it. Or bread pudding may be made plain, without apples, other fruit, or nuts. In any case, it's always nice to decorate the top of the pudding with nut halves.

TOTAL PREPARATION AND BAKING TIME: $3\frac{1}{2}$ to 4 hours, including 2 hours' simmering time for apples.

1. Place apples in stewing pan with brown sugar, spices, 2 tablespoons butter or margarine, and enough water to cover. Simmer until soft enough to mash into a coarse sauce—anywhere from 1 to $2\frac{1}{2}$ hours.
2. While the apples are stewing, melt the $\frac{1}{2}$ cup butter or margarine and pour over the bread crumbs in a large mixing bowl, tossing to coat the crumbs. Sprinkle the mix with the vanilla, tossing for even distribution. If using spirits for flavoring, sprinkle over the crumbs, tossing again. Add the white sugar and toss. Add the milk, stirring coarsely. Add the eggs, stirring until thoroughly blended into the mixture.
3. Set bread crumb mixture aside to soak until apples are ready. (If making the pudding in advance, you can let it soak overnight. It will only get better.)
4. When the apples are ready, preheat oven to 375°F.
5. Mash the apples until you get a chunky applesauce texture. Stir the apples into the bread crumb mixture coarsely, for a marbled effect.
6. Pour mixture into 2 loaf pans.
7. Bake until the top is just risen and firm, but not a second longer, about an hour.
8. Loosen sides with a table knife, slice, and serve hot with hard sauce (recipe follows) or heavy cream.

SERVES 8

Southern-Style Hard Sauce

$\frac{1}{2}$ cup powdered sugar
2 tablespoons butter or
  margarine

Juice of $\frac{1}{2}$ lemon

PREPARATION TIME: 5 minutes, not including chilling time.

1. In a food processor, blend powdered sugar and butter or margarine.
2. Add lemon juice gradually, pulsing to blend. A thick, smooth paste will form.
3. Using a rubber spatula, remove all sauce to a storage container. Let chill in refrigerator for an hour or more (sauce will harden).
4. Serve in dollops over hot slices of bread pudding. Sauce will melt and soak in, adding a delicious piquant note to the dessert.

MAKES ENOUGH SAUCE FOR 2 LOAVES BREAD PUDDING

THE MENU

Here we go again: that long accelerating slide from Hallowe'en to New Year's which has come to be known inclusively as The Holiday Season, and which usually leaves me in about the same condition as The Big Slide on the playground did when I was five. By which I mean, facedown in the sand, crying, with skint knees and a burnt butt.

I think maybe they call it The Holiday Season because, by blurring the time frame, they can make it seem sort of normal to begin your Christmas shopping a week or so before the advent of The Great Pumpkin. It isn't normal, of course. It's sick, sick, sick.

And you know what the beginning of shopping season means. It means that for the next sixty days we are going to be bombarded with advertisements showing us rosy warm extended-family gatherings, radio music about rosy warm extended-family gatherings, and movies showing us families who may suffer problems and misunderstandings, but whose problems and misunderstandings will of a certainty conclude, come the Yule, in a rosy warm family gathering.

Actually, when I was a boy, the whole Butler/Niland clan convened every Christmas in the Big House in Alligator. I don't know how warm and rosy it was, but I loved it. Cousins and second cousins and aunts and great-uncles and wives and husbands and sisters and brothers of wives and husbands— they came from all over. Some still lived in Mississippi, but many came a fur piece—California, Washington, D.C., and I don't know where all else. They brought the whiff of other worlds, other lives. I'll never forget the year one of my distant cousins showed up in *a red sports car,* an MG. That was sinful almost in itself, and none of us was surprised a few years later when she and her husband got the first divorce the clan had ever seen.

THERE ARE TWO essential components of a classic Southern Thanksgiving meal. You have to have a turkey, of course, but that isn't especially Southern. Everybody has turkey. And people either already know how to cook their turkey or they can read the instructions on the package. Basically, you just roast it till it gets really good, making sure it doesn't dry out.

But the two essentials, the sine qua non, as we Southerners like to say, are giblet gravy and cornbread dressing. Dressing, mind you, not stuffing. Your dressing is going into a baking pan, not the turkey, and will be served on the side.

I know people who wrinkle their noses in disgust at the thought, but giblet gravy is among the most succulent and delectable sauces ever devised. It's called giblet gravy because it contains little nuggets which are the chopped innards of the turkey—the giblets. And which are also why some people wrinkle their noses at the thought. But the resulting gravy will be a glorious golden color, as savory as a sunny day, and, ladled over your turkey and your cornbread dressing, will convince you that beauty, truth, and love do in fact exist and should be given thanks for.

I wonder if those gatherings really happen anymore. I'm not talking here of the loss and grief that accompany even the warmest and rosiest of families. I'm not talking buried secrets, Freudian rivalries, the bitter feuds that only a forced and extended closeness can sustain.

I mean, practically speaking, how many families can manage the logistics and the cost of getting together now? We have a daughter in California, a daughter in Oklahoma, a daughter in Virginia, and a daughter in Japan. One of my brothers is the Andrews Air Force Base officer who, when the president steps down off Air Force One, takes his briefcase. (You can glimpse him over Harrison Ford's shoulder in a scene in *Clear and Present Danger*.) My other brother lives in Tennessee. My mother and my sister live in Jasper, Texas, which is about as far from a major airport as you can get. Not many aunts and uncles left, though I have an aunt in Jackson and an uncle in San Francisco.

We all suffer from that necessity that forces our kids to go to school out of state and find work where they can. The economy divides us: We go where we have to to make a living, but once we're there, we find we don't quite make enough to pay the fare to come home very often.

So what are you gonna do when those sentimental ads start socking it to you? How you gonna avoid the holiday blues? We've wound up, as I'm sure a lot of people have, parceling out the time. We'll go to one place for Thanksgiving, and maybe a sister can join us; somebody can head this way for Christmas, and maybe somebody else can join them. It isn't perfect, but it's the best we can do, and we will take, with gratitude, what we can get.

And what seems to hold it all together is the menu.

Our Thanksgiving menu is fixed. Turkey, of course. Cornbread dressing smothered in giblet gravy. Ham maybe, especially if it's a Petit Jean ham. Cranberry sauce, the smooth kind you slice into glistening rounds, not the rough stuff with the crushed berries. Butterbeans for sure (my contribution, as you might guess). Black-eyed peas. Rolls, preferably the brown-and-serve readymades that come in the cellophane-wrapped cardboard box. Sweet potatoes topped with marshmallows (I have protested the marshmallows for years, but I get nowhere). Green-bean casserole (canned onion fritters and mushroom soup—need I say more?).

And the desserts—pumpkin pie, apple pie, bread pudding, peach cobbler, pecan pie . . .

The menu is our history together. It is the ritual of our memories and our love. It speaks to us of the ones who aren't there, some because the trip was impossible this year, others because the trip is now and forever impossible. It isn't just our favorite food. It is our lives.

Our compromise this year is San Francisco, where daughter Sherri lives and works. From Santa Fe, we're closer than ever before, and we get a great deal on tickets, and maybe my uncle can join us, and maybe Catherine can fly in for a day, though this is the busiest time of year for her.

Thanksgiving in San Fran. It'll surely feel a little peculiar. But we're sticking to the menu. We know where we are with the menu. We've already spent hours on the phone planning how we're going to enact the menu in the brand-new setting. I will be carrying, in my luggage, cornmeal and butterbeans and cranberry sauce and other stuff we aren't sure they know how to fix in the Big Windy. Carrying food *to* San Francisco, what a riot.

Cornbread Dressing

4 medium eggs
2 cups giblet broth or chicken stock (or mixture)
1 to 2 teaspoons sage
2 teaspoons thyme
½ teaspoon fresh rosemary
1 stalk celery, chopped

1 large onion, chopped (optional)
¾ cup olive oil, margarine, or butter
1 recipe Black Iron Skillet Cornbread (see page 81)
2 cups bread or cracker crumbs
Salt, to taste

We know of good dressings made with such extras as quartered boiled eggs, chopped drained oysters sautéed in butter, chestnuts, pecans, tart apples sliced very thin, chopped and sautéed mushrooms, and sausage. All of these are legitimate and can produce wonderful dressing. Our tradition is a plain dressing with no extras.

TOTAL PREPARATION AND BAKING TIME: 1½ hours.

1. Preheat oven to 350°F.
2. In a large bowl, beat eggs and combine with giblet broth or chicken stock (or mixture). Beat in spices.
3. Sauté celery and onion in oil, margarine, or butter.
4. Crumble cornbread, then combine it and bread or cracker crumbs with egg-broth mixture. Pour in sautéed vegetables and mix thoroughly. Taste for seasoning and add salt as needed. (If you are using canned chicken stock, remember that it will be somewhat salty.) The mixture should be lightly moist. Add more broth or stock if it is too dry.

5. Put mixture into lightly greased large black iron skillet. Press lightly but do not pack down.
6. Place in oven and bake until lightly browned, about 50 minutes to an hour. Serve hot with giblet gravy (recipe follows).

SERVES 8

Giblet Gravy

Neck, heart, liver, and gizzard of turkey
2 stalks celery, chopped
1 bay leaf
6 to 12 whole peppercorns

Juices from roasted turkey
Salt and freshly ground pepper, to taste
Flour for thickening

TOTAL PREPARATION AND COOKING TIME: 1 hour, not including roasting of turkey.

1. Commercial turkeys usually come with the neck and innards stuffed into the body cavity, often in a separate bag. Remove these and, in a 2-quart saucepan, cover them all with water.
2. Add celery, bay leaf, and peppercorns and simmer until the neck meat pulls away from the bone easily.
3. Remove the neck and innards, allowing the broth to continue simmering.
4. When neck and innards have cooled sufficiently, remove all possible meat from neck bone and chop innards into small pieces, the size of a pumpkin seed or thereabouts. These fragments of meat and innards are, in Southern parlance, the "giblets," which give the gravy its name.
5. Remove bay leaf and peppercorns and reserve as much of the broth as desired to make cornbread dressing (page 194), then return neck meat and chopped innards to the saucepan with the remaining broth.

6. When turkey has roasted, pour off accumulated pan drippings from roasting pan into a large deep-shouldered skillet and add the giblets and broth and water as needed.
7. Bring to a boil, then reduce heat to a high simmer. Salt and pepper to taste as you cook.
8. Just before serving, thicken gravy with flour dissolved in cold water. This process is a matter of taste and judgment. I like my giblet gravy thick enough to cling but thin enough to ladle easily. Serve over sliced turkey and cornbread dressing.

MAKES ENOUGH GRAVY TO SERVE WITH A MEAL FOR 8

CRACKERJACK

What happened is Jayme had a craving, so I whipped up a big pot of pretty fair two-bean country chili (garbanzos and pintos were the beans, in case you're curious). But as the chili was bubbling and simmering and chuckling to itself, and filling the house with that wonderful spicy aroma, I began to have a craving of my own.

I needed some crackers. You know what for, don't you?

I needed some crackers to crumble into my chili. Because that's what you did with soup and chili when I was growing up. You crumbled soda crackers into the bowl, stirred the mess around, and ate as fast as you could, while some of the cracker fragments were still crunchy. Our version of *ribollita,* I suppose. Them fancy I-talian chefs had nothing on us.

Cracker crumbling goes way back in our family. Depending on whether you wanted a bedtime dessert or an afternoon pick-me-up, you would crumble graham crackers or saltines into a big cold glass of milk and eat the result with a spoon. Happy times!

As I got older and more sophisticated, I developed the ability to have my milk with the crackers on the side, uncrumbled. What is it about crunch that we like so much? The genetic memory of the crackling of small bones? But all that crunch and saltiness, washed down with big cold swallows of milk—it became one of my favorite afterschool snacks.

So when the cooking chili kicked in my cracker reflex, I realized I had also been craving crackers and milk for quite some time. This is where the story gets a little weird.

You know you're not a normal American, let alone a normal Southerner, when you start making your own crackers. But that's the necessity I faced. The chili was already well under way, we were in our comfortable clothes, the night was dark and cold and neither one of us wanted to go back out, and yet there was not a store-bought cracker in the house. Well, a few year-old packs of melba toast, but that's hardly the same thing.

The problem is — and I don't think about this very often, but every now and then a situation arises that forces it to my attention — the problem is that we've gotten almost completely away from prepared foods. Oh we keep a bag or two of blue corn chips around in case avocados ever go on sale and a guacamole mood strikes us. We bought a couple of boxes of See's chocolates in San Francisco, pieces from which serve as occasional desserts. A few cans of black-eyed peas, but we cook them some more. I buy hamburger buns whenever we're grilling burgers. Ice cream. No point making ice cream myself, because I'm never gonna do better than Ben & Jerry's.

But no Eggos, Lean Cuisine, Ding-Dongs, Ruffles. No bean dip, party mix, powdered doughnuts, macaroni and cheese. And no soda crackers.

It isn't really a matter of principle, except insofar as principle means the way you actually prefer to live. It is, strangely enough, a matter of convenience. I find all those bags and boxes and trays of overpriced, couch-potato browse — how could you *underprice* it? — increasingly boring and increasingly tedious to deal with. It is, I swear, easier to make what you want when you want it, make it from scratch, than it is to pile in the car, waste a dollar's worth of gas, trudge the aisles of the store, stand in interminable lines while the inevitable person with fourteen items in the ten-item, cash-only lane makes out a second check, having screwed up the first one.

And after all is said and done, what you're really doing is blowing hours' and hours' worth of hard-earned money on what is essentially a cartload of puffed-up nothing. What I see when I look at a shopping bag full of Cocoa Puffs, Hamburger Helper, and Keebler's Chocolate Lover's Chip Deluxe isn't food, it is hours of my life vanishing into smoke.

The way I feel is that while you're making something yourself, you're actually living. Whereas every minute spent shopping for junk food is an extra minute in hell.

So, yes, I made my own crackers, and they were way better than store-bought. I made two batches, actually. And am I going to give you the recipe, in case you feel the same way I do?

Is a bear Catholic? Does the Pope—

Ahem. What I mean to say, of course I'm going to give you the recipe. The recipe is a variation on my basic pie-crust recipe, with extra salt and a touch of leavening. If you remember the pie-crust recipe (see page 21), what you do is cut butter into unbleached white flour in a one-to-three ratio. A good batch of crackers, for example, would take a cup and a half of flour and half a cup of butter.

Since this recipe is for crackers, not crust, add a pinch of baking soda, a teaspoon and a half of baking powder, and a teaspoon of salt to the flour *before* you cut the butter in. When you've gotten the flour-and-butter mix to corn-meal consistency, add just enough buttermilk to make the mix hang together and ball up, probably a quarter of a cup to start, then more as needed to get the right consistency. Roll the dough as thin as you like—I usually go about an eighth of an inch. Decorate however you want, with a sprinkle of salt or herbs or seeds. I went with black sesame seeds this particular night, rolling them in just a little so they would stick. It made for a snappy-looking cracker with a great taste.

Bake them at about 375°F until done, turning them halfway through the process. It shouldn't take you more than fifteen minutes of baking time all told.

Which is a good thing because that bowl of chili is just waiting for a batch of fresh, crisp, rich-tasting, homemade, crumbling-style crackers.

Just Plain Chili

2 pounds lean ground beef
1 bell pepper
6 cloves garlic
2 tablespoons olive oil
Freshly ground pepper, to taste

3 tablespoons cumin
1½ tablespoons chile powder
1 can tomatoes (28 to 32 ounces)
Salt, to taste

More or less chile powder and cumin may be used, according to taste.

TOTAL PREPARATION AND COOKING TIME: 2¾ hours.

1. Light coals in grill.
2. While coals are setting, 30 to 45 minutes, form ground beef into large patties.
3. Clean, deseed, and chop bell pepper. Mince garlic.
4. In a large deep-shouldered skillet, heat olive oil, milling in fresh pepper to taste. Add bell pepper and sauté 5 to 7 minutes. Turn heat off and stir in minced garlic.
5. Grill patties over coals until medium-rare, no more than 5 minutes on each side.
6. Turn heat on high under skillet and place patties in skillet with garlic, oil, and pepper mixture. Break up patties into small pieces with spatula and brown meat thoroughly. Add cumin and chile powder, and mix in thoroughly. Add tomatoes. Mash and break up tomatoes with spatula and mix in thoroughly. Add enough water to cover all ingredients, reduce heat to low, and let simmer 2 hours or more. Salt to taste while simmering, being careful not to oversalt.

SERVES 6

Homemade Crackers

1½ cups unbleached white flour
1 teaspoon salt
⅛ teaspoon baking soda
1½ teaspoons baking powder

½ cup butter or margarine
½ cup buttermilk
4 tablespoons sesame seeds

Poppy seeds, black sesame seeds, large-crystal salt, or various herbs may be substituted for the sesame seeds.

TOTAL PREPARATION AND BAKING TIME: 30 to 35 minutes.

1. Preheat oven to 375°F.
2. In a medium bowl, combine flour, salt, baking soda, and baking powder.

Cut in butter or margarine until the mix is the consistency of cornmeal. Add ¼ cup of the buttermilk gradually, cutting in, adding more as needed until dough balls up and comes away from wall of bowl.

3. Roll out on floured board as thin as possible (⅛" or less recommended).

4. Sprinkle with sesame seeds and go over with rolling pin one more time to embed. Cut dough into desired shapes.

5. Place on cookie sheet and put in oven and bake for 10 to 15 minutes, until lightly brown, turning once while baking.

6. Remove to wire rack and let cool until crisp. Serve with chili, soup, or as appetizers with spreads or dips.

SERVES 6

THE RECIPE

This time of year, fruitcakes are among the most despised of American phenomena, right up there with lawyers and street mimes. Actually, some of my best friends are lawyers, and I don't have much to fear from mimes. They are, after all, primarily a big-city infestation. I can't remember seeing a single one the whole time we lived in Conway, Arkansas.

But I have to admit I have an unreasonable bias against fruitcakes. I *worry* about a dessert with a greater specific gravity than the nickel-iron core of the planet. I'm repelled by the way brilliant bits of jellied fructoid cling to my teeth. I'm suspicious of any supposed digestible that can exist for decades without undergoing any detectable change of state.

But in our family, when I was growing up, we had a variation I purely loved. It was heavy and dark and richly flavored. It had raisins and pecans, but it wasn't overly sweet, and it contained no citron at all. We called it nutcake.

Nutcake originated with my grandmother, but eventually it spread to other members of the family. By the time I was a preteen, my father was claiming it as his holiday specialty. Now my youngest brother, Pat, mails all of us a nutcake for a present every Christmas.

It must have been a fairly inexpensive treat: flour, eggs, butter, sugar. We gathered the eggs from our own chickens — this was back when everybody had chickens. Truth to tell, one of the things I like about this peculiar town we live in now is that it is still not too sophisticated, at least not in our part of town, to have done away with chickens in the yard. Mornings we hear, from a couple of blocks away, the reveille of Julio Franco's roosters, from down by the arroyo.

Like as not the butter had been churned that morning and given to us, an unofficial fringe benefit offsetting the low clergyman's salary. Raisins didn't

MY GRANDMOTHER'S NUTCAKE

THIS NUTCAKE REQUIRES "the recipe"—the official version calls for "a wineglass of wine or whiskey," but as you see, wide latitudes were allowed. If you don't have any "recipe" around your house, I guess you'll have to go to the place my father and grandfather always talked about when we asked where they got it: "I got it at the gittin' place," they always said.

cost much, and pecans were free—this was back when you gathered them from your own trees or gleaned them in buckets from the groves after the commercial pickers had finished. Yes, nutcake was cheap and plentiful, but when it was in season, we thought we ate like kings.

There was only one problem. It was a problem whose solution varied from year to year, calling forth our greatest creative resources. And it was a problem whose solution, I now realize, became one of our fondest annual traditions.

The problem was finding the recipe. Not "the recipe" as in a set of instructions for mixing and baking the delectable, but "the recipe" as in my grandmother's euphemism for the booze, the sauce, the spirits, the liquor. You needed the recipe to flavor the batter in the first place, and then you needed the recipe to soak the completed product, so that it would grow moister and more complex and more wonderfully redolent as it aged.

But we were a preacher's family, remember. A *Baptist* preacher's family. And as everyone knows, Baptists have a powerful affinity for strong drink, and therefore rate it as prime among evils, ahead of even dancing, playing cards, and wearing natural fibers.

The whole state was dry, so the recipe had to come to us fortuitously, through mysterious channels. We looked for it without looking, we expected it without planning. We had to be patient, and exist in faith: It was Godless alcohol we needed, and we counted on God to provide it. The recipe might be a bottle of Beaujolais a wealthy deacon had brought back from an unusual trip to France, a bottle he handed over explaining that he and his would never drink it. How did he know we needed it? Word got around. Or maybe a bootlegger would leave a jug on the step, his conscience-offering for the year. Somehow, back then, I never wondered what happened to the rest of the jug once the nutcakes were all done and wrapped.

One year my grandfather Doc came home with most of a fifth of gin, claiming he had found it in the ditch beside the road. And somehow, back then, I never wondered how it might happen that anybody in Delta Mississippi would toss most of a fifth of gin out the window.

I know what you're thinking. Beaujolais? Gin? In a holiday nutcake? Listen, those were the very best nutcakes of all, and I don't think it's just nostalgia speaking.

Nostalgia plays its part, though. Looking back, I see that the search for the recipe added as much flavor to our lives as it did to the nutcake. It was our tacit admission of the rest of the truth, our tiny romance with sin. In the days of the Nativity, in the season of the coming of the Spotless One, we giggled and whispered and flirted with the Devil. The recipe was forbidden, and it was OK. It was dangerous, and yet it was perfectly harmless.

We lost my grandfather more than a decade ago. We lost my grandmother just this year, after a long and painful decline. It cannot redeem the suffering of her last decade, but I feel compelled to lift a glass of the recipe as I write this.

I feel compelled to say to her, although I think she cannot hear me—so far have I fallen—that I loved her nutcake, that it was Christmas to me.

Granny's Nutcake (The Recipe)

1 pound (2 cups) sugar
½ pound (1 cup) butter or
    margarine
6 medium eggs
½ cup black molasses
4 cups unbleached white flour
1 teaspoon baking soda

½ teaspoon salt
2 teaspoons nutmeg
1 teaspoon cinnamon
1 pound raisins
1½ pounds pecan halves
6 ounces wine or whiskey
    (or other "recipe")

TOTAL PREPARATION AND BAKING TIME: 1¾ hours.

1. Preheat oven to 200°F.
2. If using butter, let soften first.
3. Using a beater, cream together sugar and butter or margarine in a mixing bowl. Add eggs one at a time, beating in slowly. Beat in molasses.
4. In another bowl, sift together flour, baking soda, salt, nutmeg, and cinnamon.
5. Slowly beat the dry mixture into the wet mixture. Add raisins and pecans and stir well. Add wine or whiskey and stir with a rubber spatula until thoroughly mixed.
6. Line bottom of round cake tin (about 8" in diameter and 3" deep) with wax paper. Pour in nutcake batter.
7. Place in oven and bake for at least 80 minutes. Cake is done when a toothpick comes out clean. To store, soak lightly with more wine or whiskey.

SERVES 12

THE DOUGHNUT THINGY

I read somewhere once that the word *doughnut* derives from *dough* and *naught,* the old word for zero. Makes sense to me. Doughnuts don't look like nuts and they don't taste like nuts. They do look like naughts, though I don't know what a naught would taste like.

You notice I can't bring myself to use the modern spelling, *donut.* Purely hate those cute/ignorant shortcuts: Kwik-Klean. U-Sak-Em. Rite, nite, altho. I freely admit there's no consistency in my attitude, since I'm willing to accept "nut" for "naught."

Doughnuts may look like naughts, but they certainly don't have zero calories. In fact, as far as health is concerned, they're probably the, ah, naughtiest things you can eat.

Think of it: a batter of pure starch, with maybe some sugar added. And then this stuff is dropped into deep hot fat and frizzled to a fare-thee-well. And then they take it out and rinse it in a sugar glaze, or cover it with powdered sugar, or drown it in chocolate frosting.

Then you eat about half a dozen, yum, yum. What's that sound? Bet you didn't know you could actually *hear* the plaque settling in your coronary arteries.

But is there anything on earth more warm and sweet and pillowy than a fresh doughnut? Has there been anything since your momma's milk that delivered more of a rush to your gastric juices and pleasure centers? And never mind the sugar crash that follows in about ten minutes, when all the light of the world goes dark and your head goes *whonk* against the tabletop.

Friends, I've quit eating doughnuts. By and large, I've just quit. As retrograde as I am, as staunchly contemptuous of this angst-ridden yuppie preoccupation with a pale imitation of well-being, as much a lover of fat and frolic in food as I am, I have had to give up on doughnuts. It isn't that I don't believe in glorious exceptions to generally good practice. It's just that the price is too high. I'd rather keep having cheese on my burgers, real cream in my coffee, a nip of Ben & Jerry's. And truth to tell, I've gotten to where I don't like that sugar crash at all. I don't like spending a whole day purifying myself, waiting to get my energy and clarity back.

The only time I've eaten a whole doughnut in the last decade was when I was involved in commencement because of my former job at Hendrix College in Conway, Arkansas. Someone would spring for a few boxes that would sit on the counter of the registrar's office or out in the atrium of the administration building, and we'd all have two or three with our coffee or orange juice, just what we needed before going out to suffer in the blazing sun in 100 percent humidity in a black robe for three hours. Our theory was that the whole process was so exhausting and thankless anyway that it didn't matter how much additional damage you did to yourself.

But now Jayme and I have went and bought this doughnut thingy. It's a plunger-operated red-and-white plastic device that must date from the forties. We picked it up at an antique shop in Albuquerque. It came in its original box, and there were three recipes on the box. I've tried out one of the recipes so far, the one for French doughnuts.

I don't know what makes them French, unless it's all the eggs. What you do, you set a cup of water boiling with a couple tablespoons of butter. Then you whisk in a cup of flour very quickly, keeping the mix cooking on low heat. In moments it will pull away from the wall of the pan. At this point, the directions say to gradually beat in four eggs. What I do is dump the whole mess into the blender and blend it. Then I fill the bowl of the thingy, hold the peristaltic end over the skillet, and plunge the plunger, which drops rings of dough into the hot grease—and *Voila!* Le doughnuts française! Great with a sprinkling of powdered sugar, they have a delicate spongy texture. And surely, with all that egg protein, they're better for you than regular doughnuts. (You can even leave out some of the yolks, using two whites in place of one whole egg.)

Now I know most of you don't have a doughnut thingy. But there's a reason I've gone into all this detail. I've discovered that the recipe also makes wonderful crepes. Just pour the batter out onto a griddle or into a lightly buttered black iron skillet, turn once, fill with something appropriate, sprinkle with powdered sugar, and lace with a thread of maple syrup. I've been filling our crepes with some Danish strawberry-rhubarb jam and some cream-cheesy drained yogurt. Very very good of a lazy Sunday morning. More comfort food, something warm and satisfying to get you through the next few impatient weeks till the equinox, those difficult weeks when you look out the kitchen window and it looks bright and warm in the fine sunlight, and you itch to get out there and toss a baseball or dig in the yard, but you know better because when you went out for no longer than it took to bring the paper in, you damn near froze your ears off.

As for me, I've got plenty of stuff to keep me busy indoors. I've got two more recipes to master. It's probably only the store-bought doughnuts that are bad for you, don't you think? A person probably wouldn't gain any weight if he made the doughnuts himself, at home.

I mean, really, he probably wouldn't, would he?

French Doughnuts or Crepes

....

1 cup water
2 tablespoons butter or margarine
1 cup unbleached white flour
4 medium eggs

Cooking oil for deep-frying or 1 tablespoon butter for griddle
Powdered sugar for dusting
Crepe filling of your choice

TOTAL PREPARATION AND FRYING TIME: About ½ hour.

To make batter:
1. In a saucepan, bring the water to boil. Add butter or margarine. Turn heat to low.
2. When butter or margarine has melted in water, rapidly whisk in flour, letting mix continue to cook on low.
3. When mix pulls away from the pan, turn heat off and transfer to blender. Crack in eggs and blend until batter is smooth.

To make doughnuts:

1. Heat oil for deep-frying as you prepare the batter.
2. Fill doughnut maker with batter and drop doughnuts one at a time into hot oil. Turn when lightly brown on bottom, remove when lightly brown all over.
3. Drain on paper and dust with powdered sugar.

To make crepes:

1. Turn griddle on high and melt 1 tablespoon butter.
2. Reduce heat to medium and pour batter in pancake-size circles on griddle.
3. Turn when lightly brown on bottom and bubbles are forming on top. Lightly brown the other side and remove. Add filling of your choice.

MAKES 6 DOUGHNUTS OR 4 CREPES

THE FOSTER FLAP (AND OTHER
FILLING FOLDOVERS)

Those crepes I was talking about, the ones I started making because of the doughnut thingy, have become such a staple around our house—Jayme is finishing one up even as I write these words—that a lengthier and more detailed treatment seems in order. They're easy to whip up and easy to digest, so that they make a perfect hot breakfast for the harried worker in a rush to get to the office.

But there's more to them than the merely utilitarian. They're such light yet satisfying things—delicate, delicious, and festive—that they seem especially suited for spring. And spring *is* on the way, I have it on authority. I imagine garden parties, brunches on the patio, happy guests sluicing down mimosas and scarfing up these little beauties as fast as the chef can flip them.

I'm calling them flaps now. For one thing, it gets a little awkward repeating "those crepes I started making because of the doughnut thingy" every time I want to talk about them. For another, that's what Jayme calls them, egg flaps. I've pretty much perfected the recipe, and I'm ready to give you some details.

For one portion, begin by boiling slightly over half a cup of lightly salted water in a saucepan, adding a teaspoon or so of butter. When the butter has melted and the water is rolling vigorously, use a small whisk to gradually beat in a quarter cup of unbleached white flour. Continue whisking over low heat until the mixture stiffens and comes away from the pan.

At this point, you might let the batter cool a few minutes while you make other preparations—the filling for the dish, table settings, whatever. After the batter has cooled, beat in one whole egg and the white of another egg, continuing to beat until the batter is perfectly smooth. I prefer using a small whisk for this process, too, but if you're making more than one flap, you'll probably want to use a blender. *Much* quicker and no loss of quality.

When the batter is thick and smooth — and it will be surprisingly thick, considering how little flour is in it — put a pat of butter in a skillet or on a griddle and heat it until the butter is almost sizzling. Then pour the golden batter out to make a round flat pancake-size pool. Gradually turn the heat down as the batter firms up. When the flap is firm enough that you can lift one side with the spatula, and the top is dry enough not to run when you do so, you're ready to flip it.

If you're an experienced crepe chef and you're using the right sort of skillet, you can probably manage this trick with a flick of the wrist. I don't figure I'll be a real cook until I master this technique, but I have not, I confess, mastered it. I lack both the equipment and the talent, so I usually use two spatulas, cradling the flap carefully, then flipping it in one sudden and, if I am lucky, continuous motion. The tissues of the flaps are fragile, so expect to tear a few up while you're practicing. The good news is they're just as good, and almost as lovely, in fragments.

I cook the other side on very low heat for only about three minutes, then turn the heat off and let the residual heat of the skillet finish the job.

At this point, you're basically done, and yet the fun is just beginning. The possibilities for fillings are endless. A simple smear of strawberry preserves is wonderful. Lately I've been using some of this new sugar-free, all-fruit jelly, apricot being a particular favorite. (As usual, the stuff costs more, because they've done less to it.)

Fresh fruit works really well, and so you can take a seasonal approach to the flap. I've sautéed thin apple slices, sprinkled them lightly with brown sugar and cinnamon. Most recently I've mixed sliced fresh strawberries — lightly sugared the night before and left in a bowl to draw that bright scarlet nectar — with sliced fresh banana.

Perhaps Jayme's favorite filling is a bananas Foster variation. Slice a small banana lengthwise, brown the halves lightly on both sides in a pat of butter, sprinkle them with cinnamon, and arrange them in a semicircle on one half of the flap. Then deglaze the skillet you browned the bananas in with just a jot of rum or brandy and decoct the resulting juice over the filling.

Whatever filling you've selected, fold the flap in half over it to make a crescent, and set the crescent in the center of a bright or bold plate—I like to use our black dinnerware, because the colors stand out so strongly. Then, with a tea strainer, sprinkle a spoonful of powdered sugar over the whole arrangement, the whole plate.

Lace with a touch of maple or pecan-flavored syrup—just the lightest touch—and you've got a dish as fine and fancy as any you could buy in a restaurant with *Maison* in its name. And if you're not at a garden party or a brunch, if you're off to the office once again—well, you know, there's something to be said for starting out with a bit of brightness and pleasure. There's a message for the inner self in beginning the day with art and delight.

The Foster Flap

1 cup water
½ teaspoon salt
4 tablespoons butter or
  margarine
½ cup unbleached white flour
2 medium eggs and 2 medium
  egg whites

2 small bananas
Cinnamon for sprinkling
1 ounce rum or brandy
Powdered sugar for dusting
4 to 5 tablespoons maple
  syrup

Any number of fillings may be substituted for the bananas Foster, including avocados, cheese, other fruits, and jams or jellies. The powdered sugar and syrup are optional.

TOTAL PREPARATION, COOKING, AND SERVING TIME: 30 to 45 minutes.

1. In a saucepan, bring the water to a boil.
2. Add salt and 1 tablespoon butter or margarine. Turn heat to low. Rapidly whisk in flour, letting mixture continue to cook on low heat until it comes away from wall of pan.

3. Transfer mixture to blender and add 2 whole eggs and the whites of 2 more eggs. Blend until batter is smooth.
4. In a skillet, heat 1 tablespoon butter.
5. Peel and slice bananas in half lengthwise and sauté slices in butter, turning once, until just brown on both sides. Remove bananas from skillet to plate and sprinkle with cinnamon.
6. Deglaze skillet with rum or brandy and reserve juice in a small bowl.
7. In skillet, melt 1 tablespoon butter or margarine.
8. When butter is hot, pour in half of batter to cover bottom of skillet. Brown lightly on one side, about 3 minutes, then turn. When flap is lightly browned on both sides, transfer to plate.
9. Repeat with 1 tablespoon butter or margarine and remaining batter.
10. Layer half the banana slices on one side of each flap and pour small amount of reserved juice over bananas.
11. Fold flaps over into semicircles, center on plates, dust with powdered sugar, and trickle with maple syrup.

SERVES 2

CAN'T BEAT A FAJITA

We've been buying a fair number of these top sirloins lately.

Yep, I'm off on another red-meat kick. Can't help it, werewolf season approaches again. My eyeteeth, dogteeth, and on back are growing, are telling me it's time to rip and tear. My gullet is aching for the slather of slick corpuscles. I'm as bad as Bubba the straw-colored tomcat, moaning at the back door. Neutered and three-legged and flatheaded though he may be, he can tell it's spring, and so he needs to get out and chase birds. Get in a few fights, get his ears bloodied.

I'd settle for a two-inch thickly peppered porterhouse seared almost crusty over the coals, bloody raw in the middle. That and a side of fries with ketchup, and a Mickey's widemouth chilled so cold it's snowing inside like one of those glass paperweights with a winter scene in it.

Not that you can get a Mickey's widemouth anymore. You can get a Mickey's, and it still tastes pretty good, and it still comes in the green barrel-shaped bottles, but now all they have is those sorry-ass narrownecks, like everybody else. Oh the vanished goods of yesteryear. Why would you quit making such a wonderful item, what could the marketing strategy possibly be?

But I digress. I was talking meat. Top sirloin.

On our budget, you don't eat porterhouse all that regular. And although I love a big fat medium-rare grilled cheeseburger, I can't eat one more than every other day without getting bored. Now top sirloin is not a fine cut of meat — don't let the "sirloin" fool you — but it is a whole lot less gristly and a whole lot more tender than round steak or flank steak, and a whole lot moister than lots of other cuts. You can trim the fat and the intersectional sheathing from it pretty easily, and what's left, while it won't exactly melt in your mouth, won't give you jaw strain gnawing it in two, either. And lately we've been finding some pretty good prices on large packages of top sirloin, $2.59 to $2.99 a pound, cut about an inch thick, which is a pretty nice slab.

One thing I do with top sirloin is flour it, brown it, and simmer it a long time in a red wine sauce, and lo and behold, medallions of beef. Another thing I do with it is cube it and braise it and simmer it with selected vegetables to produce a hearty beef stew. Another thing is chicken-fried steak, and another is a kind of fast-food variation, steak fingers. Sliced in thin strips, it makes a good stir-fry dish, variations on Mongolian beef.

But the thing we've been enjoying the most lately is fajitas. For sloppy, messy, drippy, savory, pure food-in-the-hand, bite-down pleasure, you can't beat a fajita.

Actually, the way I do it, it's a kind of stir-fry dish itself — a Mexican stir-fry that you wrap up instead of draping over rice. It has, also, the advantage that you can make the whole thing in a black iron skillet. As you are probably aware by now, I believe that anything you can make in a black iron skillet, you *should* make in a black iron skillet.

Trim the fat and the muscle sheathing, like I said. Slice the meat in strips about a half inch thick, maybe less. Clean a bell pepper and slice it into thin strips. If you feel like some visual excitement and want to splurge, do some yellow and red bell pepper strips, too. You may want to do some onion slices as well. I loosen and remove the skin on three or four cloves of garlic myself, using that trick of pounding each clove under a knife blade, and then I mince the garlic pretty fine. Salt and pepper the beef strips on both sides. Set a thin layer of canola oil almost to smoking in the skillet, drop the strips in, stir lightly, flip them over for a moment, then stir, take them out, and drain them. You want them just barely seared, so they'll stay tender. They'll cook completely through in a matter of moments, so it doesn't take much time. What I'm saying, Joe, don't leave them on the heat too long.

Now drop the bell pepper and onion or garlic in the skillet and repeat the process, including the draining. You won't get all the garlic out, but that's fine. Here comes the fun part. Shake in some chile powder to taste (I'll make the distinction again: pure ground chiles, not chili powder, which is the mix with the cumin and cayenne already in it), some cumin ditto, maybe some more fresh-ground black pepper, some sea salt, some white flour. Brown this mixture momentarily in what little grease remains. Deglaze almost immediately with whatever leftover wine you have, from French red to California white to that two-year-old third of a bottle of sake. Add enough water to keep the roux from being too thick and lumpy, and simmer just a few minutes.

You know the rest of the drill. A covered basket of steamed flour tortillas. Some sour cream or your local sour-cream equivalent. Maybe some guacamole. Fill 'em, sluice 'em with your sauce, wrap 'em, bite 'em. Ease that bestial craving.

Now if you only had a *real* Mickey's widemouth at hand.

Steak Fajitas

1 pound top sirloin
Salt, to taste
Freshly ground pepper, to taste
2 tablespoons canola oil
½ red bell pepper, deseeded and sliced into strips
½ yellow bell pepper, deseeded and sliced into strips

3 to 4 cloves garlic, minced
1 teaspoon chile powder
1 teaspoon cumin
1 tablespoon unbleached white flour
⅓ cup wine (red or white)
4 flour tortillas
½ cup sour cream

One small onion, sliced into strips, may be substituted for the garlic.

TOTAL PREPARATION AND COOKING TIME: 40 to 45 minutes.

1. Remove any fat and sheathing from top sirloin and slice into strips (about ½" thick by 4" long). Dust beef strips with salt and pepper.
2. Heat canola oil in skillet till a drop of water sizzles on contact.
3. Rapidly stir-fry beef strips, bell pepper strips, and garlic and remove to drain. (Some garlic bits will remain.)
4. Dust skillet with chile powder, cumin, and flour and stir rapidly with spatula to form a roux.

5. When roux begins to brown, deglaze with wine and stir with spatula to form thick sauce.

6. Layer steamed tortillas with meat and bell pepper and drizzle with sauce. Add sour cream to taste and roll tortillas into tubes. Eat with your hands and a lot of napkins.

SERVES 2 TO 4

THE GRASS OF THE FIELDS

Not quite nine o'clock of a brilliant Saturday morning, and I'm at the kitchen window, hands covered in flour again, kneading tortilla dough. I'm looking at the patch of strawgrass in the front yard, tall and bearded and waving in the wind.

I'm thinking how beautiful the grass is, how happy I am to be here at just this moment, making our breakfast and drinking fresh hot coffee.

I'm also thinking how I'm gonna kill that grass. Root it up, hoe it out, bury it under huge rocks. Because, beautiful as it is just now, it doesn't fit in with our plans. We want a low-maintenance yard, a landscape that suits the high desert. We didn't move a thousand miles to spend our middle years slaving over a scrap of green.

I feel no division in these two attitudes, no divorce in the heart. I appreciate the immediate beauty of that grass no less.

It has its plans. I have mine.

Humans and grass have a long history together. Wheat is mutated and domesticated grass. Did our domestication cause it to mutate, or did we choose to domesticate it because it had undergone such a favorable change? Regardless, the dough in my hands is genetically linked to the grass along my walk.

Normal grass is haploid, if I remember correctly, and wheat is diploid at least, perhaps in some cases quadruploid and octoploid, if those are meaningful words. Which is to say that there has been a doubling or redoubling of the DNA material. This is what has given wheat its larger and meatier head, its easier-to-husk kernels. And all of this has happened in company with humankind: In some way or other, through selection or cultivation or the strangest of affinities, we have changed wheat. And it has changed us back. It probably changed us from hunter-gatherers to agriculturalists.

One of the tiniest side effects of this whole interaction is me, of course: looking out this window, thinking about grass and wheat and eating and making plans.

I wonder if something has plans for me the way I have plans for the grass and the tortilla. I figure something almost certainly does. Something. I don't mean God exactly. I don't mean a superior being, because I don't feel superior to the grass. I just feel like I'm in a frame of reference that's going to wax its little chlorophyll ass.

I don't mean the argument from design, or the ecstasy of sensing yourself a part of some grand and universal all-for-the-best. Though I would be glad to feel that way if I could.

I just mean something: a pattern, an energy, a framework I can't see, heading my way with a cosmic weedeater in its hands. I'm sure, in such an event, I would complain, if it gave me time to complain. But for the life of me I can't see as how I would have much grounds to.

I do see that this is another Easter poem, I'm sorry, I mean essay. I didn't know that when I started it. Wheat, bread, the staff of life got me there.

I think when Jesus took the bread and broke it and said, Take, eat, this is my body, he was realizing the identity of all life, that the meat of the grass is the meat of the fish of the sea and the fowls of the air and beasts of the land and the apes that walk on two legs. And he was realizing the essential tragedy of this broken world, that life eats life to live. That he was surrendering to the process, and in that surrender performing an act of worship for the whole of existence.

That he was echoing, in a beautiful and heartening way, Solomon's sad lament that we are as the grass of the fields. The day turns and it vanishes. The moon rises, and where is it?

I'll just nevermind for the time being, if you don't mind, whether the historical Jesus actually said those actual words. In spite of my Baptist upbringing, I've managed to lose most of my certitude. I'm as ready as the next person to suppose God probably doesn't exist. But I can't lose Jesus. They introduced us too early, and now, even if he is a fiction, he won't go away.

Don't think I'm all that surrendered to the process myself, though.

I'm hoping for a few more tortillas filled with the meat of plant eaters. A few more sunny windy spring mornings at seven thousand feet, with grass waving and hot coffee at hand. The sound of one or another of our daughters' voices on the telephone on just a few more of those lazy TV-watching evenings at home when you're not really paying attention to what you're watching. A few more of Jayme's incomparable smiles.

But I will say—and I know it's a romantic notion because I've had it since I was a teenager—that when something or other does include me out, I'd want to be not buried or burned but lost somewhere in the woods or the desert or the mountains or the water where my flesh could feed the life around me. Where I could, in some small way, repay the grass its favor.

BIG PLANS FOR BIG BEND

Jayme and I are heading to Big Bend. Again. Finally.

Big Bend draws us with an almost biological longing, the same sort of urge that sweeps the geese into their migrations. I can see, anytime I want to, just by closing my eyes, the notch of the Window, that narrow canyon opening on the blue lake of the rest of the world. Can feel the blown-back spray of the creek that runs through the canyon and falls a quarter mile to desert floor. I can hear the peregrine falcons in the big air just off the south rim, where you can see all the way to Mexico, the blue peaks of the Sierra del Carmen, sixty miles away.

I still laugh when I remember our children picking up their set-up tent to run it across to a superior and suddenly vacant campsite, anxious to get there before someone else grabbed it. Just as they got to the middle of the road, a ranger's pickup came into view. They must have felt guilty, as if they were doing something illegal, because they all, immediately and simultaneously, dropped the tent right there in the road, and scurried inside it to hide.

There are cabins at Big Bend. There's even a lodge. But we like being in the campground. We know just which juniper tree we want to be under.

And naturally, I can't think about camping without thinking about camp food. I imagine we'll spend most of next week packing, and most of that packing will involve food. I'm not going to describe the way we pack for camping. It's the one part of camping I could do without, and truth to tell, I don't like to think about it if I don't have to.

What I *do* like to think about is camp food.

Camp food! Baked potatoes black on the outside and raw in the middle. The big thick steak you drop in the coals trying to get it off the wobbly grill, so

OVER THE NEXT ten days, Lianne put so much gear together you would have thought they were preparing for an assault on Mount Everest. She liked to use the old metal and plastic milk cartons left over from twenty-odd years ago, when her father would bring them home from his job, though he wasn't supposed to. All these years she had held on to them, her only heirlooms.

She filled four of them with food and kitchen supplies—trail mix, peanut butter, boxes of crackers, dried fruit, packets of dehydrated vegetables for stews, soup mixes, powdered drinks, graham crackers, boxes of cookies, canned tuna, canned corn-beef hash, canned mandarin orange sections, canned green beans, jellies, jams, syrups, oatmeal, biscuit mix, coffee, the old tin drip coffeepot, enameled camp mugs, a couple of black iron skillets, camp pots and camp pans and camp silverware, long-handled spatulas and serving spoons and forks for cooking over a fire, a washpan, a scrubber, biodegradable detergent, washrags, plastic sacks of all sizes, some for their empty cans, cartons, their paper, eggshells, sodden coffee grounds, orange and banana peels, greasy used paper plates (which I forgot to mention above before they ate off them), and ziplocks for used food and extra empty vegetable bags to put rocks and pinecones and other treasures in, and bags to hold the bags, and army-green folded-over sheets of tear-off twist-ties with which to seal the bags. The refrigerator stuff went in at the last minute, in the big red ice chest— bacon, eggs, butter, milk for Charles, thick bars of baker's German chocolate, cheeses, wines, frozen juice, fresh bread, fresh fruit, fresh vegetables.

And that was only the food and kitchen supplies. What about the tent in ripstop nylon, the tent poles, stakes, guys, rain cover, the slickers, the sleeping bags, bedpads, pillows, matches, the stubs of used candles in old Pringle's tubes, the Coleman stove, the Coleman lantern, white gas for the stove and the lantern, flashlights in all sizes and descriptions, the battery-operated reading lamp, the medical kit with its Band-Aids, gauze, sterile solutions, disinfectants, insect repellents, pain relievers, antihistamines, pseudoephedrine pills, salves, unguents?

What about the huge box of baking soda, good for making a paste to put on beestings and antbites, also for brushing your teeth, deodorizing the tent, and cleaning the coffeepot. What about the citronella candles to keep the bugs off? What about the picks, axes, shovels, hammers, knives, the walking sticks, the twine and rope and visqueen and old vinyl tablecloths for setting things on, the toilet paper and Handi Wipes and paper towels and soap and bath towels and hand cloths, what about the booze, the books, the clothes?

Listen, she had clothes for mountain-hiking, river-rafting, evening-sitting when it got cooler and you wanted to keep the mosquitoes off your ears and ankles, she had clothes in case they wanted to drive into a town to eat, clothes to go square-dancing in, she had sunhats, tractorcaps, pith helmets, visor shades, she had twelve-year-old low-top tennis shoes, cowboy boots, hiking boots, river-waders, nice little go-anywhere flats, shower sandals, she had bandanas in six different colors and sizes, the most prized of course the big giant old-fashioned red one.

Then of course there were plastic bags full of maps, road maps to get there with, topo maps of the local area, national forest maps, maps of the entire length of the Buffalo. Oh, I could go on and on, but I won't, because [she] don't think it's one bit funny. [As for Charles, he] had seen it all before, and he knew better than to say anything.

—from *Living in Little Rock with Miss Little Rock*

that it has that just-right grittiness. The skillet-cooked dessert that is supposed to be apple crisp but that turns out to be apple limp. Marshmallows whose incandescence is sufficient to land a jumbo jet on a dirt road at midnight during an eclipse. The famous peanut-butter-and-ant sandwich, a perennial snacktime favorite. And that one successful meal after all your plans have *gang* continually and unremittingly *agley,* the one which comes at just the right moment and tastes better than all the concoctions of all the chefs of New Orleans, and which is usually Vienna sausages up in the rocks with crackers and a slug or three of good tequila.

Actually, though, I have had some *good* experiences with camp food. One of the best meals I ever had camping was in Big Bend, way back fifteen years ago almost to the day: a beef stew Provençale cooked up by one of my all-time favorite people, a silver-haired gentleman we all chose to refer to as Pappy. Way I remember it, we came back from a fourteen-mile round-trip hike to the south rim, weak and famished, and this wonderful ungodly fabulous aroma was drifting over the campground. First time I ever saw anybody put black olives in beef stew. Later on I repaid him. Saved his life with an orange during another long hike.

Fresh fruit. We should definitely take fresh fruit. It won't stay fresh long—there will come a day when we have to eat three bananas each, or do the unthinkable and throw the last half dozen away. Still, we're going to need those bananas for potassium for all those fourteen-mile hikes. And apples for our apple limp. The citrus fruits will bear up well, especially if we keep them cool. As Pappy can tell you, nothing tastes better than an orange in the middle of the desert. And limes and lemons for those camp margaritas.

Well, maybe *something* tastes better than an orange in the middle of the desert.

Trail mix! I believe the idea behind trail mix is condensed nutrition to keep the pack light and refurbish all those megacalories you're burning up as you ascend to Laguna Meadow and beyond. But never you mind how the serious backpackers do it. In our family we had four kids, counting Jayme, and so trail mix evolved into a beautiful and trifold symmetry, a perfection of three elements and three elements only: raisins, roasted peanuts, and M&M's. And then you pick out all the M&M's. On the way to the campsite. If you actually have any trail mix left by the time you climb out of the car at the park, your camping trip is off to an inauspicious beginning.

Chocolate. Yes, definitely chocolate. Miles and miles and miles of chocolate.

And coffee! Man, there's a whole book to write just about camp coffee. Nothing like that first cup, the one that gives you the courage you need to face the Coleman stove one more time and fight it to a draw over the question of whether or not you're going to have a hot breakfast. Before that, the sleepy negotiation over who's going to get up and make the coffee, usually decided by who has to pee the worst.

There's a lot more to say. I have not yet begun to consider all the perils and delights of camp food. But I gotta go. Got some big-time packing to do.

IT'S A DOOZY IF YOU TOP
IT WITH PIZZAZZ

I think I've finally learned the craft of homemade pizza. Now there's nothing at all wrong with having a good old greasy mass-produced American pizza delivered to your door just as the movie starts and she gets through shaking the martinis.

Nothing except that it always seems to cost at least seventeen dollars, especially since you're a decent human being with kids of your own and the college student delivering the pizza is working for minimum wage and so you make sure to add on a reasonable tip.

It takes me probably two hours to make a pizza from scratch, and my time is definitely worth better than eight and a half an hour. So no way am I arguing that making your own pizza is a paying proposition. But you probably understand by now why it's worth it anyhow.

One of the problems I have had with pizza-creation in the past is getting the crust right. Proud as I am of my breadmaking skills, until recently I had never created a really superb pizza crust, the kind that chews *and* crunches and tastes even better the next day when you heat it up. All my crusts in the past tended to be either too hard and crunchy or too limp and floppy.

There's nothing more discouraging than having a tectonic-plate-size slab of cheese slide to the floor, dragging your mushrooms and bell peppers and tomato sauce with it just a second before you introduce the point into your open and salivating mouth. Unless it's grinding your way through a crust with all the texture and flavor of Styrofoam-coated cardboard.

I had read somewhere that a shortcut to a good crust was to roll out biscuit dough real thin. Well, I've tried that technique a number of times, and I'm here to say it leaves a lot to be desired, even when the dough you start with is that good old homemade buttermilk biscuit variety.

No, for a really good pizza crust, you have to go to yeast. There's just no way around it. But that's not all the technique you need. I'd made yeast-rising dough for pizza crust before, and while it sometimes seemed an improvement on crusts made with biscuit dough, it was still less than satisfactory. It was either too breadlike or too dense and chewy. And I still suffered from the Onerous Unforgivable Problem of the Floppy Point.

Finally I read or heard somewhere that the trick to making really good French bread was to use no oil, and I decided to try the same method on pizza crust.

Bingo!

So here's what you do. You take a packet of yeast and a teaspoon of sugar and stir them into a half cup of very warm water and let them sit till the yeast is activated, a matter of minutes. Meantime, you put two cups of unbleached white flour in a bowl and mix in a teaspoon of salt and two teaspoons of sugar. Meantime meantime, you preheat the oven to 120°F or so, and meantime meantime meantime you plop a couple of tablespoons of butter on the pizza pan and put the pan in the oven to melt the butter. By now your yeast is ready, high and foaming, and you pour it into the flour bowl and begin mixing with a rubber spatula or some such, adding more warm water until you get the right consistency of dough. It won't take much more water—you want a light, moist dough, sticky but not gluey. Now you turn the dough out on a big floured board and knead it. Your oven is probably plenty warm, so turn it off.

I use the Chinese sword-forging technique for kneading dough: I fold it in half and flatten it out and fold it in half again. Repeat the process ten times and you have a thousand layers of gluten fibers. Do it twenty times and you have a million of them.

When the dough is silky soft but no longer sticky, put it back in the bowl and put the bowl in the warm oven to rise. When it has risen, anywhere from thirty minutes to an hour, knead it again. Sometimes, in honor of tradition, I throw the dough, using centrifugal force to widen and flatten it, but I'm not very good at the technique, so after a little throwing, I finish out with a rolling pin.

Fit the dough into the pizza pan, trim the edges—and then there's one last trick, which solves the floppy-point problem, and which is also essential for pie crusts, and which they never tell you in the cookbooks. Prebake the crust at 375°F before you add the toppings. Not all the way done—you don't want it brown at all—but until it begins to acquire some firmness and crispness, no more than five to seven minutes.

You'll have a pizza crust good enough to eat by itself. But of course you don't want to do that, you want to add all kinds of toppings. For which you now need some recipes.

I've developed a couple of doozies (check out the sidebar). Doozy is a word, by the way, which comes from the popular nickname for the Deusenberg automobile. Deusenbergs were in such favor at one point that if something was really good, really impressive, it was a Deusy.

So I read, anyhow. I don't quite date back that far.

I do date back far enough that I have very conservative ideas about what goes onto a good pizza. There's a new restaurant in town here, Pizzazz, supposed to be quite good, which offers all manner of unusual pizzas, including the smoked salmon pizza. I'm a big fan of smoked salmon, and I believe my friends who tell me the restaurant is four-star. But I don't know.

Sounds kind of fishy to me.

I don't approve of chili pizzas, free-range chicken pizzas, or even Canadian bacon pizzas. And I think people who eat pizzas with pineapple on them should be required to wear badges so that those of us who care about standards will not mistakenly start up a culinary conversation.

The word *pizzazz*, by the way, comes from the old Pizzazzamotive automobile, which had unusual horsepower for a 1920s V-3. So that when anyone showed a lot of friskiness, a lot of get-up-and-go, they were said to have a lot of pizzazz.

I think the two sorts of toppings I've developed may fairly be said to have pizzazz—pizzazz in sufficient quantities to activate the most jaded taste buds, although the recipes themselves are simple and basic. The trick is in the cooking—or in not overcooking, I should say. One of the advantages of my method is that, by prebaking the crust, you cut down the baking time for the pizza itself to a short enough period that your cheese doesn't get burnt and leathery.

WE BEGIN, OF course, with garlic. Everything begins with garlic. In the beginning God created garlic. And then He said, Man that smells good. I think I want a pizza tonight.

Feel free to vary the ingredients according to what you like and don't like, but I use garlic, bell pepper, mushrooms, fresh tomatoes—three or four Romas, because they remain firmer—dried oregano and tarragon, and fresh basil.

You may have noticed that this pizza is not especially heavy on tomato sauce—in fact, there is only as much as you generate from the fresh Romas in your own skillet. As much as I like the fruit of this particular vine, I get tired of super red, super tomatoey pizzas and chilis and pasta sauces and barbecues. But if you have a craving, here's a variation on the recipe you'll probably like. After deglazing, add a can of tomato sauce, a can of tomato paste, and generous amounts of water, then simmer a good long time, until the sauce is rich and thick, what Jayme calls red sauce. Add the other ingredients as before, and Voila! (Naturally, since you are cooking the sauce for a longer period, you'll have to adjust the time when you begin prebaking the crust.)

To anchovy or not to anchovy? This, actually, I am willing to accept as a matter of taste. Some people just can't stand them, but Jayme and I both feel anchovies make the perfect finish, that wonderful wicked burst of fish oil and saltiness. Simply scatter them across the top after all the other ingredients, making sure you get a roughly equal distribution.

Follow all of the steps in the following recipe, maintain a proper respect for tradition, choose one of the topping variations from the sidebar, and you will have yourself a hot, rich, redolent, and not only satisfying but absolutely scrumptious homemade pizza.

The word *scrumptious,* by the way, derives from the brief but intense popularity of Albert Scrumpt's famous 1934 Scrumptomobile, the only three-wheel-drive convertible ever to . . .

Homemade Pizza with Yeast-Rising Crust

For the crust:

1 packet yeast

3 teaspoons sugar

³⁄₄ cup warm water

2 cups unbleached white flour

1 teaspoon salt

For the topping:

5 to 8 cloves garlic

1 bell pepper

¹⁄₂ pound mushrooms

3 to 4 Roma tomatoes

5 to 6 leaves fresh basil

4 cups part-skim mozzarella

2 tablespoons olive oil

¹⁄₂ cup red wine

1 tablespoon dried oregano

2 teaspoons dried tarragon

Salt and freshly ground pepper, to taste

Flour for thickening

TOTAL PREPARATION AND BAKING TIME: 1³⁄₄ hours.

1. In a small bowl, combine yeast, 1 teaspoon sugar, and ¹⁄₂ cup warm water. Stir until dissolved and let sit to activate.

2. In a large bowl, combine flour, salt, and remaining 2 teaspoons sugar. When yeast is activated, pour yeast water into flour mixture, working in with rubber spatula and adding more warm water as needed. When necessary, work dough with hands. Dough should be springy and moist, but neither sticky nor too stiff.

3. Turn dough out on floured board and knead thoroughly.

4. Return dough to bowl, cover bowl with wet cloth, and set in warm place to rise.

5. While dough is rising, prepare other ingredients. Peel garlic and slice very thinly. Clean and dice bell pepper. Clean and slice mushrooms.

6. Drop tomatoes in boiling water for 30 seconds, remove, and peel. Then dice them coarsely.

7. Mince basil leaves. Grate or shred mozzarella.

8. Set burner to high heat. Add 1 tablespoon olive oil, mill in pepper to

taste, then add garlic and mushrooms and sauté till mushrooms are just browning.

9. Remove garlic and mushrooms to bowl, then add bell pepper to skillet. Add more olive oil if needed.

10. Sauté bell pepper till just tender and remove to bowl with mushrooms and garlic.

11. Sauté diced tomato very rapidly, no more than a minute, and remove to bowl with other vegetables.

12. Deglaze skillet with wine. Add basil, oregano, and tarragon. Let mixture simmer 5 to 10 minutes, salting and peppering to taste. Thicken mixture with a little flour dissolved in water.

13. Return vegetables to skillet, mix in, and turn heat off.

14. When dough has risen, roll out into a circular shape (slightly larger than 15" pizza pan) on a floured board.

15. Preheat oven to 375°F.

16. Fit dough circle into greased pizza pan, and trim excess. Let crust rest and rise for 5 minutes.

17. Place in oven and prebake for 5 to 7 minutes.

18. When crust is slightly dry and just firm to the touch but has not browned at all, remove from oven.

19. Spread with prepared sauce, top liberally with mozzarella, and return to oven. Bake until cheese is melted and crust is brown, about 15 to 20 minutes. Serve topped with grated Parmesan.

MAKES A SINGLE 15" PIZZA

SIX SECRET HERBS AND SPICES

I've been preoccupied lately, real preoccupied.

Even the routine duties of life have been a burden since I've had to handle them all by myself. Jayme's been out of town for her aunt's funeral. It is has been the season for that sort of news, I'm afraid. Then there's the house and yard. Been doing considerable work on the house and yard. House and yard are about to kill me. My grandfather had his last heart attack trying to crank a balky lawnmower. I made up my mind I wasn't going to go the same way, but sometimes I wonder. Practically rebuilt the cotton-picking house last week, while somehow keeping just barely ahead of all those job-related deadlines and preoccupations. Began waking up at five, four, three in the morning, working all day, sometimes till as late as nine or nine-thirty.

I couldn't help noticing that, while I was on this binge of concentration and effort, my eating patterns changed. Not surprising. Day after day went by in which I felt I couldn't spare even half an hour to whip up a good meal, much less write letters, shine my shoes, go to committee meetings, cut my fingernails, or watch television.

What happened was food had changed over from meditation to mere fuel. I would stand at the refrigerator and drink five swallows of milk right out of the jug just to get my stomach to shut up so I could focus on what I was doing and get back to work. Or I would carve off a couple of ounces of cheese and cram them down before I zoomed off to teach class—a midflight refueling just in order to keep from getting light-headed (more light-headed than usual) while I was lecturing about comma splices and misplaced modifiers and garbled syntactical structures.

I didn't abandon my high-protein tendencies entirely, but neither did I spare the time to be especially careful. I ate what was handy, what was already made. Evenings I leaned toward fast food, comfort food. Had most of a big box of Kentucky Fried one night—good, greasy, hot. Did myself up a couple of real meals, too—burgers on the grill, my own version of fried chicken, chili. But heavy emphasis on short preparation time and short eating time. I wasn't trying to learn anything, and I wasn't trying to enjoy anything. I was just trying to keep the engine running.

Now I know this pattern is not news to many Americans. Our insanely congested lives force perhaps most of us to live this way. Meditation is a luxury in the dreamless society, in the corporatized society, in the mechanized society. I complain, but I'm luckier than some, can count on coming into, every so often, a small patch of Wide Time. Time that meanders on like a great big wide slow river under the moon. Time you drift down like Huck and Jim on the raft (and didn't they have some good eating?).

But many people aren't so lucky. For many people, maybe most, time and urgency are the same thing. We really ought to do something about that situation, don't you think? Humans aren't meant to live that way. It isn't good for us. The stupid thing is that, socially speaking, it isn't even *productive*. Which is the only excuse for hurrying up, to produce more and better.

All human activities can be engaged in meditatively or urgently. Who was it who said something to the effect that the urgent always drives out the important? If we can either write a poem or go to a committee meeting, we wind up going to the committee meeting. A month later we can't remember what happened at the committee meeting or why it was so urgent.

And we don't have a poem, either.

What do I mean when I say that normally food is meditation for me? I mean that I think about what I'm doing while I'm doing it. I mean that I enjoy a before, a during, and an after. I plan what I'm going to eat and what's going to be in it and how I'm going to cook it and how I'm going to serve it, and I think about how I'm going to enjoy it. And all of those activities are also ways of getting in touch with my own life, of thinking about who I am and what I want and why I want it and what I owe to other people and what I owe to the other life of this earth.

I think about what my body actually needs, as opposed to what I may have a craving for. Do this sort of thinking often enough, and you quit having crav-

CREAM GRAVY WITH pan-fried chicken was a staple of my youth. Happened every Sunday. You had it over rice or mashed potatoes, with English peas, rolls, and iced tea.

A mastery of gravies goes a long way to cementing your reputation. Keeping a few simple principles in mind, there's no reason ever again to serve up a lumpy or tasteless gravy.

There are two basic approaches to gravy: the roux approach and the flour-in-water approach. In the roux approach, as the name implies, you get your color by browning a little flour in hot oil, and you produce the gravy with whatever liquids you apply to the roux.

In the flour-in-water approach, you already have the stock for your gravy in hand, and you thicken the stock by adding flour dissolved in cold water to it while it simmers.

You've seen an example of the first approach in the recipe for tomato gravy (page 14) and an example of the second approach in the recipe for giblet gravy (page 195). In the first approach, all the color usually comes from the browning of the flour, and all the flavor from whatever fluids you use for deglazing. In the second approach, you are most often using a stock that has cooked off a meat dish, such as roast turkey or pork roast or pot roast. As a result, all the color and flavor come from the color and flavor of this stock. Cream gravies are basically gravies whipped up from a roux you

ings and start enjoying true appetite — defined as when your desires match up with your needs. Eating my KFC this past week, I realized that pigging out was just the other half of treating food as mere fuel. You treat your body as a machine long enough, you start having deficiencies, you start having inconsolable hungers. Americans binge, I suspect, because they are by and large denied true pleasure. I don't have any large social answers, though. All I have is recipes.

Like the fried chicken I mentioned earlier, a small victory over my obsessions. What I did was sprinkle a bunch of breasts with some dried dill, fresh-milled black pepper, salt, a touch of chile powder, a touch of cumin. Then I create in the skillet that you have fried something in (so that scrapings from the frying are included and add a bit of extra savor). Cream gravies, therefore, are usually mild in flavor (unless you add seasonings) and do not carry much flavor of the meat. The famous sausage gravy that some people like to serve over biscuits is an example.

Nobody says you can't combine the two approaches, and I often do, adding chicken stock to a roux made from fried-chicken scrapings, for example, and then thickening further with flour dissolved in water. This produces a more *chicken*-flavored chicken gravy than cream gravy. Sometimes, the juices from a roast are not dark enough to my liking, and I create a dark roux with flour and butter in order to add color and texture to my gravy.

Because it refers to gravy, I will leave you with a little poem, a pastiche upon a stanza from a very famous (and very bad) poem, one that those my age had to memorize in school. See if you can recognize the original. (Hint: Pay attention to the sound, not the meaning.)

THE MENU
Rice with veal, lightly garnished,
And the gravies, hot and cold.
Just a tart, too crusty, warmish.
Whatnots floating in a bowl.

dredged the pieces in flour and fried them in canola oil, ten minutes on a side. Drained them on a brown paper sack and had a feast.

Didn't take all that long, the way I did it, but it returned me to childhood Sunday afternoons. I'd been missing fried chicken, and somehow, as good as the Colonel's was, it hadn't made up for the loss I was feeling. And of course, since this was a sort of Southwestern take on my childhood favorite, it brought past and present time together for me.

So here's to meditation, the sixth spice.

Even if we have to work like the devil to get to it.

Pan-Fried Chicken

1 fryer chicken, cut into pieces
Salt and freshly ground pepper,
   to taste

Flour for coating
6 tablespoons cooking oil

For variations in flavor, rub the chicken with selected herbs and spices before flouring. For Southwestern pan-fried chicken, rub the chicken with a mix made from 1 teaspoon chile powder, 1 teaspoon cumin, and 1 teaspoon dried dill.

TOTAL PREPARATION AND FRYING TIME: 40 minutes.

1. Salt and pepper chicken pieces to taste. Dredge in flour, or shake in paper bag with flour.
2. Heat oil in large skillet.
3. Beginning with skin side, brown chicken in oil till deep brown on both sides, 10 to 15 minutes on a side.
4. Remove and drain on paper. Serve hot for Sunday dinner with gravy (recipe follows), mashed potatoes, English peas, and rolls or biscuits, with iced tea as a beverage.

SERVES 4

Pan-Fried Cream Gravy

Oil and cracklings from frying
   chicken (or other meat)
2 tablespoons unbleached
   white flour

Salt and freshly ground pepper,
   to taste
1 cup milk

This recipe will actually make an excellent cream gravy from any pan-fried meat, including pork chops and chicken-fried steak.

TOTAL PREPARATION AND COOKING TIME: 15 minutes, not including frying the chicken.

1. After you have finished frying the chicken (or other meat), add flour, salt, and pepper to skillet on medium heat and with a spatula form a roux.
2. When roux begins to brown, rapidly blend in milk with spatula, pouring about ¼ cup at a time. If gravy is too thick, thin with water or more milk. When gravy is smooth and golden, it's ready to serve.

SERVES 4

A GRACE FOR THE OLD MAN

We didn't quite make it to that expected Christmas dinner.

I suppose that, as the eldest son, apostate that I am, whenever what's left of our family gets together again, I'll be the one saying grace over meals.

My father died last week. He had been a Baptist preacher for forty-five years. He had been married to my mother for fifty-three years. I never saw a man more uncomplaining or less afraid of mortality, except perhaps Ben Kimpel. My father would have been the last man to describe himself as humble or virtuous, but he had served faithfully, and he seemed to imply that his passing was a trivial matter, of no very great concern to the world at large.

Those of you who have lost someone so near and so instrumental—you may suppose how things are for our family, for my mother, my sister, my brothers. It isn't my purpose to speak of such matters here. But I have never been efficient at separating one facet of my life from the others. I eat every day, as you do. I eat while I live, I eat in order to keep living, and as I am freshly reminded, I die while I eat. Now that my father is no longer here to sustain his name, I feel a need to sustain it, momentarily, for him, to carry it into places it might not otherwise be heard, to whisper it in every corner of my own brief existence.

Jack Armand Butler is his name. His, too. He had it first.

The Butler tribe ate like field hands. Which is what they had been, essentially: field hands in their own fields. They grew and separated, and only my Uncle Alfred remained on the land. He hosted the family reunions. Christmas dinner was a true feast. I could recite the litany of dishes, but you're familiar with most of them. I could describe how a dozen or so adults sat at the great table and more than a dozen children were scattered to card tables, but odds are you're familiar with that, too. I could tell how the most significant graduation of my life was the graduation from the card table to the big table, and you might remember a similar passage.

My father was the youngest of eleven, and the last to go. I like to think of him as a boy, claiming, eventually, that same seniority. I like to wonder when he moved up to the big table.

When he became a preacher, our subset of the family moved into a life in which eating was, if anything, even more important than it had been before. When was the last time you saw a skinny preacher? My father developed an affinity for the lost places, the out-of-the-way country churches, back in the days when most Southern Baptists were poor and unsophisticated and genuine. Before we became dominant and found out about money, political power, and TV makeup. Even after the transformation of the sect in the last half of this century, my father managed to find pockets of isolation, tiny islands in which the old ways survived.

The members of his pastorates were field hands as well, or at least small farmers. We got paid in produce more than once, and we had Sunday dinner in someone else's home as often as we had it in our own. If I sometimes appear to claim connoisseurship of fried chicken, chicken and dumplings, mashed potatoes with gravy, butterbeans, ham with redeye gravy, leatherneck green beans, crowder peas, black-eyed peas, cornbread, fresh tomatoes, fried green tomatoes, tomato gravy, biscuits, sweet rolls, pot roast, fried okra, sweet potato pie, pecan pie, lemon icebox pie, chocolate pie, I hope you will forgive me. I have sampled so many variations from so many splendid kitchens, have been offered the heroism of so many anonymous platters.

So OK, so I couldn't resist the litany after all.

It was the food that was the glory of our difficult early years. And of course it was the food that killed my father, if one must attribute blame. He became as round as any minister, and the weight and the fat wrecked his heart and plagued him, in later years, with diabetes. It was wonderful and touching to see him, in his last decade, lose the extra mass. Here was an old man, frail and gaunt and white-haired, and every time I looked at him, I saw the lean young airman of the wedding photos, the eagle-eye Bible pilot of my nightly dreams.

I parted company with all that eating somehow, though never with the love of food. The meals, like the practice of the faith, seemed to me to become less

ACROSS FROM THE TREATMENT CENTER IN BEAUMONT, TEXAS

The halt, the lame, the aged, the infirm—
they come to Luby's for the buffet lunch.
The limbless lift their forks, the jawless munch
with special fittings. Nothing comes to term
for these few minutes, no tumor, virus, germ
consumes us. We consume the blue cheese, ranch,
the thousand island, chew the chicken, french
fries, fishcakes, okra, mud pie, we slug back warm
iced tea. It's dinner-on-the-grounds, almost,
almost reunion. The hum of family talk,
laughter at favorite stories, the clink of silver.
And we hum and clink and talk. *Show me that river,
take me across.* Such spirit, old man. Such Ghost.

You won't use your chair when we go. You stand up and walk.

real. The word *processed* loomed ever larger in our lives. Even my mother went to canned biscuits, to individually wrapped slices of cheese food-product. Pies were whipped up with Jell-O and Dream Whip and Ritz-cracker crusts. And who can blame them, after a life of hard labor? Convenience may be more signal, finally, to those who have earned it, than some young Puritan's version of reality.

Still, whenever we went back for a visit, it was always reunion, it was always a feast. I felt honored once to attend dinner-on-the-grounds at his last small church, Bethany (from which he resigned a month before his death). One of the last meals we had together was at the Luby's cafeteria in Beaumont, Texas, where my mother and I had taken him for another course of treatment for yet another of his manifold late ailments. And I felt honored there, too.

My father had a wonderful ending. You and I should be so lucky. Doing better than he had in some time, he invited my mother out on a date (his description). He was, apparently, feeling frisky. They went to a restaurant just a few blocks from their house, and they partook of what his eulogist, another preacher from that world that I remember so lovingly but can no longer inhabit, described as "one of his favorite dishes—Mexican food."

After they'd eaten, my father told my mother how happy he was.

And then he was gone.

If I were to offer a prayer, I might say a lot of things. I might say thank you for this good man, for the family he built. I might say thank you, Lord, for the peace and satisfaction you gave him at last. Thank you for letting us get over all the awkward years, the times of separation and bitterness and disappointment. Thank you for letting us remember how we loved each other, for letting us at last and finally come full circle.

But just now all I really want to say is thank you for letting him finish his meal.

THE ORIGINAL ALLIGATOR FRUITCAKE

Life goes on. And on and on.

We don't, but life does.

Grief, I find, is a remarkable thing, stranger even than I had suspected. There is a curious exhilaration in it. There is, at least, if you have found resolution with the person you have lost. I suspect that grief is a crueler thing entirely without that satisfaction.

And I haven't really lost my father. He visits me in dreams. He visits me as a young rowdy, as an old preacher. He visits me fat and black-haired and forbidding, and he visits me thin and frail and white-haired and leaning on his cane. The other night he sat in the back of a pickup drinking whiskey with me, and he sang this song:

> I bought it because I need it,
> I drank it because I bought it,
> I'm drunk because I drank it.

You can tell me these aren't real, that they are just smokes in the brain, nighttime phantasms. But I know better. I know the man, and it's him.

Another peculiar thing about grief is that it doesn't *replace* the other emotions. It coexists with them. It and the other more usual emotions move through each other the way bright rings move through each other on the surface of still, wide water.

So I suppose it isn't strange that I find myself, so soon after my father's funeral, thinking of fruitcakes. Christmas, after all, is not quite here. And I suppose it is even less strange, given the reminiscences of the last dozen days, the near-perpetual recall of old dear times, that I am thinking of fruitcakes in connection with Alligator, Mississippi.

Yes, I know. Fruitcakes. Yes, I remember what I have said about them in the past.

I dread them, too, as much as you do. Denser than U-238, and maybe more dangerous. I'm not convinced citron isn't radioactive. I know for sure it glows in the dark, and the red kind makes Superman do weird things and the green kind takes all his powers away. And isn't it the same stuff they set fire to in order to drive off mosquitoes?

That's what people do in the summertime. They burn the fruitcakes they didn't eat last winter, and those flying pests just drop right out of the air.

I admit to all these feelings, but here's the way it came down this year. Jayme has a sneaking affection for fruitcakes. Well, not so sneaking. The worst, heaviest, oldest, jammiest fruitcake ever misbegotten upon a defenseless universe—it could find a friend in Jayme. Come holiday season, all sorts of biological imperatives kick in for her. They do for me, too, but most of my holiday biological imperatives say to head for the hills until it's all over.

Jayme now. She needs to go shopping. I mean, really *needs* to. She needs to prepare seven or eight meals huge enough to feed the 81st Airborne, should they choose to drop in. She needs to build ribbons and bows and wreaths and light candles.

It's all pretty wonderful, really, and thank God that a few grumps like me have had the good fortune to hook up with people who really know how to live.

Except for that one scary and terrible compulsion.

She needs to eat fruitcake.

Cognizant of the situation, this year I resolved that one of her presents was going to *be* a fruitcake. But a really good fruitcake. One of the world's great fruitcakes. A fruitcake you could be proud to pass down to your children and your children's children. Well, the recipe anyhow, since this fruitcake, unlike most in its genre, was going to be edible. Not merely edible, but scraping-the-last-crumb-off-the-wax-paper delicious.

So what do you do when you've committed yourself like that, and you have to deliver? What do you do when you're outside your comfort zone, your normal run of resources?

You get back to your roots, that's what you do. You call on the wisdom of the tribe.

When I get ready to make my second trillion dollars, I'm going to publish a food book. Another food book. I've got a fund of recipes, and I'm going to write a little text to go with the recipes, and then I'm going to sit back like Uncle Scrooge and watch the greenbacks cascading into my money vault.

Because, friends, the fund of recipes I am speaking of comes from a little green book sitting on my cookbook shelf. A book called *Alligator Round-Up*. It contains all the Butler clan's special recipes going back seventy years or more. My father's among them.

To make an Alligator fruitcake literally by the book, you need six eggs, four sticks of butter, two cups of sugar, two and a quarter cups of all-purpose flour, four tablespoons of frozen orange juice concentrate, four cups of chopped pecans, a cup of chopped candied cherries, a cup of chopped pineapple, and a "cup of chopped mixed fruit" (don't ask me).

Naturally, I made a few changes. I had already determined that I was going to use sun-dried cherries in whatever fruitcake I concocted, so I did about half a cup of those instead of candied cherries. I was planning to try for a bit of the citron effect without actually using citron, so I looked for dried pineapple, but never found any. Wound up using about half a cup of dried mango instead. Actually, I was going to concede a little citron to Jayme's compulsions, the green stuff for holiday color, but I never found any of that, either. I couldn't quite believe I was supposed to put four cups of pecans in the cake, so I only did three cups. And I didn't have any orange juice concentrate. That worked out fine, though, because I did have some leftover orange juice, and what I did was, I microwaved the dried fruit briefly in enough juice to cover, and by the time the fruit had finished absorbing fluid, I had a couple of ounces of thick syrupy juice left over.

I had to make changes in the cooking instructions, too, because we live in a much thinner atmosphere. But you probably won't have to compensate for that, so I'll tell you the way the book told me.

Chop the fruit and nuts, and add one and a quarter cups of the flour (I stirred it all together to coat the fruit and nuts). Cream the butter and sugar, then add the eggs one at a time. Add the orange juice. Mix the remaining ingredients — the other cup of flour and the flour-fruit-nut combination — line the bottom of a pan with wax paper, and bake at 275°F for two hours.

You'll notice this is a low temperature and a long cooking time. Don't want your fruitcake to go through any traumatic changes. You want it to meditate slowly on its glorious transformation. What *Alligator Round-Up* doesn't tell you is what size pan. I used the eight-inch cake tin that I planned to present the cake in anyway, lining not merely its bottom but the sides as well, and it turned out to be exactly the right dimensions, the cake rising just to the top of the tin.

Now that I think of it, I'm willing to bet that this fruitcake recipe was the basis for my grandmother's nutcake, which, over the years, became my father's nutcake. Jayme said I could tell you that the result is definitely worth the wait. And she knows her fruitcakes.

I mean, look at who she married.

The Original Alligator Fruitcake

4 tablespoons frozen orange
  juice concentrate
8 tablespoons water
½ cup sun-dried cherries
½ cup chopped dried pineapple
  or mango

3 cups chopped pecans
2 ¼ cups unbleached white flour
4 sticks butter or margarine
2 cups sugar
6 medium eggs
Rum or whiskey for soaking

TOTAL PREPARATION AND BAKING TIME: 2½ hours, not including soaking time for cherries.

1. Reconstitute orange juice with the 8 tablespoons water. Soak cherries in juice until they absorb all but about 4 tablespoons of it.
2. Pour off extra orange juice into a small bowl.
3. Preheat oven to 275°F.
4. In a large mixing bowl, combine pineapple or mango and pecans with cherries and 1¼ cups of the flour. Stir this mix together.

5. Cream the butter or margarine and sugar together in a mixing bowl, then beat in the eggs one at a time. Stir in the remaining orange juice, then mix in the remaining cup of flour and the flour-fruit-nut mixture.
6. Line the bottom of a round baking tin (about 8" in diameter and 3" deep) with wax paper and pour in the batter.
7. Place in oven and bake for 2 hours or until a toothpick comes out clean when inserted. Before storing, lightly (or heavily) soak with rum or whiskey.

SERVES 12

SNOW CREAM

It was maybe the best New Year's of my life, coming off the saddest Christmas. Not the unhappiest Christmas, you understand—just the saddest.

We've been through a long dry spell in Santa Fe. No surprise, we're living in the desert. But this drought has gone on for two years. No monsoon season in July and August. That's what they call it here, monsoon season. Regular afternoon thundershowers that cool things down and freshen the air and set double rainbows glowing over the Sangres. But when the rainy season doesn't come, the high-pressure cell locks in, and the temperatures soar, and the trees die.

Then, this fall, no snow. We waited. And we waited.

No snow in October, when it usually starts.

No snow by Thanksgiving, when the ski resort was planning to open.

No snow by Christmas.

No snow in the mountains means no water in the rivers in spring. And that means the ground stays hotter, and that might mean another high-pressure cell sets up and drives all the rain-carrying winds away for yet another year, like a bad-tempered parent chasing away the children who love her and only want to cheer her and make her feel better.

Finally, the next-to-last night of the year, we had a light snow. Not much, but enough to give us a white New Year's Eve, and some hope for the future.

We had been thinking, Jayme and I, that we might head downtown to the bar in the El Dorado Hotel and meet up with a few friends. As the evening approached, though, we could tell we wanted to stay home. It wasn't that sort of thing where you slouch in your chair and watch really bad and really boring specials on TV and have five or six or seven and watch the ball drop all by yourself and then you feel really depressed because you're such a loser.

This was a much nicer stay-at-home.

We had icy martinis around six, hers with Tanqueray Sterling because gin gives her problems, and mine with Boodles, that most juniper-driven of all the genevers. And we talked and laughed and had a good time. Then we whipped up some guacamole to have with blue corn chips, and switched over to margaritas because they went with the guacamole and we were planning to have burritos with chili for a midnight meal and what the hell, don't we live out West anyway?

And we laughed and talked some more. Then about ten-thirty we put on our triple-option Columbia all-weather coats and our boots and our ski mittens and went walking. We went all over the neighborhood, looking at the snow in the yards, looking at the holiday lights. Around here, everybody leaves them up all twelve days of Christmas, until Epiphany.

We walked down to the arroyo, and then we walked down *in* the arroyo. And almost nobody else was out, and it was cold and clear, and the windows were all lighted with people staying warm and you hoped happy. And you could feel the year coming, the new year. You could feel it gaining speed in the big empty night, rolling toward you like the ghost of the grandest tidal wave that ever was, but this one bringing something exciting and not wreckage.

And I realized that this was where it happens, Time. It happens Outside.

We got back with five minutes to spare, and cracked a bottle of Moët & Chandon, and watched the ball drop, and stood out on our steps and toasted each other and the change, and listened for a while to cheers in the distance and watched fireworks over the rooftops toward the Jemez range.

Then we had our burritos, and finished with some eggnog, and finally went to bed about two o'clock. And slept late, and woke up to more snow. This time it was really coming down. It came down most of the day. Dry, light, feathery stuff. Beautiful stuff. It came down in heaps and drifts. And since we still weren't through celebrating because it still wasn't Epiphany—we do all twelve days of Christmas—we walked in that snow, too.

We went out and *skied* in it.

And because I'm a Southern kid who has never gotten enough of it, I remembered a great way to celebrate snow. I remembered something I'd had maybe half a dozen times in my life, which was the number of times it snowed in Mississippi over two decades: snow cream.

When I was a kid, we made it with Pet milk, which is still the classic and, some would say, only way. But a few years back I came up with a superior recipe. The next time there's a good snow where you are, whip some heavy cream and a little sugar very stiff and very sweet, with vanilla to taste. Then slowly beat in as much of the cold powdery stuff as it takes, a little at a time, until the whole is very smooth and firm.

Dust it with cinnamon or nutmeg if you like. Eat it with a spoon.

It will taste like the ice cream the angels eat. It will taste as light and fresh and promising as the New Year itself, as the kind of time that happens Outside.

Snow Cream

1 cup heavy cream	4 cups fresh cold dry snow
3 tablespoons sugar	Nutmeg or cinnamon, to taste
Vanilla extract, to taste	

Appropriate amounts of artificial sweetener may be used instead of sugar.

TOTAL PREPARATION TIME: 10 minutes (or all winter if you're waiting for snow).

1. In a mixing bowl, beat the heavy cream until peaks begin to form, sprinkling in the sugar and vanilla during the last part of the process.
2. Go outside, find a clean spot, and collect the snow. Immediately beat as much of the snow as required into the whipped cream, until the mixture is very light, cold, smooth, and firm.
3. Dust with nutmeg or cinnamon if desired. Serve immediately.

SERVES 2

AT THE GENEROUS TABLE

We're going to Truchas again, dinner at a friend's home. I've mentioned him before, Alvaro Cardona-Hine. He and his wife, Barbara, run a gallery high up on the llano, and from their courtyard you can see one of the most beautiful vistas on the planet. Sweeping views of the Jemez range in the west and the Sangre de Cristos range in the east, the long spectacular light.

I'm always exhilarated when a jaunt to Truchas is in the offing, and it isn't just—or even mostly—because I know I'm likely to see such a sunset as must have happened at the end of the first day of creation, or the wandering tribes of mist in the green valleys. It's because of the moments we are about to share with our friends. We go to Truchas fairly frequently, and Barbara and Alvaro come down the mountain to visit us. A lot of shared dinners, a lot of laughter.

I know that we're going to get there, and we're going to be welcomed in from the chilly air of late afternoon to a snug warm adobe home. That we're going to be welcomed in with smiles and cries of pleasure, that the jokes and compliments and teasers will begin immediately.

I know that we will be led into the living room and seated around the big wooden coffee table. Barbara will begin brewing pungent black or green or herbal tea, and a pot of honey will be brought to the table, and cheeses and crackers and slices of apples will be present, and Alvaro will ask if you want a glass of the El Patron or the Il Tesoro or any of one of the several bottles of remarkable mescals he has been exploring lately. He has, as usual, found something wonderful, and nothing will do but that you, his friend, must immediately share it to the fullest.

Dinner will be a vegetarian feast, half a dozen dishes, pastas and beans and ratatouilles and fine bread and fresh vegetables, and the wine will flow, and the talk will flow, and there will be desserts, and there will be espresso, cups and cups of espresso, and there will be liqueurs . . .

It is such a generous table. Such a generous home.

I think Alvaro is one of the master painters of the age. If I had a fortune, I would spend a fortune on his paintings, and on a place to hang them. Always, before dinner, after an hour or so around the coffee table with the tea and the mescal, we plead to go back into the studio. And in the studio, in the beautiful disorder that is the heart of grace and order, there are always paintings, paintings, paintings. Paintings on easels. Paintings leaned up against walls and against other paintings. Paintings that have recently been hung. There are small paintings and huge ones. Bird paintings both spooky and funny. Sutra paintings. Landscapes, ineffable landscapes.

I will see seven new pieces that break my heart, that bring me to tears of joy. There is such a welling-up in Alvaro's being. Such an unstoppable flow. It is not as though he does not suffer difficulty, sorrow, and pain. Like most of the rest of us, he has experienced more of the bad heavy dark than he requires. But at his table, and in his art, none of it shows.

And I think how none of us can create generosity for ourselves. How we can create it only as a gift for others. And I think how such utter generosity is at the center of the art I most love. It gives, and it gives, and it gives. It gives with a merry heart, it gives without let or hindrance or reservation, without fear of judgment, resentment, misunderstanding, envy, rejection.

Then I think of us, the guests at the generous table. What can we do, how can we behave? You've seen the varieties of response. You've seen the shamed, self-effacing guest, the one who is continually embarrassed to be the recipient of such benevolence, who protests over and over, No, not me, really, I've had too much already, please, no more. You've seen the status-conscious, glancing around the table at the others, taking offense because someone else is served first or because someone else is enjoying more of the host's attention at the moment, someone who has not known the host nearly as long and therefore should not be as welcome. You've seen the cost-counters, the score-keepers, the ones who are tallying the probable cost of the evening and prorating it among the visitors and thinking when it will be necessary to reciprocate and who to invite. You've seen the self-absorbed, refusing this or that delight, carefully styling their responses to sallies long since forgotten in the whirl of the conversation, thinking ahead to their other plans for the evening, when they will have to leave.

There's only one fit way to sit at the generous table, though, isn't there? There is only one grace you can offer the perfectly generous host. And that grace is acceptance, wholehearted happy acceptance. Blessings shower on your head past all reason and past all deserving. Celebrate the abundance abundantly. Break bread freely with your friends. Take, and eat.

INDEX

Note: Page numbers in *italics* refer to official recipes.

apples
  bread pudding, *188–89*
  pie, 56–58, *58–59*
avocados, 94–96
  creperritos, breakfast, 98–100, *100–101*
  Guacamole, Jayme's Onion-Free, 96–97
  Sandwich, World's Best, 95–96, *97*

bacon
  Pork-and-Bean Sandwiches, Postwar, 48–49, *49–50*
bananas
  Foster Flap, The, 210–12, *212–13*
barbecue
  Chicken, Jayme's Amazing Oven-Baked, 72–74, *76–77*
  Pork Ribs, Mosey Froghead's Country-Style, 70–72, *74–75*
barbecue sauce, 68–72
  leftover, 74

basil
  pasta with egg dressing, *162*
  pizza with yeast-rising crust, homemade, 226–29, *230–31*
beans
  butterbeans. *See* butterbeans
  Sandwiches, Postwar Pork-and-48–49, *49–50*
beef
  Chili, Just Plain, *199–200*
  Meatballs, Elena Lester's Authentic Greek, 135–37, *137–38*
  Meatloaf, Four-Meat Piñon Country, 114–16, *116–17*
  steak fajitas, 214–16, *216–17*
beer
  -batter onion rings, 172–73, *174*
  homemade, 177–78
biscuits
  buttermilk, 9–12, *13*
  Shepherd's Winter, 122–23, *124*
  tomato gravy and, 12, *14*
  two-to-one rules, 9–10
blackberries, wild, 40–43, 132–33
  cobbler, 42–43, *43–44*

black iron skillet
  care and feeding of, 15–20
  Cornbread, 79, *81*
  Pie Crust, Universal, *21–22*
  quiche. *See* quiche
bread
  French, *182–83*
  fry, 151–52
  pudding. *See* bread pudding
  sandwiches. *See* sandwiches
  sourdough, dill-garlic, 179–80,
    181–82
  toast, garlic and dill, 77
bread pudding, 186
  apple, *188–89*
  hard sauce for, Southern-style,
    189–90
butterbeans, 52–53
  country-style speckled, *53–54*
buttermilk
  biscuits, 9–12, *13*
  Cornbread, Black Iron Skillet, 79,
    81
  corncakes, skillet, 157–58, *158*
  crackers, homemade, 199, *200–201*
  sourdough bread, dill–garlic,
    179–80, *181–82*

cabbage, 65–67
  Chowchow, Mom's, 82–83, *84*
  coleslaw, 66, *67*
cake
  fruitcake. *See* fruitcake
  Nutcake, Granny's (the recipe),
    202–4, *204–5*

strawberry shortcake, 107–9, *109–10*
capers
  chicken Kiev, capered, 168–70,
    170–71
catfish, 60–62, 66, 67
  light, 62, *63*
cheddar cheese
  Oysterfellers Rock 'n' Roll, 140–41,
    141
  Pork-and-Bean Sandwiches, Post-
    war, 48–49, *49–50*
cheese. *See specific types of cheese*
cherries
  Fruitcake, The Original Alligator,
    244–45, *245–46*
chicken
  fingers, 74
  Kiev, capered, 168–70, *170–71*
  Oven-Baked, Jayme's Amazing,
    72–74, *76–77*
  pan-fried, 234–35, *236*
  pâté, chicken liver and pork, 180,
    183–84
  pot pie, 89–91, *91–92*
  stewed, with buttery dill
    dumplings, *92–93*
chicken livers
  pâté, pork and, 180, *183–84*
chile peppers, 152–53
  rellenos, 153
chili, 152, 197
  Just Plain, *199–200*
Chowchow, Mom's, 82–83, *84*
cilantro, 113
  meatless loaf, 118–20, *120–21*